# VARIETIES OF QUESTIONS IN ENGLISH CONVERSATION

# STUDIES IN DISCOURSE AND GRAMMAR

EDITORS

SANDRA A. THOMPSON
*University of California at Santa Barbara*
*Department of Linguistics*
*Santa Barbara, CA 93106*
*USA*

and

PAUL J. HOPPER
*Carnegie Mellon University*
*Department of English*
*Pittsburgh, PA 15213*
*USA*

*Studies in Discourse and Grammar* is a monograph series providing a forum for research on grammar as it emerges from and is accounted for by discourse contexts. The assumption underlying the series is that corpora reflecting language as it is actually used are necessary, not only for the verification of grammatical analyses, but also for understanding how the regularities we think of as grammar emerge from communicative needs.
Research in discourse and grammar draws upon both spoken and written corpora, and it is typically, though not necessarily, quantitative. Monographs in the series propose explanations for grammatical regularities in terms of recurrent discourse patterns, which reflect commmunicative needs, both informational and socio-cultural.

Volume 3

Elizabeth G. Weber

*Varieties of Questions in English Conversation*

# VARIETIES OF QUESTIONS
# IN ENGLISH CONVERSATION

ELIZABETH G. WEBER

JOHN BENJAMINS PUBLISHING COMPANY
AMSTERDAM/PHILADELPHIA

1993

**Library of Congress Cataloging-in-Publication Data**

Weber, Elizabeth G.
   Varieties of questions in English conversation / Elizabeth G. Weber.
      p.   cm. -- (Studies in Discourse and Grammar, ISSN 0928-8929; v. 3)
   Includes bibliographical references and index.
   1. English language--Interrogative. 2. English language--Spoken English. 3. English language--Variation. 4. Questions and answers. 5. Conversation. I. Title. II. Series.
PE1395.W43      1993
425--dc20                                                                                    93-5764
ISBN 90 272 2613 X (Eur.) / 1-55619-369-6 (US) (alk. paper)                                     CIP

© Copyright 1993 - John Benjamins B.V.
No part of this book may be reproduced in any form, by print, photoprint, microfilm, or any other means, without written permission from the publisher.

John Benjamins Publishing Co. · P.O. Box 75577 · 1070 AN Amsterdam · The Netherlands
John Benjamins North America · 821 Bethlehem Pike · Philadelphia, PA 19118 · USA

To Sandy Thompson

To Sandy Thompson

# Table of Contents

**Preface** ..................................................................................................... xi

**Chapter 1 The Problem: The Relationship between Discourse and Grammar**
    1.1. The Linguistic Problem ........................................................... 1
    1.2. Assumptions about the Relationship between Linguistic Form and Communicative Meaning ........................................................ 2
    1.3. Goals ........................................................................................ 4
    1.4. Morphosyntactic Form ............................................................ 5
    1.5. Intonation ................................................................................. 7
    1.6. Approaches to Language in its Social Context ...................... 9
        1.6.1. Emotive Theory of Ethics ............................................ 9
        1.6.2. Speech Act Theory ...................................................... 9
        1.6.3. Discourse Analysis .................................................... 11
        1.6.4. Conversation Analysis .............................................. 12
        1.6.5. Other Disciplines ....................................................... 15
    1.7. Conclusion ............................................................................. 16

**Chapter 2 Analytical Procedures and Principles**
    2.1. General Procedures ............................................................... 19
        2.1.1. The Database ............................................................. 19
        2.1.2. Reasons for Studying Utterances Doing Questioning ........ 20
        2.1.3. Selectional Criteria for Utterances Doing Questioning ....... 20
    2.2. Organization of the Data ....................................................... 22
        2.2.1. Morphosyntax ............................................................ 22
        2.2.2. Intonation ................................................................... 26
        2.2.3. Communicative Functions ........................................ 27
    2.3. Analytical Procedures ........................................................... 28
    2.4. Organization of Conversation ............................................... 29
        2.4.1. Sequence Structure .................................................... 29
        2.4.2. Turn-Taking Procedures ............................................ 29
        2.4.3. Repair Phenomena .................................................... 30
        2.4.4. Preference Structure .................................................. 33
    2.5. Summary ................................................................................ 38

**Chapter 3  Methodology**
- 3.1. Data .................................................................................................39
  - 3.1.1. Conversations ..................................................................39
  - 3.1.2. Transcription Notation ....................................................43
- 3.2. Coding Procedures.........................................................................46
- 3.3. Conclusion .....................................................................................55

**Chapter 4  Declarative Questions: Morphosyntactic Patterns**
- 4.1. The Problem of Declarative Questions..........................................57
- 4.2. Data ................................................................................................58
- 4.3. Morphosyntactic Patterns of Declarative Questions .....................59
  - 4.3.1. Declarative Questions with No Associated Marker .............59
  - 4.3.2. Marked Declarative Questions........................................60
- 4.4. The Interpretation of Declarative Questions with No Associated Marker...............................................................................................73
  - 4.4.1. Intonation and Declarative Questions with No Associated Marker................................................................................73
  - 4.4.2. Gesture and Declarative Questions with No Associated Marker................................................................................75
  - 4.4.3. Accessibility of Information and Declarative Questions with No Associated Marker..............................................75
- 4.5. Next-Turn Repair Initiators and Declarative Questions with No Associated Marker .........................................................................77
- 4.6. Distributive Facts ...........................................................................79
  - 4.6.1. Marked Declarative Questions........................................80
  - 4.6.2. Declarative Questions with No Associated Lexical or Morphosyntactic Marker ..................................................85
- 4.7. Summary of Distributive Facts ......................................................89

**Chapter 5  Declarative Questions: Function**
- 5.1. Multiple Functions of Declarative Questions................................91
- 5.2. Functional Distribution of Declarative Questions ........................91
- 5.3. Next-Turn Repair Initiators (NTRI's) ............................................92
- 5.4. Requests for Confirmation.............................................................94
  - 5.4.1. Marked Requests for Confirmation in Terms of A-events and B-events .....................................................................96
  - 5.4.2  Requests for Confirmation Which Have No Associated Marker..............................................................................102
- 5.5. Declarative Questions Not Interpretable in Terms of A-Events and B-Events ................................................................................106
  - 5.5.1. Topic/Sequence Solicitations........................................107
  - 5.5.2. Request for a Reason ....................................................108
  - 5.5.3. Uptakes...........................................................................110
  - 5.5.4. Knowledge Gaps ...........................................................113
  - 5.5.5. Candidate Understandings ............................................115

|        | 5.5.6. Arrangements | 116 |
|---|---|---|
|        | 5.5.7. Narrator Checks | 117 |
|        | 5.5.8. Criticism | 117 |
|        | 5.5.9. Topic Continuation | 118 |
|        | 5.5.10. Reported Questions | 118 |
| 5.6.   | You're Kidding | 119 |
| 5.7.   | Conclusion | 120 |

**Chapter 6  Nonclausal Questions: Morphosyntactic Patterns**

| 6.1. | The Problem of Nonclausal Questions | 123 |
|---|---|---|
| 6.2. | Data | 124 |
| 6.3. | Morphosyntactic Patterns of Nonclausal Questions | 125 |
|      | 6.3.1. Nonclausal Questions with No Associated Marker | 126 |
|      | 6.3.2. Marked Nonclausal Questions | 127 |
| 6.4. | The Interpretation of Nonclausal Questions with No Associated Marker | 138 |
|      | 6.4.1. Next-Turn Repair Initiators and Nonclausal Questions | 138 |
|      | 6.4.2. Accessibility of Information and Nonclausal Questions | 138 |
| 6.5. | Distributive Facts | 138 |
|      | 6.5.1. Marked Nonclausal Questions | 139 |
|      | 6.5.2. Nonclausal Questions with No Associated Marker | 142 |
| 6.6. | Summary of Distributive Facts | 150 |

**Chapter 7  Nonclausal Questions: Function**

| 7.1 | Multiple Functions of Nonclausal Questions | 151 |
|---|---|---|
| 7.2. | Functional Distribution of Nonclausal Questions | 151 |
| 7.3. | Next-Turn Repair Initiators (NTRI's) | 152 |
| 7.4. | NTRI's and Preference Structure | 164 |
| 7.5. | Other Functions of NTRI's | 169 |
| 7.6. | Candidate Solutions to Same-Turn Repairs | 172 |
| 7.7. | Functions of Nonclausal Questions not Implicated in Repair | 173 |
|      | 7.7.1. Topic/Sequence Solicitations | 173 |
|      | 7.7.2. Preferred Responses to Pre-Announcements | 177 |
|      | 7.7.3. Backdowns | 180 |
|      | 7.7.4. Candidate Understandings | 181 |
|      | 7.7.5. Try Questions | 185 |
|      | 7.7.6. Other Functions | 186 |
| 7.8. | News Receipts | 187 |
| 7.9. | Conclusion | 189 |

**Chapter 8  The Many-to-Many Relations of Lexical and Morphosyntactic Markers of Question Function**

| 8.1. | Introduction | 191 |
|---|---|---|
| 8.2. | Lexical and Morphosyntactic Markers | 192 |

|  |  |  |
|---|---|---|
| 8.3. | Misinterpretations | 202 |
| 8.4. | Distribution of Markers in Declarative Statements | 205 |
| 8.5. | Conclusion | 208 |

**Chapter 9   Conclusions**
|  |  |  |
|---|---|---|
| 9.1. | Introduction | 211 |
| 9.2. | Goal 1 | 211 |
| 9.3. | Goal 2 | 212 |
| 9.4. | Functional Explanations of Morphosyntactic Patterns | 214 |
|  | 9.4.1. Declarative Questions | 215 |
|  | 9.4.2. Nonclausal Questions | 216 |
| 9.5. | Universals of Question Function | 217 |
|  | 9.5.1 Question Marking Strategies | 218 |
|  | 9.5.2. Implication for Typological Studies | 219 |
| 9.6. | Typical Questions | 219 |
| 9.7. | Implications for Other Areas of Language Study | 220 |
|  | 9.7.1. Descriptive Linguistics | 220 |
|  | 9.7.2. Speech Act Theory | 221 |
|  | 9.7.3. Formal Linguistics | 221 |
|  | 9.7.4. Cognitive Science | 221 |

Notes .................................................................................................. 223

Appendix ............................................................................................ 227

References ......................................................................................... 231

Index .................................................................................................. 243

# Preface

This book is based on the research I did for my dissertation in linguistics (University of California, Los Angeles 1989). It is, simply put, an attempt to examine how linguistic form is utilized by speakers to create and interpret meaning. This goal requires that as much attention be paid to meaning as linguistic form. To get at the meanings created by participants in interaction, I utilized the principles and procedures employed by conversation analysts. Although this work is not itself conversation analysis, it has come about, in large part as a result of my studying how conversation is organized functionally by participants.

Combining the divergent perspectives of two fields — in this case linguistics and conversation analysis — is always a challenge. The results of this study, I believe, justify the difficulties inevitably involved in explaining the value of conversation analysis to linguists, and the linguistic value of the work to conversation analysts. The conversational data on which this study is based have revealed unexpectedly transparent correlations between form and meaning.

My thanks are due to the many teachers and colleagues I have had the good fortune to know during my years at UCLA, especially Manny Schegloff, Raimo Anttila, Jack Du Bois and Sandy Thompson. My debt to so many other scholars, especially the late Dwight Bolinger, can only be suggested by my citations.

I would also like to express my sincerest appreciation to Jerrie Campbell for her efforts in preparing this manuscript for publication.

# Chapter 1

# The Problem: The Relationship between Discourse and Grammar

## 1.1. The Linguistic Problem

Throughout the history of western thought, many ideas about the nature of human beings, the world and the relationship between them have been stated in terms of dichotomies. Philosophers have split the person into mind and body: the knower has been opposed to that which is known. The facts of nature have been contrasted to the values which arise from our experience in the world. It is not surprising to find, therefore, that attempts to understand the nature of language have also given rise to a dichotomy — linguistic form vs. communicative meaning.

Once a split has been conceptualized, it remains the task of philosophers to explain the relationship of the separate parts. Within linguistics today, there are several positions regarding the relationship between linguistic form and communicative meaning. Crucial decisions follow from assumptions about this relationship, *e.g.*, decisions about the relevance of data and the appropriate analytical method. Before discussing the assumptions about the relationships which ground this study, I will first briefly discuss linguistic form and communicative meaning.

Linguistic form may be realized acoustically as spoken language, manually as signed language or graphemically as written language. This study will deal only with spoken language. Spoken language may be analyzed with respect to its form on different levels, *e.g.*, phonetic form (the level of the inventory of sounds in the language); phonological form (the level at which sounds in the language combine into words) or morphosyntactic form (the level of word order and morphological marking). Intonation, a factor which is so closely connected to the form of an utterance, must be taken into consideration in any study of spoken language. Pike (1945) makes the following observation:

> Every sentence, every word, every syllable, is given some pitch when it is spoken. Even a sound in isolation is produced by vibrations whose frequencies constitute its pitch. There are no pitchless sentences (p. 20).

Although the role of intonation in realizing the meaning of an utterance is not as crucial as nonlinguists might assume, intonation does play a crucial role in the functional interpretation of an utterance in some cases in the data (Couper-Kuhlen 1986).

Linguistic forms realize different types of meaning (referential or propositional meaning, affective meaning, interactive or social meaning). Bolinger (1977) notes various facets of the term "linguistic meaning" in the following:

> Linguistic meaning covers a great deal more than reports of events in the real world. It expresses, sometimes in very obvious ways, other times in ways that are hard to ferret out, such things as what is the central part of the message as against the peripheral part, what our attitudes are toward the person we are speaking to, how we feel about the reliability of our message, how we situate ourselves in the events we report and many other things that make our messages not merely a recital of facts but a complex of facts and comments about facts and situations (p. 4).

This work focuses on one aspect of the relation between linguistic forms and the meanings they bear.

## 1.2. Assumptions about the Relationship between Linguistic Form and Communicative Meaning

The general goal of this study is to examine the relationship between linguistic form and communicative meaning, *i.e.* how speakers capitalize on linguistic forms to realize social meanings. The first assumption of this work is that meanings are only interpretable in terms of a context. This is an assumption about the nature of meaning which, of course, goes beyond language-in-use.

The second assumption is that linguistic forms relevant in any examination of the relationship between form and meaning are only those which occur as linguistic behaviors produced by participants in response to their needs in natural situations. These linguistic forms can be contrasted both to stretches of talk and particular individual morphosyntactic forms produced for the specific purpose of gathering data.

These two assumptions limit this study's data to particular instances of naturally occurring spoken language situated in the context of discourse. This guarantees that the linguistic context in which morphosyntactic forms are situated is also part of the data. Thus, to a certain extent, the analyst has access to the same linguistic context as the participants who produced and interpreted the talk. Given the assumption that the meanings of a linguistic form are interpretable in relation to its context (including its prior discourse context), this limitation is essential. Note: not all linguists make these assumptions; consequently, they are not constrained to use the same kind of data (language produced in the course of naturally occurring interaction).

The third assumption is that linguistic utterances are purposive — the means by which speakers satisfy their needs in interactional situations. Through their utterances, speakers achieve their interactional ends. These ends are inextricably bound to the needs continuously emerging in the ongoing talk as it exists in real time. Every linguistic production inherently exhibits a judgment by the speaker as to what s/he should do in the existential interactional situation. Each linguistic utterance produced in interaction is an action by the speaker. Each utterance is understood to be indexical to the prior text and the present context. It is immediately interpretable in terms of the interaction-so-far and subsequently interpretable in terms of the interaction which follows.

The final assumption of this work is that the structure of linguistic forms (as instruments of communication) reflects the communicative ends of speakers. Grammar is assumed to emerge from discourse. Discourse becomes the pattern model for grammar (García 1975, 1979; Thompson 1983, 1987a, 1987b; Du Bois 1985, 1987a, 1987b, 1992; Hopper 1987, 1988; Hopper and Thompson 1980, 1984; Hopper, 1987, 1988; Geluykens, 1992; Hopper and Traugott (forthcoming)). Benveniste articulated this view of grammaticization in his dictum: *Nihil est in lingua quod non prius fuerit in oratione* (1966:3, cited in Laberge and Sankoff 1979:419). In other words, morphosyntactic types are motivated by the patterns of the *token aggregate, i.e.,* the patterns produced in individuals' actual speech *(parole)*. Du Bois (1984) articulates this view of the relationship between discourse and grammar as follows:

> Once we see that the grammaticization of new structure *depends* on variability, it becomes clear that this need cannot be fully satisfied by the lexicon, which after all is a collection of types in language. In speaking, new combinations are produced (as tokens) in variable profusion. But this variability is ordered, in accordance with the general consistency of speakers' goals, plus the requirements of the current language system.... Since the production of discourse is driven by speaker goals, the new patterns are suffused with functional implications from the outset....Discourse is thus capable of providing patterns already imbued with functional significance as models for potential grammar.

Because discourse is motivated by speakers' goals, the morphosyntactic patterns emerging from an examination of tokens found in discourse are defined in terms of the use of these tokens. Discourse use involves factors of both information flow and interactional goals (Schiffrin 1987:6; Goodwin 1987:19n; Ford and Thompson (forthcoming)).

## 1.3. Goals

In this study, my first goal is to demonstrate that morphosyntactic form correlates with the communicative function "doing questioning" when this function is identified on the basis of the sequential structure of the talk[1] (Goody 1978, Owen 1984, Stenström 1984, Schiffrin 1987). Coulthard (1977) describes the problem of the relation between discourse and grammar as the interface between form and function:

> The difficulty is to explain how a relatively small number of grammatical options can realise a relatively large number of discourse functions, and how both listener and analyst can successfully recognise which function is being conveyed (pp. 14-15).

Morphosyntactic form alone cannot account for the meanings interpretable from a linguistic form. The sequential position and intonation of a linguistic form in the talk is crucially significant for its functional interpretation. The issue, then, is how morphosyntactic options interact with both intonation and sequential position in production and interpretation. In short, if the relationship of linguistic form and discourse function is one of many forms to a single function and a single form to many functions — the issue is how speakers encode the messages they intend and how recipients interpret those messages with regard to their function. In this study, I will attempt to describe how speakers use morphosyntactic form to do the social action of questioning and how recipients use the same form to interpret these utterances.

The term *question* applies ambiguously to interactive function and morphosyntactic form. Commonly this term refers to some utterances which are doing questioning as well as to those which exhibit specific grammatical forms, *viz.*, interrogative forms. Note: any linguistic form in the data which is interpretable as doing questioning has been included in the corpus. The criterion by which forms were selected, therefore, is a functional one. If a linguistic form serves the function of asking a question, it was included. The application of this criterion resulted in a corpus of *functional questions* realized by a variety of morphosyntactic forms. In addition to the expected interrogative forms, the corpus includes utterances realized by declarative clauses, particles, single words and phrases.

The problems involved in identifying questions are addressed by Bolinger in his study *Interrogative Structures of American English* (1957). He notes:

> The Q[uestion] is an entity that is often assumed but seldom defined. The confidence of the assumption betokens something that is reacted to in a fairly consistent way by all speakers. The difficulty of definition betokens a complex which is not only made up of a number of ingredients, but whose ingredients may vary as to presence or absence or proportionate weight. If there were no such variation there would not be a complex in the linguistic

> sense: a given allophone may be acoustically complex, but — considered as a type rather than as a sound — its components are relatively constant and it is therefore linguistically simple; a phoneme on the other hand comprises possibilities not all of which need always be present, or always be present in the same proportion. Q's are complex in the latter sense — so much that countless borderline utterances cannot be classified, except arbitrarily, as Q's or N[on-]Q[uestion]s (p. 1).

Note: the analytical principles identifying linguistic forms as doing questioning will be presented and discussed in Chapter 2.

My second goal is to consider how the structure of the morphosyntactic forms which do questioning are *motivated* by their function. This goal is related to the assumption that syntax is motivated by discourse use (García 1975, 1979; Thompson 1983, 1987a, 1987b; Du Bois 1985, 1987a, 1987b, 1992; Hopper 1987, 1988; Hopper and Thompson 1980, 1984; Bentivoglio and Weber 1986; Weber and Bentivoglio, 1991; Hopper, 1987, 1988; Geluykens, 1992; Hopper and Trangott (forthcoming)). The temporal character of spoken language is an important element in demonstrating this relation (see also Chapter 9).

## 1.4. Morphosyntactic Form

There are four major morphosyntactic clause types in English. A clause consists of a subject and a finite verb (with the exception of the imperative clause). The four clause types are: declarative, interrogative, imperative and exclamatory.

Quirk *et al.* (1985:803) define declarative clauses as those clauses in which the subject is present and (generally) precedes the verb, as in the following:

> Pauline gave Tom a digital watch for his birthday.

In English, syntactically interrogative clauses are signaled by word order and morphology. Quirk *et al.* (1985:803) define interrogatives as those clauses marked in one of two ways:

- *yes-no* interrogatives: the operator (*do*) is placed in front of the subject:

  > Did Pauline give Tom a digital watch for his birthday?

- *wh*-interrogatives: the interrogative *wh*-element is positioned initially:

  > What did Pauline give Tom for his birthday?

Quirk *et al.* (1985: 803) define imperative clauses as those clauses which normally have no overt grammatical subject and whose verb has the base form, as in:

> Give me a digital watch for my birthday!

Exclamatory clauses have an initial phrase introduced by *what* or *how*, usually with the subject-verb order, as follows (Quirk *et al.* 1985: 803):

> What a fine watch he received for his birthday!

Quirk *et al.* also identify four major semantic types which are normally associated with the four major syntactic clause types:

| Syntactic Clause Type | Semantic Type |
|---|---|
| Declaratives | Statements |
| Interrogatives | Questions |
| Imperatives | Directives |
| Exclamatives | Exclamations |

Although direct association between syntactic and semantic class is the norm, the two classes do not always match (Quirk *et al.* 1985:804). In other words, there is not a one-to-one correlation between syntactic clause type and the function it serves in the discourse.

Many linguists, conversation analysts and philosophers have observed this same noncorrelation between syntactic clause type and discourse function (Sinclair and Coulthard 1975, Pike 1975, Schegloff 1984, Coulthard 1977, Searle 1969, 1975, 1979, Bolinger 1982, 1989, Geluykens 1989a, 1992, Kim 1992, Green 1989, Tsui 1991, Ashby 1988, Schiffrin 1987). Pike (1975) illustrated this point with the following diagram:

| Role of Sentence Nucleus: | Class of Sentence Nucleus |||
| --- | --- | --- | --- |
|  | Declarative Clause | Interrogative Clause | Imperative Clause |
| Statement | 1 | 4 | 7 |
| Question | 2 | 5 | 8 |
| Command | 3 | 6 | 9 |

**Diagram 1.1.**
Adapted from Pike (1975)

Note: it is possible for any major clause type in English to serve any discourse function. Examples for eight of the nine cells representing form/function correlations are presented in the Appendix. The diagonal line depicts those form/function correlations most frequently associated by speakers, *i.e.*, the statistical norm. Sinclair and Coulthard (1975) state that questions can be realized by a declarative, interrogative, imperative or moodless structure. On the other hand, syntactically interrogative forms can serve functions other than doing questioning; for example, they can communicate requests, commands and/or invitations (see also Bolinger 1989, Geluykens 1988).

## 1.5. Intonation

In considering the relationship between linguistic form and communicative function, it is necessary to discuss the role of intonation. The function of doing questioning can be served in discourse by practically any kind of morphosyntactic form; likewise, such forms can assume any intonation contour. Bolinger (1982) states that any intonation that can be applied to a declarative form can also be applied to *yes/no* interrogatives; further, *wh*-questions will admit any intonation contour with a terminal rise, just as they will with a terminal fall. Although a terminal rise in intonation is often referred to as question intonation by linguists and nonlinguists alike, "it must not be thought that the rise is a pure grammatical symbol for interrogation, for questions neither require nor monopolize it" (Bolinger 1972:28). This position is clearly stated by Pike (1945, cited in Bolinger 1972). He maintains that the meaning of intonation has to do with feeling and attitude, not with syntax:

> ...popular non-linguistic tradition would seem to claim that there is a question pitch as distinct from a statement pitch; all questions are presumed to use the first of these two, and, as a corollary, the question pitch would not occur on statements. The evidence fails to support the assumption. There are many more contours than one for question and for statement. Specifically, it was a marked surprise to me to find that there are many different contours which can be used on questions, and that for any contour used on a question I could usually find the same one used on a statement; likewise, for all — or nearly all — contours used on questions. In other words, there appeared to be no question pitch as such (p. 59).

Over 40 years later, Bolinger (1986) still insisted on the independence of grammar from intonation:

> Intonation has more in common with gesture than with grammar..., though both gesture and intonation are tremendously important *to* grammar, as their lines intersect (p. viii).

Cruttenden (1986:59) states that "there is no such thing as 'question intonation' although some tones may be more common on questions than others." His first point is exemplified in the text by a *yes/no* question realized by four different tones: high-rising, low-rising, high-falling and low-falling. His second point (some tones may be more common on questions than others) is equally as important.

Throughout this study, it must be kept in mind that there is no such thing as unambiguous question intonation and that some tones may be more common on questions than others. The consensus of linguists who study intonation is that intonation cannot, *in itself,* unambiguously identify morphosyntactic forms as doing questioning (Couper-Kuhlen 1986, Bolinger 1986, 1989, Geluykens 1987, 1988, 1989b, Brown 1980). This does not mean, however, that intonation plays no role in the functional interpretation of any particular utterance; nor that there are no typical correlations between morphosyntactic forms and intonation contours for utterances which do questioning in discourse. It does mean, however, that there are *multiple* factors relevant to the interpretation of an utterance and that the *interaction* of these factors is important. The interaction of three factors — morphosyntactic form, intonation and sequential position — is the problematic issue for linguists who wish to specify the relationship between form and function.

When the relationship of morphosyntactic form and intonation to question function is at issue, it is important to distinguish whether the relationship is in the "real world" or in the "linguistics' world." In the real world where people talk and sometimes ask questions, intonation and morphosyntactic form are inseparable.[2] In this world when people produce an utterance, what they say (words in a certain order) and how they say it (the intonation contour) constitute the utterance. The particular interpretation of an utterance in regard to its communicative function is grounded in the experience of its morphosyntactic form spoken in its particular intonation contour. The spoken utterance is experienced whole, without seams, in regard to its morphosyntactic form and its intonation contour.

In the linguistics' world, morphosyntactic form and intonation are separable analytically; therefore, an utterance may be considered from the perspective of its morphosyntactic form apart from its intonation contour. For example, the morphosyntactic form of an utterance can be described without mentioning its intonation. This kind of description may include the following: syntactic clause type, the order of constituents, features of the subject (person, number), features of the verb (tense, polarity), etc.

In summary, the distinction between utterances in the real world (which are produced and experienced as a unity) and utterances in the linguistics' world (linguistic forms analyzed in terms of individual linguistic factors) is significant when the relationship between morphosyntactic form and intonation is considered in realizing communicative function. This study analytically focuses on the role of morphosyntactic form in the interpretation of utterances doing questioning. There are no *general* claims made about the relative weight of morphosyntactic elements, intonation contour or sequential position. In Chapter 8, however, I will present *particular* instances in which a change in one or more factors can change the functional interpretation of the utterance itself. (Intonation patterns associated with declarative clause questions will be discussed in Chapter 4.)

### 1.6. Approaches to Language in its Social Context

This section reviews:

- Philosophers who have recognized the social function of language;
- Linguists who have recognized that the functional aspects of language-in-use are relevant to linguistic analysis;
- Sociologists who have described the uses of language-in-interaction; and
- Other disciplines which have studied language in its social context.

#### 1.6.1. Emotive Theory of Ethics

Philosophers who are concerned with the meaning of evaluative words (Ogden and Richards 1923) and the emotive theory of ethics (Ayer 1936, Stevenson 1944) have proposed that evaluative terms are used to express emotion. Thus, they recognize that language serves social functions. Urmson (1968) presents a review of the literature which serves as the basis of the emotive theory of ethics.

#### 1.6.2. Speech Act Theory

Philosophers who write about the philosophy of language (Austin 1962, Searle 1969, 1975, 1979) have noted various aspects of the form/function problem (speech-act theory recognizes the functional aspect of language). In *Speech Acts* (1969), Searle hypothesizes that to speak a language is to engage in rule-governed intentional behavior:

> The form that this hypothesis will take is that speaking a language is performing speech acts, acts such as making statements, giving commands, asking questions, making promises, and so on; and more abstractly, acts such as referring and predicating; and secondly, that these acts are in general made possible by and performed in accordance with certain rules for the use of linguistic elements (p. 16).

Searle describes the form/function problem in terms of meaning, *viz.*, how things mean what they mean and how hearers understand what is meant. He identifies the unit of linguistic communication as the speech act which is a function of the meaning of a sentence. There are necessary and sufficient conditions for the performance of particular speech acts. From these conditions, rules are established for the use of linguistic devices which define a speech act as a particular type. The problem lies, first in determining the conditions relevant to each particular type of speech act and then in extracting the rules which give the sentence its force of action (illocutionary force).

Linguistic devices signal the differences among particular kinds of speech acts, although not in a one-to-one relationship; and utterances can realize more than one particular type of speech act. The particular force of action of any speech act is generated by the interaction between rules relating to linguistic forms and necessary and sufficient conditions (Owen 1984).

In *Expression and Meaning* (1979), Searle deals with the question: "How many ways of using language are there?" (p. vii), *i.e.*, how many types of speech acts can be realized? Searle proposes that there are five general ways of using language; utterances can be assertives, directives, commissives, expressives and declaratives. In assertives, the speaker tells people how things are. In directives, the speaker tries to get them to do things. In commissives, the speaker commits him/herself to doing things. In expressives, the speaker expresses his/her feelings and attitudes. In declaratives, the speaker brings about changes in the world via utterances.

Because utterances can be categorized as belonging to more than one category of speech-act type, the problem is: How do speakers and hearers know which particular speech act is in force? In other words, how do speakers produce the form which will accomplish the speech act they intend, and how do hearers understand which particular type of speech act is in force?

Searle's formulation of the form/function problem springs from certain assumptions about the relationship of meaning and linguistic form. Meaning is inherent in the form itself; it is in some way "given," rather than negotiated. The problem is: How do hearers manage to understand the meaning? This "given" meaning is actually the literal meaning of the utterance. This notion of meaning relates to the idea of a null context (see Garfinkel 1967, Rommetveit 1974).

The literal meaning is contrasted with the speaker's intended meaning in any particular context. Because the force of action (or illocutionary force) of a speech act (what it is doing) is a function of its meaning, the force of an utterance is also somehow inherent in its form. This force, then, will vary with the intended meaning. Thus, speakers and hearers must move from the literal meaning of an utterance to its implied or intended meaning. This concept can also be stated as the force of action of speech acts. Speakers and hearers must move from the direct force of an utterance to its indirect force, *i.e.*, what the utterance may be doing in any particular context.

The work of philosophers who have developed the speech-act approach to language is relevant in this study because these writers clearly recognize that using language involves doing something. In *How to Do Things with Words* (1962), Austin states that the proper object of study is not the sentence but the utterance in its speech situation.

Searle also notes that as a social action, the utterance is the basic unit of communication:

> The unit of linguistic communication is not, as has been generally supposed, the symbol, word or sentence, but rather the production or issuance of the symbol or word or sentence in the performance of the speech act. To take the token as a message is to take it as a produced or issued message. More precisely, the production or issuance of a sentence token under certain conditions is a speech act, and speech acts ... are the basic or minimal units of linguistic communication (p. 16).

The speech-act approach to language, however, is different from the present study because speech-act theorists base their work on language *not* produced by participants in interactional situations. It is, rather, language which is supposed to constitute plausible responses for hypothesized contexts. Because this study concentrates on the relationship between linguistic form and communicative function, the forms examined are those in real time actually responsive to the ongoing existential communicative situation constructed by the participants. In this sense, the data consist of real talk while the speech-act philosophers study imagined talk.

This difference in the origins of data has significant consequences for functions ascribed to linguistic acts. The function of any utterance is crucially dependent upon its sequential position in the talk in which it is produced because functions (*e.g.*, questions and answers) are interactional units, not linguistic or grammatical units (Sacks 1965, Sinclair 1966, Schegloff 1984, Coulthard and Brazil 1979:88, Owen 1984:46-48).

When language is isolated from the communicative situation, it is impossible to discover what speakers are doing or how the language is being used. Interactional functions cannot be attributed to individual sentences when plausible contexts are merely imagined. In an analysis of remedial exchanges in English conversation, Owen (1984) concludes that it is simply not possible to analyze a transcript of a conversation in speech-act terms, *i.e.*, speech-act theory does not offer any techniques for discovering the acts which are being performed (see Turner 1975). In terms of remedial exchanges (consisting of primings, apologies and responses), it was not possible to assign primings and responses an illocutionary function. These functions were discoverable only on the basis of their sequential position in the talk.

*1.6.3. Discourse Analysis*

Anthropologists and linguists, as interested in meaning as form, recognize functional aspects of language, *e.g.* Malinowski (1923, 1935), Firth (1935), Pike (1954), Bolinger (1952, 1954, 1977). Sinclair and Coulthard (1975) review the literature relevant to issues of language function and the structure of discourse. Prior to 1975, very little work within linguistics was concerned with language-in-context, the functional aspects of particular utterances or the functional structure of the discourse as a whole.

Givón (1979) reviews the scant early work on discourse. In 1966, Sinclair proposed that only by examining "real" utterances in the context in which they were produced can their meanings be understood. Friedrich (1979 [1966]) employed the notion of the context of speech events. Weinreich (1980 [1964]) conducted semantic research and recognized the importance of discourse for the study of meaning. The sociolinguistic approach of Labov (1964, 1966, 1972a, b) made the study of everyday talk a central concern. Diver (1969, 1975) and his students developed form-content analysis based on characteristics of human communication and behavior (García 1975, Kirsner 1969 and 1972, Reid 1974). Grimes (1968, 1971, 1970, 1975) and Longacre (1968, 1972) pioneered work on the organization of texts above the level of the sentence. Bloom (1970, 1976 [1973]) examined form and function in emerging grammars via analyses of audio- and videotaped interactions of mother/child.

In regard to spoken texts, the sequential determination of discourse function was clearly recognized. Malcolm Coulthard (1977) states:

> The structure, or constraints on the next speaker, cannot be expressed in grammatical terms; however, the linguistic form of the utterance is almost irrelevant; what is structurally important is its linguistic function and it is evidence of this kind which points to the existence of another level, discourse, between grammar and nonlinguistic organization. Sequences, which from a grammatical viewpoint are a random succession of clauses of different types can be seen from a functional viewpoint to be highly structured (p. 7).

In the past decade, linguists doing discourse analysis have used both written and spoken language-in-context to describe how language actually functions. Linguists have been interested particularly in how morphosyntactic forms function in various discourse genres and how texts of different discourse genres are structured.

*1.6.4. Conversation Analysis*

Schegloff (1984) argues that making explicit the relationship between language and social action, as in speech-act theory, is misguided. He exemplifies the flaws in this approach by discussing the relationship between forms which do questioning and interrogative forms. Schegloff refers to doing questioning as an action of a certain type. If questions (as forms of action) could be described solely in linguistic terms, a bridge between language and social behavior would be possible. This view of categories of action in terms of linguistic form is misleading, he states, because interactional categories of action (questions/answers, offers/acceptances) are common-sense categories, not technical ones. In other words, questions cannot be identified on the basis of linguistic devices. Schegloff makes the point that any analysis omitting the sequential position in the discourse of an utterance will be unable to determine its use (what its recipients make of it and do about it).

For the analyst interested in language use, the first problem is identifying the utterances which are questions, *i.e.*, doing questioning in the talk. This problem is not merely academic — any participant in conversation faces the same problem. If asked a question, a participant must "answer."

To summarize, in contrast to speech-act theorists, it is not linguistic form which enables participants or analysts to make a judgment regarding the function of an utterance, rather it is the sequential organization of conversation in terms of adjacency-pair structure (Schegloff and Sacks 1973, Sacks, Schegloff and Jefferson 1974).

Adjacency pairs are sequences which are related in terms of a typology:

> The typology operates in two ways: it partitions utterance types into "first pair parts" (*i.e.*, first parts of pairs) and second pair parts; and it affiliates a first pair part and a second pair part to form a "pair type." "Question-answer," "greeting-greeting," "offer-acceptance/refusal," are instances of pair types. A given sequence will thus be composed of an utterance that is a first pair produced by one speaker directly followed by the production by a different speaker of an utterance which is a) a second pair part, and b) is from the same pair type as the first utterance in the sequence is a member of (Schegloff and Sacks 1973:296-96, quoted in Schegloff 1984:33).

Adjacency-pair sequences exhibit not only relative ordering of parts but also discriminative relationships between their parts. In other words, the pair parts belong to the same type. It is this feature of adjacency-pair organization which makes an *answer* relevant to a question, whereas an acceptance or refusal would not be relevant.

Schegloff (1984) further suggests that linguistic form is not important in the action interpretation of an utterance. Regarding questions as a category of action, he remarks:

> One consequence of this discussion, to my mind, is that not only is the path from linguistic questions to interactional ones not a straight line, but that not much may lie at its end. For a substantial part of what we might expect to be available to us as understanding of questions as a category of action is best and most parsimoniously subsumed under the category "adjacency pairs"; much of what is so about questions is so by virtue of the adjacency-pair format. And what distinguishes questions from first pair parts of other sorts does not seem in any straightforward way to be sought from linguistic resources (p. 34).

The problem of form and function dissolves when function is interpreted solely from sequential position. For the problem to exist, the interpretation of function must be dependent on or related to linguistic form. The problem lies in explicitly stating that relationship. The conversation analyst's approach represented by Schegloff (1984) assumes that linguistic form is *not* significant for the interpretation of communicative function. (Communicative function is interpreted on the basis of an utterance's sequential position in the talk.) Participants are constrained to construct their utterances "to show attention to, and understanding of, their placement." In other words, an utterance is constructed to demonstrate that its speaker has attended to the prior utterance or sequence of utterances.

Schegloff makes the following argument to support this claim. In considering questions realized by interrogative forms, the problem is not only the issue of how an interrogative form can do something other than questioning, but also how it does questioning. Even in those cases where an utterance doing questioning is realized by an interrogative linguistic form, the form *itself* cannot account for the function because such forms can also realize other functions (invitations, requests, commands). Schegloff uses the same reasoning to propose that functions (categories of action) are interpretable in terms of adjacency-pair structure and not linguistic form. Linguistic form stands as a "last resort" function. Interpretive procedures may rely on form as a last resort to resolve ambiguity.

Schegloff and Sacks (1973) discuss the placement of utterances. They state that in some instances, placement considerations alone are crucial to determine function:

> Past and current work has indicated that placement considerations are general for utterances. That is: a pervasively relevant issue (for participants) about utterances in conversation is 'why that now', a question whose analysis may ... also be relevant to finding out what 'that' is. That is to say, some utterances may derive their character as actions entirely from placement considerations (p. 299).

Further, participants can find an answer to be an answer *only* by reference to its sequential placement, *i.e.*, after a question. No appeal to phonological, syntactic, semantic or logical features of the utterance will identify it as an answer.

Goffman (1981) notes that a problem with Schegloff and Sacks' formulation is that questions will have to be determined in the same manner (by reference to sequence). This concept also does not allow that what followed a question was not an answer to it; whereas, utterances following questions can fail pointedly as answers, can be meant to fail as answers and can be understood as not being proper answers.

Further, although answers may not be marked by phonological, syntactic, semantic or logical features (which help recipients decide if an utterance is an answer), they are indeed typically marked (Bolinger 1957:6-7):

...to say that an answer of a sort can certainly be provided to a prior question without employing the conventional markers of an answer (and that the slot itself must be attended, not what apparently gets put into it) need not deny that answers will *typically* be marked phonologically, syntactically, semantically, etc. and that these markers will be looked to as a means of deciding that what has been said is an answer (p. 51).

Because participants do not recognize questions by reference to their answers, we can still ask how they do recognize or interpret an utterance as a question when they hear one being done. Questions and answers, as discussed above, are a pair type subsumed under the category of adjacency pairs. The production of a first-pair part by a speaker makes the production of a second-pair part by a recipient relevant. The operation of this type of structure in conversation requires "the recognizability of first pair part status for some utterances" (Schegloff and Sacks 1973:296). Recipients must recognize the first-pair part status of an utterance in order to produce a relevant second-pair part from "the pair type of which the first is recognizably a member" (Schegloff and Sacks 1973:299).

The existence of insert sequences (Schegloff 1972) demonstrates that questions can be produced immediately after other questions; and as such are not misinterpreted by their recipients as answers to the prior question. The placement of an utterance after a first-pair part doing questioning does not necessitate that the utterance be interpretable as an answer, nor does it preclude that the utterance is interpretable as a question. Some questions have another question as their preferred answer, as in *You know what? What?* (Sacks 1972a:230).

In these cases, how do recipients know the utterance following a question is not an answer but another question? This is, of course, a participant's problem as well, but not one which causes any real difficulty — participants recognize questions even when they appear after other questions. Participants in conversation, then, must not rely on sequential position alone in order to interpret an utterance's function. Schegloff and Sacks (1973) suggest that the problem of recognizability for questions can be handled "constructionally, as when the syntax of an utterance can be used to recognize that a question is being produced" (p. 296). In this study, I will examine how syntax interacts with sequential position in the production of utterances doing questioning.

*1.6.5. Other Disciplines*

The study of discourse has not been limited to linguistics. Such disciplines as anthropology, semiotics, poetics, psychology, sociology and communication research have all investigated language-in-use, both written and spoken. Van Dijk (1985) presents the historical background and relevant literature for the analysis of talk produced in a social context. In his comprehensive introduction to *Discourse and Dialogue* (the third volume of *Handbook of Discourse Analysis*), the author traces the development of the study of language in its interactional context within sociology and anthropology. Within these fields, the following areas have all been concerned with discourse: phenomenology, cognitive sociology, microsociology, ethnomethodology, symbolic interactionism, the sociology of everyday life, formal sociology and the ethnography of speaking (Schiffrin 1987:1-2, 11-12).

## 1.7. Conclusion

When the interactional function of an utterance is described as question function or doing questioning, many linguists recognize there is no one-to-one relationship between morphosyntactic form and communicative function. While interrogative forms are associated typically with doing questioning, any morphosyntactic form in the appropriate context can serve the same function. The communicative function doing questioning has been far too undifferentiated to be of any value in examining the relationship of form and function in discourse.

Stenström (1984) confirms that a variety of morphosyntactic forms can function as questions; and both rising and falling intonation co-occur with these various forms (see also Geluykens 1987, 1988, 1989b). Schiffrin (1987) comments on the relationship between speech acts and morphosyntactic form as follows:

> This lack of fit between act and syntactic form suggests that interactionally situated language use is sensitive to constraints quite independent of syntax (as, indeed, many speech act theorists have shown (p. 32).

Given the variation in morphosyntactic forms which do questioning in discourse, how do the so-called *nontypical* morphosyntactic forms get interpreted as doing questioning? Although lexical elements may serve as indicators of question function (Bolinger 1957, Stenström 1984), how do nontypical morphosyntactic forms *without* lexical indicators get interpreted? If the morphosyntax of the form does not suggest question function, how is the interpretation made? Note: this final question involves the interaction of morphosyntactic form, sequential position and the role of intonation in the interpretation of question function.

Being a pragmatist, I assume there is no difference which does not make a difference. Given this, I cannot happily accept that the morphosyntactic form used to do questioning makes *no* difference, *i.e.*, that different forms are functionally interchangeable. Thus, we may also ask why speakers choose one question form vs. another — in other words, what discourse environments condition the choice of different question forms (Stenström 1984).

My initial assumption was that different morphosyntactic forms must correlate with different functions, however subtly. If gross functional classifications like doing questioning did not show obvious correlations with morphosyntactic form, I projected that perhaps a close examination of the data would reveal more finely grained patterns (Goody 1978). On the basis of the literature, I assumed the nontypical question forms (noninterrogative questions) would exhibit no correlation with morphosyntactic elements which might play a role in their interpretation as questions. The literature clearly maintains that with the exception of certain lexical indicators such correlations do not exist; and this lack is treated as a problematic issue. An examination of naturally occurring conversational discourse reveals, however, that noninterrogative question forms do correlate regularly with morphosyntactic elements which may play a role in their interpretation as questions.

Linguistic form and question function exhibit correlations which are more transparent than the literature would lead us to believe. In terms of several simply specified procedures well established in the linguistic literature, noninterrogative question forms (without morphosyntactic elements which may play a role in their interpretation as questions) are, indeed, interpretable as questions.

In this study, I will describe a number of lexical and morphosyntactic elements which realize, or are closely associated with, noninterrogative forms functioning as questions. The relevant elements occur either within the noninterrogative forms, immediately prior and/or subsequent to them. In this work, I will refer to these lexical and morphosyntactic elements as "markers associated with question function." These markers[3] are associated with question function by virtue of the fact that they co-occur with noninterrogative forms which function as questions. *This terminology makes no claim that the lexical or morphosyntactic element itself is occasioning or forcing the interpretation of the form as a question.*

In the "real world," an utterance is experienced as a "package" in regard to its morphosyntactic form, its intonation contour and its sequential position in the discourse. Morphosyntactic elements which realize, or are closely associated with, an utterance are available as a resource for the recipient to interpret the utterance. Any morphosyntactic element which realizes, or is closely associated with, a noninterrogative form doing questioning is playing some role in the interpretation of that utterance. The element is relevant to interpretive procedures by virtue of the fact that it is part of the utterance which the speaker constructs to realize question function at that moment in the conversation. It is a part of the design of the utterance "package."

In summary, this study will show that recipients in conversation have access to a variety of lexical and morphosyntactic elements as well as intonation and sequential positioning when interpreting noninterrogative morphosyntactic forms which do questioning. These variables interact to unambiguously signal question function. Thus, for noninterrogative utterances doing questioning in this study, there is a good correlation between linguistic form (in conjunction with sequential position and intonation) and communicative function.

# Chapter 2

# Analytical Procedures and Principles

## 2.1. General Procedures

In this study, I will examine the relation between morphosyntactic form and communicative function by analyzing *noninterrogative* functional questions in English conversational data. I will:

(1) Identify all those linguistic forms in the data which do questioning on the basis of their function in the talk;
(2) Classify all the functional questions in the data on the basis of their morphosyntactic form as interrogative questions, declarative questions or nonclausal questions;
(3) Discuss the role of morphosyntactic form in the interpretation of declarative questions and nonclausal questions, *i.e.*, *noninterrogative* questions; and
(4) Examine the interactional goals these forms satisfy, *i.e.*, examine their uses in the interaction.

*2.1.1. The Database*

The database is composed of audiotaped English conversations among participants who know each other as acquaintances, friends or family members. The data can be classed as follows:

- Face-to-face and telephone conversations which have been collected and transcribed by others and have been provided by Emanuel Schegloff; and
- Dinner-table conversations collected and transcribed by Elizabeth G. Weber and/or Marian Shapley (see Chapter 3 for a detailed description of each conversation and for coding procedures).

"Conversation" is all those forms of talk-in-interaction which do not involve some special rights/obligations/constraints. These conversations were not produced for research purposes but occurred in the course of natural (vs. laboratory) interaction. Because all but one of the face-to-face interactions have *not* been videotaped, a record of the visual dimension of the interaction does not exist. To date, however, there is no evidence that audiotaped data are seriously inadequate as objects of linguistic analysis (Owen 1984:3-4; see also Goodwin 1979).

In telephone conversations, the participants and the analyst are limited, of course, to the audio portion of the interaction. No evidence exists that telephone conversations (as opposed to face-to-face ones) are an inadequate source for studying language-in-use.

## 2.1.2. Reasons for Studying Utterances Doing Questioning

I have chosen utterances which do questioning as the object of this study for several reasons:

(1) Functional questions appear quite frequently in everyday conversational discourse;

(2) They are relatively easy to identify using one's native speaker capacities in conjunction with the analytical techniques of conversation analysis. Note: those utterances which are ambiguous for the analyst with respect to question function are also ambiguous for the participants. (The ambiguity of such utterances is itself an additional source of insight into the relationship of linguistic form and question function.)

(3) Noninterrogative forms which do questioning are frequently cited in the literature as prototypical examples of the form/function problem discussed in Chapter 1.

## 2.1.3. Selectional Criteria for Utterances Doing Questioning

The criteria for selecting forms in this study are not morphosyntactic (inverted word order/presence of a *wh*-word), rather they include linguistic utterances of any syntactic form which can be interpreted as doing questioning in the interaction. In initially approaching the data, therefore, I had to look for instances of doing questioning without a preconceived notion of which specific functions would be involved in doing questioning. From the instances of the phenomena which I recognized, a profile of their functions began to emerge.

A phenomenon is not necessarily discoverable by the analyst in every instance it occurs. While developing a characterization of doing questioning, constant reexamination of the data is necessary — other instances of the phenomenon may become visible where previously opaque, allowing other aspects of function to be revealed. Thus, the selection process evolved over time and was intrinsically responsive to its own development. In short, selecting forms which are doing questioning was not a single task, nor was it based on preconceptions about how doing questioning is used in interaction (*e.g.*, requesting information) or what forms are used.

Accordingly, a broad concept of the action doing questioning was helpful. Utterances which are doing offers, invitations, requests, jokes, etc. in a question format are included in the data (Bolinger 1957:3-5). Note: this concept of doing questioning is broader than that which is held by conversation analysts.

Question/answer sequences constitute a particular adjacency-pair type which is distinguished from other adjacency-pair types such as invitation/acceptance or rejection, request/grant or denial, offer/acceptance or refusal (Chapter 1). The examples in this text are a broad sample of the kinds of utterances included in the data as doing questioning. For each example, the reader can evaluate the classification doing questioning while acquiring a concrete sense of the kinds of utterances included in the data.

The analysis of the data was influenced by an ethnomethodological analytical approach according to which speakers construct utterances which are doing questioning in such a manner that these utterances can be recognized as questions. In other words, utterances are recipient-designed (Sacks 1971). If a speaker wants to ask a question and receive an answer, s/he must do so in such a way that a recipient can interpret the utterance as a question. This approach suggests that recipients respond to utterances on the basis of what they interpret them as doing. In responding to questions, recipients construct their utterances in ways that can be recognized as responses *even if* these utterances do not constitute answers. There are, of course, ambiguous cases in which doing questioning may be only a possible interpretation. Finally, analysts are also native speakers and, therefore, can identify utterances constructed to be recognized as doing questioning, utterances which are constructed to be recognized as responding to questions and utterances which are ambiguous.

An examination of the participants' behavior to see if *they* considered the utterance to be doing questioning played a crucial part in deciding whether an utterance was selected for this study. In other words, was the utterance constructed by the speaker to be recognized as doing questioning? Was the recipient's response constructed to demonstrate that it was responding to a question? The recipient's response may have been constructed either to demonstrate that it is doing answering or to show an orientation to the utterance as a question in some other way. For example, the recipient might respond by professing ignorance (*I don't know*) when asked a question soliciting information. Of course, the only way to select an object which is doing questioning is to recognize it as such. The analyst must utilize his/her own interpretive capacities to describe:

- How questioners construct utterances so that recipients recognize them as doing questioning;
- How they respond if their questions are ignored;
- How recipients construct answers;
- How they evade answering; and
- How questioners respond if their questions are ignored (Bilmes 1985).

The issue of the data cannot be separated from the issue of usage. Particular kinds of interactional uses emerging from any analysis of data are grounded in the kinds of interactions which are the source of the data. Interactions are characterized by different speech exchange systems and different turn-taking systems. Family members talking over dinner use different turn-taking rules from participants in a courtroom or in a doctor-patient interaction during a medical examination (Tannen 1981b, Drew 1985, West 1984). Consequently, the ends to which speakers may exploit morphosyntactic form in a courtroom or a medical exam may differ significantly from those at a dinner party.

## 2.2. Organization of the Data

In considering the relationships between linguistic forms and communicative functions, discourse analysts must choose some system of classification to describe the forms and the functions. Linguistic forms are describable in terms of their prosodic organization and their syntactic organization. The communicative functions which linguistic forms realize must also be classified. Specifying the prosodic, syntactic and functional organization of the data is itself problematic (Coulthard 1977:x). With regard to the prosody, one of a number of possible systems of transcription must be chosen. Depending on this choice, certain features of the talk will be included in the data and others, excluded. With regard to the morphosyntax, a hierarchical order of organizing structure must be selected — syllable, word, phrase or clause. With regard to the functional classification of the data, the number of functional units, as well as their size, is an issue.

### 2.2.1. Morphosyntax

Utterances in the data which were identified as doing questioning were first classified either as constituting or not constituting a syntactic clause.

*2.2.1.1. Syntactic Clauses.* A subject and a complete finite verb phrase are the traditional criteria for clause structure, with the exception of imperative clauses without a subject. Those questions which fit these criteria were further classified by clause type. Note: the data consist of interrogative clauses and declarative clauses;

therefore, functional questions were never classified as imperative or exclamatory clauses.[1]

*Interrogative Clauses*

Interrogative clauses were classified according to traditional criteria (Chapter 1):

- *wh*-questions by a *wh*-word subject + verb phrase or
  A *wh*-word in another grammatical role + subject/verb inversion
- Yes/no questions by subject/verb inversion.

Note: for *yes/no* questions, when *only* the auxiliary verb is lacking or reduced because of phonological processes, utterances which have a syntactic declarative form but are interpretable as interrogative forms (example 1) were included in the data as interrogative forms (not as declarative forms).

In the following examples, the auxiliary *do* is not produced:

(1)  H    Y' 'know what I thought you "sai:d *hh=    ⇐
     N    [°What,
     H    [for food, hhhh hhhhhhh                      HGII 16:13

There are a number of criteria which can be used to make the distinction between declarative forms and those which are interpretable as interrogatives (*e.g.*, intonation, word order, the possibility of the presence or absence of *do* or *have*). It is not possible, however, to make this distinction in every case (Holmes 1985).

In these data, ambiguous cases were excluded, as in the example below. The intonation suggests that the utterance is constructed as the declarative clause of a tag question; however, the tag was not produced:

(2)  K    Speech acts.
          You know about "speech acts,                ⇐
     M    Yeah, I'm learning, this course.       Shapley/Nel 8:38

*Declarative Clauses*

Declarative clauses were classified according to traditional criteria:

- The subject precedes the verb.

Additionally, clauses with:

- *Only* a subject which is reduced but recoverable
- Lacking a subject which is unrecoverable but with a complete verb phrase
- Prior *how come* or *how about* + declarative clause

Note: in conversation subjects are often reduced or lacking as the result of phonological processes. If an utterance has a phonologically reduced subject or lacks *only* a subject which is recoverable from its form, it was classified as a declarative clause.

Example 3 exhibits a clause with a reduced subject, and example 4 illustrates a clause with a recoverable subject. The following example introduces a new topic:

```
(3)    N    Hello:?
            (.)
       H    Hi:,
            (.)
       N    HI::.
            (.)
       H    How are you =
       N    Fi:ne how are you,
            (.)
       H    Oka:[y,
       N        [Goo:d,
            (0.4)
       H    *mkhhh [hhh
       N           [What's doing,
            (.)
       H    aAh:, noth [i     n :,]
       N               [Y' didn't g ]o meet "
            Grahame?=
                                            ⇐
                                    HG II 1:17
```

Next, the utterance is made after another participant in the conversation reaches for a cracker:

```
(4)    W    "Couldn't resi:st, "huh:.       ⇐
                                    Riggenbach 3:63
```

This utterance is realized by a declarative clause plus a particle tag. The subject is interpretable as *you*. Declarative clauses with tags are traditionally referred to as tag questions; and tag questions do not satisfy the criteria for interrogative clauses. (In these cases, "question" refers to question function not to interrogative form.) In summary, when an utterance is lacking a subject which is recoverable from the form of the utterance, but contains a complete verb phrase, the utterance was classified as a declarative clause.

There are several cases in the data of declarative clauses introduced by subordinating conjunctions (*if, then, but* (example 29)). In conversation, it is not uncommon to find declarative clauses introduced by these subordinators unassociated with a "main" clause (Schiffrin 1987, Ford forthcoming).

Quirk *et al.* (1985:803) define interrogative clauses as introduced by a *wh*-word. Their criterion has been used in this study with one exception. Utterances with an initially positioned *how come* or *how about* plus a declarative clause have been classified as declaratives marked by a prior *wh*-word (example 62).

*2.2.1.2. Nonclausal Forms.* Nonclausal forms are distinguished from independent clausal forms by:

• The absence of both a subject and a complete finite verb phrase.

Nonclausal questions may be realized by particles (*huh*), words, *wh*-words (*who, what*) or phrases. We have seen that when an interrogative clause only lacks an auxiliary verb, it is still classified as an interpretable interrogative. Similarly, when a subject is reduced or lacking, the utterance is still classified as a declarative clause. When the subject and the auxiliary verb are both lacking in an utterance, however, it is classified as a nonclausal form, as in example 5:

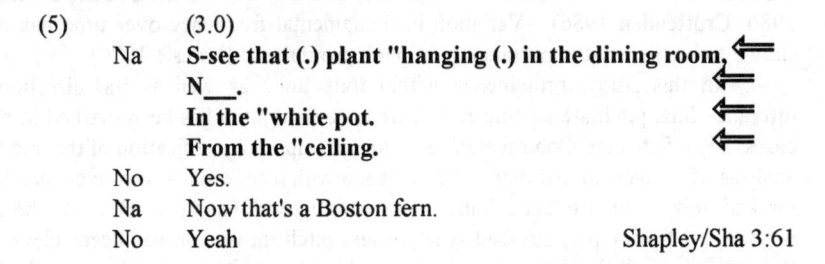

(5)          (3.0)
     Na    S-see that (.) plant "hanging (.) in the dining room, ⇐
            N__.                                                  ⇐
            **In the "white pot.**                                ⇐
            **From the "ceiling.**                                ⇐
     No    Yes.
     Na    Now that's a Boston fern.
     No    Yeah                                    Shapley/Sha 3:61

Note: this utterance has not been classified as an imperative clause even though it lacks a subject and the main verb is in its base form. The semantics of the verb *see* preclude the interpretation of this utterance as an imperative (Quirk *et al.* 1985:827). Rather, it is interpretable as an interrogative clause — *Do you see....* Because utterances are classified according to clause structure on the basis of their actual form and not their interpreted form (with the above mentioned exceptions), this utterance was classified as a nonclausal form because it lacks both a subject and a finite verb.

## 2.2.2. Intonation

A variety of communicative functions has been ascribed to intonation — the expression of emotion, the conveyance of a sense of completeness vs. incompleteness or certainty vs. uncertainty, the marking of important information and the organization of interaction, e.g., competition for the floor (Shapley 1987). Several types of intonational cues are discussed in the literature.

Register refers to basic pitch level and is measured over a stretch of discourse rather than in a single clause or intonational unit. This dimension has been associated with emotional interpretation (sorrow or joy) (Fónagy 1978).

Intonation contour refers to the relative heights of earlier or later pitch peaks and is usually measured over the duration of a clause. Bolinger (1986) associates various contour patterns with basic meanings (finished vs. unfinished). A larger intonational unit, a period of pitch peaks over time, has been associated with the organization of information on a particular topic in discourse. These informational units are measured over several utterances in reference to pitch peaks and have been termed paratones (Fox 1973), tone sequences (Brazil 1985), prosodic groups (Gibbon 1984) and subordinating sequences (Crystal 1969).

Consisting of one nuclear or phrasal stress, tone units characterize continuous speech (a prominence and optional nonprominent material precede and follow the unit) (Crystal 1975, Pierrehumbert 1980, Halliday 1985).

Pitch level, loudness, duration and tempo have been associated with the perception of stress. Perceived stress, or prominence, is linked to changes in the acoustic variables of fundamental frequency, intensity and duration (Couper-Kuhlen 1986, Cruttenden 1986). Variation in fundamental frequency over time has been shown to be the most important cue to pitch prominence (Lehiste 1970).

In this study, prominence within tone units as well as the direction of utterance final pitch are significant.[2] Utterance final pitch has been marked in most cases. (See Schuetze-Coburn et al 1991 for an empirical justification of the auditory analysis of conversational data.) Prominence within tone units, however, has been marked only in the utterance doing questioning in each example. Because the data is collected from tapes, stressed syllables and pitch movement has been relevant in the analysis of all the data. Prominence within tone units has not been marked on every utterance because such markings inhibit readers unfamiliar with transcripts. This is significant because it has always been my goal to make this work as accessible as possible to both linguists and nonlinguists (see Du Bois et al. 1992).

Linguists have been unable to reach a consensus on the best way to represent prominence and pitch direction within tone units. Cruttenden (1986) cites a number of systems in use among linguists to mark intonation: Pike 1945; Trager and Smith 1957 [1951]; Halliday 1967, 1970; O'Connor and Arnold 1973; and Cruttenden 1986. Nonlinguists have also added even more options for representing intonation. Many ethnomethodologists, for example, follow the transcription notation devised by Gail Jefferson (Sacks, Schegloff and Jefferson 1974). Note: no matter how detailed a transcript is in regard to intonation, it never captures the essence of the interaction (Ong 1967, 1977, Esau 1982). My initial exposure to conversation analysis convinced me of this. Despite the many insights from the transcript, which was coded for prosody according to Jefferson's notation, the light and playful nature of the entire interaction was totally absent. Only listening to the tape revealed that aspect of the interaction.

*2.2.3. Communicative Functions*

Studies of language-in-context also differ when classifying what an utterance is doing in discourse. Searle (1979:vii) rejected Wittgenstein's suggestion that language has countless functions and proposed that five general categories of speech-act functions were sufficient to describe language use: assertives, directives, commissives, expressives and declaratives. Conversation analysts utilize common-sense categories: offer, request, acceptance/rejection, complaint, invitation, compliment and agreement/ disagreement; and they do not discuss the number of possible functional categories.

In an approach to discourse analysis represented by Sinclair and Coulthard (1975) and Coulthard (1977), the category *act* is postulated. Acts are defined by their function in the discourse in a very general way; and function encompasses what the act responded to in the prior discourse and initiates in the subsequent discourse (Coulthard 1977:104). For example, the act *elicitation* functions to request a linguistic response, while the act *directive* functions to request a nonlinguistic response. Although acts are very general descriptions of social actions, at a secondary stage of analysis, a concept of "delicacy " may be applied to general classifications. By means of this concept, finer distinctions can be made among acts of the same general type if the responses to the acts initiated warrant a distinction. This system of discourse analysis makes use of only 22 types of acts.

Goldberg (1983) proposed categorizing utterances as moves relating the referents in the utterance to the referents in the prior utterance or utterances. The four move types postulated are:

- Introducing,
- Reintroducing,
- Progressive-holding, and
- Holding.

This system of assigning discourse function relies on participant-tracking in the discourse.

The present study differs from some other studies because it does not impose a preconceived set of functions on the data. Functions which emerge from an examination of the data involve both the organization of information and the management of social relationships. The examination of any form takes into account as many of the preceding sequences as the analysis can justify. In other words, I have no preconceived notions as to how much of the preceding talk may be relevant for the analysis of any particular form.

## 2.3. Analytical Procedures

The analytical procedures used in approaching the data involve four questions. The first question is the conversation analyst's question: *Why this now?* (or what is the utterance doing in the interaction). This question emphasizes the sequential, temporal structure of the talk-in-interaction and recognizes that an utterance gets its force of action from its position in a sequence. Note: interpretive procedures make crucial reference to this sequential position.

The second question is Ragmar Rommetveit's (1974) question: *What is made known?* Like the first, this question respects the indexical nature of talk. What is made known by an utterance depends on what is assumed to be known, what has made the context and what the utterance intends to make the context. *Context is what is taken for granted rather than explicitly articulated in the talk.* Information is interpreted in terms of what has gone before, how it is nested and which context it intends to activate. This concept of information is related to the information status of linguistic elements, *e.g.*, newly activated, previously semi-activated, previously already activated (Chafe 1984), but not limited to it. In this sense, information involves what gets said in relation to what has or has not been said and potentially what could be said (Tyler 1978).

Language is not assumed to be responsive to a given social context; rather, language itself constitutes the context as well as being responsive to it. A social reality, which is partially shared and intersubjectively established, is assumed to be both a prerequisite and a consequence of communication. This social reality is the context to which the talk is indexical; and it is in reference to this context that interpretation takes place (Stewart 1978).

Relevancy is also an aspect of social context. What counts as relevant in any situation is not a given, but socially constructed (also Sacks 1972b). Answers to questions are so by virtue of being relevant (in some way). Some utterances following questions are understood as improper answers; therefore, a relevant answer is a matter of social accomplishment.

The third question I used in approaching the data is the linguist's question: *Why this form now?* or in what way is the form responsive to the interactional needs of the situation. This question is asking how the form in that particular sequential position is contributing to what the utterance is doing. In other words, I am asking "why a given form is effective for the job in which it is employed" (Goody 1978:2). Goody suggests that an interest in how forms do their job can be characterized as an interest in the "tactics of social interaction."

The fourth question is the pragmatist's question: *What consequences does the use of this form have?* (How does it leave its mark in the talk?) This question is asking how other participants understand specific elements of the form in the interaction (what affect it has). This question is intended to be sensitive to the form itself (Dale *et al.* 1978, Levelt and Kelter 1982).

This last question is not to be confused with the conversation analyst's interest in what participants make of an utterance, *i.e.*, how participants respond to an utterance as an interactional move or social action. By virtue of participants' responses to an utterance, the analyst is justified, in part, in categorizing the utterance as a social action. For example, the conversation analyst can describe an utterance as a first-pair part doing questioning on the basis of a recipient's production of a second-pair part doing answering. The answer shows how the recipient understood the first-pair part, *i.e.*, that it was interpreted as a question.

## 2.4. Organization of Conversation

This study makes reference to a number of important aspects of the organization of conversation which have been described by ethnomethodologists in numerous publications (Jefferson 1972, Sacks, Schegloff and Jefferson 1974, Schegloff 1979, 1981, 1984, Schegloff and Sacks 1973, Schegloff, Jefferson and Sacks 1977, Schenkein 1978, Goodwin and Goodwin 1986, 1987, 1992, Lerner 1989, 1991, Schegloff 1987, 1989, 1990, 1992, Tsui 1989).

### 2.4.1. Sequence Structure

Conversation is organized in terms of adjacency-pair structure which operates across two turns (Chapter 1). Sequences of adjacency pairs do not reflect random bits of talk; instead, they display a coherent organization. This organization is interpretable as (Levinson 1983, Heritage 1984):

- Pre-expansions,
- Post-expansions or
- Insert sequences.

### 2.4.2. Turn-Taking Procedures

The turn-taking procedures which operate in conversation have been described by Sacks, Schegloff and Jefferson (1974; Levinson 1981:296). These procedures are organized normatively so that one person talks at a time.

## 2.4.3. Repair Phenomena

Participants in conversation need to have a way of dealing with repair phenomena; and the organization of repair has been described by Schegloff, Jefferson and Sacks (1977) (see also Weber & Baltaxe in press and Schegloff 1987, 1992). Because many of the utterances doing questioning in this study are functioning to initiate repair, this aspect of conversational organization will be given an extended discussion.

Repair refers to the efforts of participants to deal with trouble in speaking, hearing or understanding. Repair is central to the work of interaction and is organized by the turn-taking system of the speech exchange system in which it occurs. Because this study is based on conversational data, the repair organization discussed is relevant to this least-constrained speech exchange system. In dealing with repair phenomena, the distinction must be made between understanding the world and understanding the talk, *i.e.*, what is said.

Repair in conversation is not error correction; therefore, it is not necessary to have a theory of error before dealing with repair. Some errors in conversation do not get repaired; and not all repairs follow an independently established error although repair may involve correction. Further, repair may be prompted by factors not considered to be errors, *e.g.*, extraneous noise.

Repairs are instigated by trouble in the talk. Trouble in speaking includes word searches, articulation difficulties, intonation or stress problems and the reordering of elements in an utterance. (Trouble in *speaking* is just one kind of troubled talk.) The distribution of repairs can be characterized in terms of turns of talk. Repairs can occur in the same turn as the trouble source, the transition space before the next turn, the next turn after the trouble source or the third or fourth turns after the trouble source. For the speaker of the trouble source, the opportunities for repair occur in the same turn, in the transition space between a turn and a next turn and in the third turn. For the recipient of the trouble source utterance, the opportunity for repair is in the next turn and fourth turn. These opportunities for repair are structured into the talk itself.

Repair can be discussed in terms of two factors:

- Who initiates it — the speaker of the trouble source or someone else;
- Who resolves it — the speaker of the trouble source or someone else.

When repair processes are initiated by the speaker within a turn, the repair is exhibited in the disruption — however minimal — of a projected turn. The repair initiator itself, once it is done, signals trouble. Repair initiators for self-initiated repairs consist of a limited set of devices. In English, these devices include the glottal stop, sound preservations and *uh*. They must show disjunction between what has gone before and what is to come. The repair itself is built to display the trouble source.

The following example exhibits a same-turn repair:

(6)  N   I did fee-   ⇐
         ah what I "felt is,   ⇐
         I pushed 'A__ to the "wa:ll,
         so that she was "always unhappy.           Weber 10 :165

When repair is initiated by a participant other than the speaker, the utterance initiating the repair occupies "one main position: the turn just subsequent to the trouble source turn" (Schegloff, Jefferson, and Sacks 1977:367). These repair initiators are *next-turn repair initiators* (NTRI's) and locate the trouble source. When a repair is initiated after the trouble-source turn by a participant in the next turn, the projected sequence of the talk is interrupted in order to deal with the repair. Repairs, then, disrupt the projected sequence of the talk. When there are multiple speakers involved in the interaction, if initiation is not done in the next turn, a participant may lose the chance to signal a problem. On the other hand, subsequent talk may clarify the trouble.

The following example includes a NTRI:

(7)  P   Is it like the first time they dated?
     J   "Huh?                                     ⇐
     P   It's like the first time that (.)
         it was like a date?                       Kinjo 6:10

In terms of sequence structure, NTRI's may be insert sequences or post-expansions. These utterances are the least restricted utterance type since they can appear any time. NTRI's locate the trouble source — the repairable element — in the prior utterance and nothing more (see also Chapter 7). Even if nothing has been actually said by another participant but only imagined, NTRI's can result. NTIR's indicate the grasp a speaker has on the trouble-source utterance, *i.e.*, how much is comprehended and how much needs to be repeated.

NTRI's have been described as echo questions in the linguistic literature. Cruttenden (1986:92) states that echoes are "most commonly questions which query the whole or some part of the previous utterance of another speaker, often with a note of incredulity...." He also notes that echo questions often take a high-rise intonation contour, while exclamations take a rise-fall. In both cases, the nucleus of the tone falls on old information. This old information, then, is interpretable as having special significance for the speaker.

In the case of same-turn repairs, the speaker is usually the one who effects the repair, although other speakers may overlap or interrupt the speaker within an ongoing turn. Repair initiated within a turn is generally completed in the same turn. Multiple repair spaces emerge as the utterance is constructed through time. In short, everything is repairable. Recipients must decide whether what comes next is more turn or is doing repair, *i.e.*, repairing something which has come before.

Transition-space repairs occur between turns — the time when it is not clearly the speaker's turn; yet, the next speaker has not begun. A transition-space repair is incremental to the previous turn. These increments in the transition space, however, do not further the interaction; instead, they "fix" a previous statement and make no claims for more turn. By definition, these repairs are self-initiated. Speakers can be oriented to possible misunderstandings within a turn, or they can become aware of them later in the transition space:

(8)  N   I don't know,
         I'm dy::ing to know what happened up the street.
         We had the who:le thing going on with my friend
         (0.2)
         **[who's up the ] "stree:t.=**           ⇐
     L   [with J___? ]
     N   =Yeah.                                    Weber 8:116

N's transition-space repair, which clarifies the referent of *my friend*, is overlapped by L's NTRI which locates trouble with the referent of *my friend*. Recipients often provide speakers with a chance for self-repair by pausing before an NTRI.

Repair can also occur at third and fourth-turn positions. Third-turn repairs are effected by the speaker of the first turn (the trouble-source) and are usually completed within the third turn. A distinction can be made between real third turns and incidental third turns which are preceded by recipient feedback, *e.g.*, *mm hm*. Example 9 exhibits a real third-turn repair and example 10 exhibits an incidental third-turn repair:

(9)  J   Is it goin to be at your house?
     B   Yeah.=
     J   **=Your apartment?=**                    ⇐
     B   =My place.=                         Schegloff NYI: 3-4

(10) B   hhh And he's going to make his own paintings,
     A   mm hm
     B   **and- or I mean his own frames.**       ⇐
     A   yeah                              Schegloff SBL 1: 1.12-10

Fourth-turn repairs constitute the recipient's last opportunity to locate the repairable. Example 11 exhibits a fourth-turn repair:

(11) P   Hello?
     L   Phil?
     P   Yeh.
     L   Josh L___.
     P   Yeah

```
L    Ah;; what've you gotten so far.
     Any requests to dispatch any trucks in any area,
P    Oh you want my daddy.                              ⇐
L    Yeah, Phi[l,
P              [Well he's outta town at a convention.
                         Schegloff CDHQ 15: Openings, 299
```

In summary, every turn gets to be a first turn, a next turn, a third turn, a fourth turn; therefore, repair opportunities constitute a sliding scale.

### 2.4.4. Preference Structure

Conversation is organized in terms of sequences which may have pre-expansions, inserts and post-expansions. Some types of pre-sequences are built to avoid rejections. This suggests that not all responses are equal. In fact, invitations and requests are built to be accepted rather than declined. Assessments are constructed to be agreed with, rather than disagreed with. Questions can be built to receive expected answers rather than unexpected answers.

When a participant in conversation is in the position of producing a response to an invitation, s/he has the choice of accepting or declining. When a participant is in the position of producing a response to a request, s/he has the choice of granting it or refusing it. When asked a question, a speaker can produce the expected answer or the unexpected answer. These alternatives, however, are not equally valued. The acceptance, the grant and the expected answer are preferred even over the real desires of the speaker. The organization of conversation which reflects the values placed on responses is known as preference structure (Sacks 1987 [1973], Pomerantz 1975, 1978, 1984, Levinson 1983, Atkinson and Heritage 1984, Owen 1984).

Preference structure may be exhibited lexically and syntactically in question forms. Quirk *et al.* (1985:808) state that *yes/no* questions can be built to anticipate either a positive or a negative answer. Positive *yes/no* questions which contain nonassertive forms (*any* or *ever*, etc.) generally are neutral in respect to affirmative or negative responses, as in the following examples from Quirk *et al.* (1985:808):

Did *anyone* call last night?
Do you live *anywhere* near Dover?
Do you suppose that *any* of the class will ask any boring questions?

When assertive forms are used in positive *yes/no* questions, *e.g.*, *someone* or *somewhere*, they may be conducive to an affirmative answer:

Did *someone* call last night?
Has the boat left *already*?

> Do you live *somewhere* near Dover?

We may say that the question has been built to prefer a *yes*. Positive *yes/no* questions may also prefer negative responses:

> Do you *really* want to leave?

The occurrence of *really* gives this example a bias for a negative response.

Quirk *et al.* (1985:808-9) also state that negative *yes/no* questions always prefer a negative response, as in the following:

> *Don't* you believe me?
> *Aren't* you joining us this evening?

Negative *yes/no* questions may contain an element of surprise or disbelief; they may also express disappointment.

Tag questions always express a bias for the expected response. If the statement is positive, the tag is generally negative — and expects a positive response. If the statement is negative, the tag is generally positive — and expects a negative response (Quirk *et al.* 1985).

In preference structure, the *question* prefers the answer, not the questioner. Preference is not a psychological construct but rather a structural aspect of language-in-use. Preference structure is demonstrated within a speaker's turn by the choice of particular syntactic and intonational variables.

Via relationships of contiguity/noncontiguity and agreement/disagreement, preference structure is expressed across speaker turns. The preference for a particular response is determined by the action realized by the utterance, *e.g.*, requests prefer grants vs. rejections, self-deprecating utterances prefer disagreements vs. agreements. The properties of adjacency pairs are constrained by these relationships. Even if recipients do not produce the preferred answer to a question, they often exhibit an orientation to that answer. In summary, respondents generally either produce the preferred response or demonstrate that the dispreferred response, indeed, is *not* the preferred one.

*2.4.4.1. Contiguity/Noncontiguity.* With regard to conversation, contiguity refers to sequence-in-time (temporal order). Two elements of the talk are contiguous if one follows the other without intervention. Speakers are able to control their own utterances to make any two elements contiguous. No single speaker, however, can control contiguity across turns. In fact, however, a preference for contiguity is exhibited across many types of adjacency pairs, including question-answer sequences. Questions select a recipient to speak at the first possible completion point. The speaker of the question must stop, and the selected person answers. It takes an action by A to end up with a question at the end of a turn. It takes an action by B to construct a turn so that the answer appears at the beginning of the next turn. A and B must design their utterances in such a way that the question and answer are contiguous. Note: dispreferred responses are often noncontiguous. They are marked by a delay as well as other elements which result in the dispreferred response being produced late in the turn.

*2.4.4.2. Agreement/Disagreement.* Questions and answers can be in a relationship of agreement or disagreement (Sacks 1987 [1973], Pomerantz 1975, 1978, 1984, Levinson 1983, Atkinson and Heritage 1984, Owen 1984, Tsui 1991). Responses agree when they realize the preference of the action which the utterance suggests, *e.g.,* invitations prefer acceptances, requests prefer grants, pre-announcements prefer forwarding responses, self-deprecating remarks prefer disagreements. Thus, agreeing answers are preferred responses while disagreeing answers are often dispreferred.

Agreeing answers occur contiguously, while disagreeing answers are often pushed late into their turns, *i.e.,* they are not contiguous. When there is disagreement, characteristic markers of a dispreferred response often result in the answer appearing late in the turn ( Sacks 1987 [1973], Pomerantz 1984, Levinson 1983, Tsui 1991). In the example below, H produces a question which is a pre-announcement; then N produces an answer which realizes the preference of the pre-announcement, *i.e.,* she produces another question which solicits the announcement:

(12)  H    Y' know w't I did last ni: [ght?
      N                              [Wha:t,                    ⇐

                                                        HG II 22: 21

Note: N's answer overlaps the end of H's utterance.

In the next example, M asks a question which issues an invitation. L produces a disagreeing response which implicitly rejects the offer:

(13)  M    You wanna come over here and have an omelet?
           (1.0)
      L    eh: (0.4)                                            ⇐
           why, you don't wanna go out?                         ⇐
      M    Well we can go out if you want           Reeves 1: 39

L's rejection of M's offer is pushed late into the turn by pauses and *eh:*.

*2.4.4.3. Summary of Preference Structure.* Levinson (1983: 334-5) gives the following characteristics of dispreferred second-pair parts:

Delays:

- Pause before delivery
- Use of a preface (see below)

- Displacement over a number of turns via repair initiators or insertion sequences

Prefaces:
- Markers or announcers of dispreferreds, *e.g., uh* and *well*
- Token agreements before disagreements
- Appreciations if relevant (for offers, invitations, suggestions, advice)
- Apologies if relevant (for requests, invitations, etc.)
- Qualifiers (*e.g., I don't know for sure, but ...*), including self-editing
- Hesitation in various forms

Accounts:
- Carefully formulated explanations for the dispreferred act

Declination Component:
- Suited to the nature of the first part of the pair, but characteristically indirect or mitigated

Responses usually agree with the preference of the action which the utterance realizes, *e.g.*, invitations prefer acceptances, requests prefer grants, pre-announcements prefer forwarding responses, self-deprecating remarks prefer disagreements. Preferred responses are generally contiguous with the first-pair part. Responses which do not agree with the preference of the action realized by the utterance show some orientation to the preferred response. They are shaped to the preference of the action realized by the utterance, independently of the facts of the world. The next example, from a dinner-table conversation, exhibits a response shaped to the preference of the question. B, as hostess, makes an offer of more soup which is being served as a first course:

(14)　B　　More?　　　　　　　　　　　　　　　　　　⇐
　　　 N　　No, I think I'll save space.　　　　　　Sh/Fer 6: 146

N refuses B's offer and then accounts for her action. In doing so, she is showing some orientation to the preferred response (an acceptance).

Dispreferred responses are generally discontiguous with the first-pair part and show regularity of structure in the initial elements of the second-pair part (example 13). When there is evidence that an answer will be dispreferred, the answer is not the sole responsibility of the second pair-part speaker. The speaker of the first-pair part may reproduce the first-pair part so that the answer will be contiguous and in agreement with the question. Getting an adjacency pair to agree and be contiguous involves both parties. The following example from Merritt (1976; cited by Levinson 1983), shows how participants manage this shared responsibility:

(15)  C   Do you have hot chocolate?
      S   mmhmm
      C   Can I have hot chocolate with whipped cream?
      S   Sure ((leaves to get))                           Merritt: 337

This example is from a service encounter. The customer first determines whether or not the shopkeeper has hot chocolate before requesting it.

A pre-disagreement can project a disagreement and provide the other participant with a chance to reformulate the question so the answer, eventually, will be both contiguous and preferred. The following example is a complete telephone conversation (provided by Emanuel Schegloff) which demonstrates how participants may construct their talk to avoid dispreferred responses:

(16)   ((ring))
       M   Hello?
       D   'lo Marcia,
       M   Yea [:h    ]
       D       ['t's) D ] onny.
       M   Hi Donny
       D   Guess what. hh
       M   What.
       D   *hh My car is sta::lled.
           (0.2)
           ('n) I'm up here in the Glen?
       M   Oh::.
           [(0.4)]
       D   *hhh
           A:nd. hh
           (0.2)
           I don't know if it's: po:ssible,
           but [*hhh ] see
               [(0.2) ]
           I have to open up the ba:nk. hh
           (0.3)
           a:t uh: (.) (in Brentwood? hh)=
                      (in fact what's)
       M   =Yeah:- en I know what you want- (.)
           en I whoa-
           en I would,
           but- except I've gotta leave in about fifteen minutes.=
       D   = [Okay
       M     [ (hheh)
       D   then I gotta call somebody else.
           right away.

```
D      (.)
       Okay?=
M      =Okay [Don  ]
D            [Thanks] a lot.=
       =Bye-.
M      Bye:.
```

After D has announced he has a problem with his car, M projects a rejection of his request for help by silence. She makes no offer to come to his assistance. D, in fact, never explicitly requests help; however, M anticipates a request and explains why she cannot grant it. Thus, M never expressly rejects the tacit request.

## 2.5. Summary

In this chapter, the general procedures underlying this study have been described. The data consist of all the functional questions in the conversations which were considered. I identified these questions by employing my native-speaker capacities in conjunction with an ethnomethodological approach to the data. All functional questions were classified by form as interrogative questions, declarative questions or nonclausal questions (particles, words and phrases). Declarative and nonclausal forms were analyzed with regard to the role morphosyntactic form plays in their interpretation as questions and their function in the interaction.

# Chapter 3

# Methodology

## 3.1. Data

The data consist of 14 conversations among speakers who know each other as family members, friends or acquaintances. Each conversation is identified by name. In this section, I will present a brief description of each conversation, including the social setting, the number of speakers, the duration of the conversation in minutes (to the nearest minute), the number of pages of transcript and the approximate number of words.

### 3.1.1. *Conversations*

**Conversation 1 — Clacia**

Collected/transcribed by: Charles and Marjorie Goodwin and Gail Jefferson
Date: early 1970's
Social setting: face-to-face (July 4th block party)
Number of participants: 6
Duration in minutes: 10
Pages of transcript: 20
Number of words: 3,260

**Conversation 2 — Ford**

Collected/transcribed by: Cecilia Ford
Date: October, 1985
Social setting: face-to-face
Number of participants: 3
Duration in minutes: 6
Pages of transcript: 13
Number of words: 2,340

**Conversation 3 — Gee**

Collected/transcribed by: Young Gee
Date: October, 1985
Social setting: telephone conversation
Number of participants: 2
Duration in minutes: 5
Pages of transcript: 8
Number of words: 1,250

**Conversation 4 — HG II**

Collected/transcribed by: Emanuel Schegloff and Gail Jefferson
Date: 1974
Social setting: telephone conversation
Number of participants: 2
Duration in minutes: 19
Pages of transcript: 46
Number of words: 7,250

**Conversation 5 — Kinjo**

Collected/transcribed by: Hiromi Kinjo
Date: October, 1985
Social setting: telephone conversation
Number of participants: 2
Duration in minutes: 5
Pages of transcript: 12
Number of words: 1,640

**Conversation 6 — Lazaraton**

Collected/transcribed by: Anne Lazaraton
Date: Oct. 1985
Social setting: telephone conversation
Number of participants: 2
Duration in minutes: 3
Pages of transcript: 5
Number of words: 470

**Conversation 7 — Mannon**

Collected/transcribed by: Tracy Mannon
Date: October, 1985

Social setting: telephone conversation
Number of participants: 2
Duration in minutes: 6
Pages of transcript: 16
Number of words: 1,680

**Conversation 8 — Riggenbach**

Collected/transcribed by: Heidi Riggenbach
Date: October, 1985
Social setting: face-to-face (gathering after a movie)
Number of participants: 5
Duration in minutes: 5
Pages of transcript: 11
Number of words: 1,400

**Conversation 9 — Shapley/Boys**

Collected/transcribed by: Marian Shapley
Date: 1981
Social setting: face-to-face (dinner)
Number of participants: 5
Duration in minutes: 30
Pages of transcript: 23
Number of words: 8,290

**Conversation 10 — Shapley/Fer**

Collected/transcribed by: Marian Shapley
Date: 1979
Social setting: face-to-face (dinner)
Number of participants: 5
Duration in minutes: 18
Pages of transcript: 18
Number of words: 6,040

**Conversation 11 — Shapley/Nel**

Collected/transcribed by: Marian Shapley
Date: 1979
Social setting: face-to-face (dinner)
Number of participants: 6
Duration in minutes: 54

Pages of transcript: 28
Number of words: 5,880

**Conversation 12 — Shapley/Sha**

Collected/transcribed by: Marian Shapley
Date: 1979
Social setting: face-to-face
Number of participants: 4
Duration in minutes: 36
Pages of transcript: 30
Number of words: 8,700

**Conversation 13 — SN4**

Collected/transcribed by: Frankel and Girton
Date: early 1970's
Social setting: face-to-face
Number of participants: 5
Duration in minutes: 12
Pages of transcript: 30
Number of words: 2,040

**Conversation 14 — Weber**

Collected/transcribed by: Elizabeth G. Weber
Date: October, 1985
Social setting: face-to-face (dinner)
Number of participants: 4
Duration in minutes: 5
Pages of transcript: 12
Number of words: 1,520

Together, these conversations constitute two hours and 34 minutes of talk, 272 pages of transcription and approximately 51,760 words. The speakers come from various parts of the country and range in age from 15 to over 60 years. There are 53 participants — 24 men and 29 women.

In this section, I have presented a brief description of the each conversation included in the database. The following section will cover how these data were coded with respect to linguistic, informational and interactional factors.

*3.1.2. Transcription Notation*

In this study, the data are represented (with a few conventional exceptions) in English orthography. This differs from the transcript notation of many ethnomethodologists who follow the notation of Jefferson (Sacks, Schegloff and Jefferson 1974) and represent the data in a pseudophonetic system. Their goal is to give the reader "equal access to all the data being analyzed" (Atkinson and Drew 1979:26, cited in Owen 1984:6). Owen (1984:5) makes the point that the data are represented in a "curious, hybrid, pseudophonetic system designed to give an accurate impression of how the original recordings sounds." In this study, references to actual phonetic realizations are given in phonetic symbols enclosed in brackets, *e.g.*, [d].

Notational conventions devised by Gail Jefferson (Sacks, Schegloff and Jefferson 1974) are also incorporated in this study. These conventions are illustrated with examples from the corpus.

**Simultaneous Utterances**

Brackets indicate overlap (simultaneous utterances or portions of utterances):

    B    May I give you a piece of [ramekin?
    M                                [yes.( )

**Sequential Utterances Not Separated by a Pause**

When one utterance follows another without any noticeable pause, the two utterances are connected by an equal sign:

    P    John, now you know that's not nice.
    J    I know it wasn't nice=
    P    =y- you apologize to that boy.=
    J    =Oh:. I will

**Alternative Hearings**

When the transcriber was in doubt as to the hearing, brackets indicate alternative hearings of a single speaker's utterance:

    M    She's [ oh no. hell no.
              [(hell no)

### Possible Hearings

An utterance or portion of an utterance placed within parentheses indicates a possible hearing of the utterance. This notation recognizes the transcriber's uncertainty as to what was actually said:

> S    She [wasn't invited to the wedding?
> M    [ (I'm gonna take her out.)

### Pauses

Pauses are estimated in tenths of seconds; (.) = a micropause, *i.e.*, a slight break in the speaker's speech rhythm.

### Lengthening

Lengthening is indicated iconically by one or more colons.

### Cutoffs

A noticeably cutoff word is represented by a dash:

> S    I don't know have you been studying lately, (0.2)
> M    No eh not at aw- not at all:

### Laughter

Within words, (h) indicates laughter.

### Aspiration

Inbreaths are represented by *hhh, and outbreaths, by hhh.

> H    *hhihhh I think I'll get the le(h)tter next yea(hhh [h)r
> N    [Yea(h)h,=
>       =hhhhh *hh You'll get a ten page lett(hh)er

### Loudness

Loudness is transcribed by capital letters.

       P     (Oh, my [God)
       J            [Yeah=he should understand the humor of it all.
       P     THAT'S NOT FUNNY=
       J     =It's fu::nny ha ha

**Low Intensity Sounds and Utterances**

A small raised circle (º) represents low intensity sounds/utterances.

       M    What's the next rank above Colonel.
              ((laughter))
              Could he get promoted.
       ( )    ((laughter))
       T     ºI don't know.
       L     ºLieutenant Colonel?
             (1.0)
       M    What comes after Colonel,

**Change in Pitch Level**

An upturned arrow (↑) represents a higher pitch level.
A downturned arrow (↓) represents a lower pitch level.

       N     but uhm (1.2)
             they really you know
             ↓ I want this one
             ↑ they went around
             and I forgot to undo ↓ that one.
             they went around and around,

**Stress**

    The term "stress" is used to indicate prominence. There are several different theoretical approaches to prominence, *e.g.*, prominence as pitch obtrusion alone, prominence based on pitch obtrusion vs. prominence based on loudness and prominence as rhythm (Couper-Kuhlen 1986). After Cruttenden (1986), I will use the term "stress" to refer to prominence "however such prominence is achieved" (p. 16).

    The notation of stress follows Du Bois *et al.* (1992). When stress is marked, the following symbols are used before those words in the utterance which bear stress. Note: stress is marked on words rather than syllables because in English lexical stress is predictable. Any unpredictable occurrences of stress within a lexical item will be marked phonetically.

- Primary stress = "
- Secondary stress= '
- Unstressed syllables are unmarked

**Terminal intonation**

Terminal intonation is indicated as follows:

- Falling intonation = .
- Level intonation  = ,
- Rising intonation = ?

(See page 28 for a discussion of which utterances are marked for terminal intonation and stress)

### 3.2. Coding Procedures

My coding procedures were guided by the belief that a phenomenon can reveal itself from itself[1]. Although my intent was to approach the data with as few preconceptions as possible, of course, the initial coding reflected my expectations as to what linguistic factors might be relevant. I attempted, however, to maintain an open attitude throughout the coding procedure with respect to noticing new and possibly relevant factors. The following two records from the database exhibit the categories coded for each question.

## METHODOLOGY

| 1 | Code | Sh/Nel | 4 | 11 | Functional type | ques | Structural Class | con | Repetition | - |

**1PP**: What is she majoring in?

**Inserted Material**: ∅

**2PP**: Latin...American studies

**Post Insert**: ∅   3rd: really, at Yale   2PP Speaker: rec   2PP Question: -   #  1

**1PP Initial**: ∅   2PP Initial: ∅   Repair: -   STRep Type: @

**Structure**: wh+v+su   **Syntactic Type**: inter

**Confirmation**: -   **Alternative**: -   **Intonation**: r   **Overlap 1PP**: -

**Overlap 2PP**: -

**1PPSp Story**: @   1PP DisMode: @   2PP DisMode: @

Record 1

| 2 | Code | W | 8 | 127 | Functional type | ques | Structural Class | stor | Repetition | - |

**1PP**: Is that? [Where is that.

**Inserted Material**: [Wasn't she gonna to go UCLA that (.) thing=

**2PP**: It's at UCLA

**Post Insert** | 3rd: yeah, okay | 2PP Speaker: | rec | 2PP Question | - | # | 1 |

**1PP Initial** | Ø | 2PP Initial | Ø | Repair | + | STRep Type | reconstruction |

**Structure:** wh su+v  **Syntactic Type:** inter

**Confirmation:** -  **Alternative:** -  **Intonation** f  **Overlap 1PP** in

**Overlap 2PP** post

**1PPSp Story** rec  **1PP DisMode:** description  **2PP DisMode:** loc. background

Record 2

The categories coded in the records are described as follows:

**Code**

These fields uniquely identify the utterance doing questioning by transcript name, page and line. In record 1, the utterance is taken from the Shapley/Nel transcript, page 4, line 11. In record 2, the utterance originated in the Weber transcript, page 8, line 127.

**Functional Type**

This field broadly classifies the utterance being coded with regard to type of first-pair part as follows:

- Question (most general category)
- Next-turn repair initiator (NTRI)
- Topicalization (initiates a topic)
- Exclamation
- Greeting
- Offer
- Joke
- Invitation
- Request
- Clause + *you know*

Since it was not clear to me at the beginning of the coding process which, if any, of these utterances were doing questioning, all clauses associated with *you know* were coded. Eventually most of these *you know* utterances were removed from the database because they did not function as questions. Note: records 1 and 2 classify the utterances coded "question."

**Structural Classification**

This field broadly classifies the utterance according to its sequential position in the talk (in an opening or closing sequence, in a story, in a pre-sequence, etc.). "Conversation" is the default case in which no particular classification is made. In record 1, the utterance is coded "conversation;" and in record 2, the utterance is coded "story environment."

**Repetition**

This field marks whether or not the second-pair part contains repeated elements of the first-pair part (whether the answer repeats elements of the question). Because what constitutes a repeated element is an open question, a broad concept of repetition was assumed. This field is coded as to the presence (+) or absence (-) of repeating elements. Neither record 1 nor record 2 exhibits any repetition.

### First-Pair Part

This field reproduces the functional question from the transcript. The question in record 1 is *What is she majoring in.* The question in record 2 is *Is that-Where is that.*

### Inserted Material

This field marks any pause and/or verbal and nonverbal interactional material between the first-pair part and the second-pair part. Inbreaths are not included unless a pause separates the inbreath from the second-pair part. Inserted material is *not* the second-pair part answer. Record 1 has no inserted material. Record 2 exhibits the following inserted material: *Wasn't she gonna go to UCLA that (.) thing.* The inserted material is produced by someone other than the speaker or the recipient of the question being coded.

### Second-Pair Part

This field contains the second-pair part example from the transcript. In record 1, the second-pair part answer is *Latin ... American studies.* In record 2, the second-pair part answer is *It's at UCLA.*

### Post Insert

This field marks any pause and/or verbal and nonverbal interactional material between the second-pair part and a third-position receipt. A third-position receipt acknowledges an answer. Inbreaths are not included unless the inbreath is separated from the third-position receipt by a pause. Inserted material is *not* the third-position receipt.
This field is coded "not applicable" (@) if there is no third-position receipt. In record 1, there is no material inserted between the second-pair part and the third-position receipt. In record 2, the inserted material is *pass the milk*. The speaker of this material is neither the speaker of the second-pair part nor the speaker of the first-pair part and third-position receipt.

### Third-Position Receipt

This field contains the third-position receipt of the second-pair part answer. It is coded as ø if there is no third-position receipt. In record 1, the third position receipt is *really, at Yale.* In record 2, the third-position receipt is *yeah, okay.*

### Second-Pair Part Speaker

This field codes who answers the question (the person to whom it was addressed or the speaker). This field codes the speaker of the second-pair part as:

- *sp* = the speaker of the first-pair part
- *rec* = the recipient of the first-pair part.

Note: this field indicates cases in which people answer their own questions. In both record 1 and record 2, the speakers of the second-pair parts are the recipients of the first-pair parts.

### Second-Pair Part Question

This field codes whether or not the second-pair part is itself a first-pair part question by (+) or (-). This recognizes instances where people answer a question with a question. In records 1 and 2, neither answer is in itself a question.

### Number of Clauses

This field broadly classifies the utterance as to its clause structure:

- LTC = less than 1 clause
- 1 = 1 clause
- MTC = 1 clause + additional nonclausal material
- 2 = 2 clauses
- 3 = 3 clauses

Utterances which do not exhibit clause structure are coded as follows:

- Particle, word, phrase
- Interpretable as a declarative
- Interpretable as an interrogative

In records 1 and 2, both questions are realized by a single clause. In record 2, the question is repaired. Only the repaired version of the utterance (*Where is that*) is coded according to clause structure.

### First-Pair Part Initial

This field codes initial material, *e.g.*, discourse markers like *well, oh, because* (Schiffrin 1987). Neither record 1 nor 2 exhibits initial material.

### Second-Pair Part Initial

This field codes initial material, *e.g.*, *well*. Neither record 1 nor 2 exhibits initial material.

### Same-Turn Repair

This field codes whether or not the first-pair part is a same-turn repair by (+) or (-). This judgment is made on the basis of the presence or absence of a repair initiator and the syntactic form of the utterance. In record 1, the question does not exhibit any signs of repair. In record 2, the question begins, is aborted and then reconstructed as a different syntactic form.

### Same-Turn Repair Type

This field labels the type of repair exhibited by the utterance (an insert repair, a reconstructed turn repair, etc.). In record 2, the question is an instance of a reconstruction repair.

### Descriptive Structure

This field codes the initial elements of an utterance up to the point at which both the subject and the verb are produced. The elements coded are the following:

- *su* = subject
- *v* = verb
- *op* = operator verb, *e.g.*, *do*
- *aux* = auxiliary verb, *e.g. are* in *are coming*
- *wh* = *wh*-pronoun, *e.g.*, *who, what, where, how, why*

Any elements produced before the subject and verb are also coded conventionally (*pp* for prepositional phrase, *adv* for adverb, etc.). In the case of repaired turns, only the final version which goes to completion is coded in the initial analysis. In record 1, the question *What is she majoring in* is described as follows: *wh + v + su*. *Wh* codes the *wh*-word *what*, *v* codes the verb *is* and *su* codes the subject *she*. In record 2, the question *Where is that* is described as follows: *wh + v + su*. *Wh* codes the *wh*-word *where*, *v* codes the verb *is* and *su* codes the subject *that*.

### Syntactic Type

This field codes clausal utterances by syntactic type (Quirk *et al.* 1985): declarative, interrogative, exclamatory or imperative. In addition to these types, the following were also coded:

- Particle
- + particle
- + tag
- + *right*
- *you mean* +
- + *you know* +
- *remember* +
- Interpretable declarative
- Interpretable interrogative
- Interpretable interrogative (*you know*)
- Interpretable exclamatory
- Interpretable imperative
- *wh*-word
- Noun
- Adv
- Prepositional phrase

In both record 1 and 2, the questions are coded as interrogatives.

### Confirmation Question

This field codes whether or not the question is seeking confirmation or disconfirmation. Neither question coded in record 1 or 2 seeks confirmation.

### Alternative Question

This field codes whether or not the question offers an alternative. Neither question coded in record 1 or 2 offers an alternative.

### Intonation

This field codes the direction of terminal intonation as follows:

- Falling = *f*
- Rising = *r*
- Level = *l*

The question in record 1 has rising terminal intonation, and the question in record 2 has falling terminal intonation.

### Overlap First-Pair Part

This field codes whether or not utterances are overlapped and, if so, by what other utterances.

If the first-pair part is:

- Not overlapped by any other utterance, this field is marked (-).
- Produced simultaneously with another utterance, this field is marked (*sim*).
- Overlapped by a previous utterance, this field is marked (*pre*).
- Overlapped by insert material, this field is marked (*in*).
- Overlapped by the second-pair part, this field is marked (*2*).

In record 1, the question is not overlapped by any other utterance. In record 2, the question is overlapped by inserted material.

### Overlap Second-Pair Part

This field codes whether or not utterances are overlapped and, if so, by what other utterances.

If the second-pair part is:

- Not overlapped by any other utterance, this field is marked (-).
- Overlapped by the first-pair part, this field is marked (*1*).
- Overlapped by inserted material, this field is coded (*in*).
- Overlapped by inserted material before a third-position receipt, this field is marked (*post*).
- Overlapped by a third-position receipt, this field is marked (*3*).

In record 1, the second-pair part is not overlapped by any other utterance. In record 2, the second-pair part is overlapped by material inserted between the second-pair part and the third-position receipt.

### Speaker of the First-Pair Part in a Story Environment

This field codes whether or not the storyteller or the story recipient produces the first-pair part. This field is not applicable to the question in record 1, while the speaker of the question in record 2 is the recipient of the story.

### First-Pair Part Discourse Mode

This field is relevant to story sequences. Discourse mode refers to descriptive material vs. event-line material. If the recipient of the story produced the first-pair part, this field codes the type of information the recipient requests from the storyteller. If the teller of the story produced the first-pair part, this field codes the kind of response the teller requests from the recipient of the story. This field is not relevant to the question in record 1, and in record 2, the information requested is descriptive information.

**Second-Pair Part Discourse Mode**

This field is relevant to story sequences. This field codes the kind of response and/or information either the recipient or the teller of the story is given. This field is not relevant to the question in record 1, and in record 2, the information provided is locative background information.

This section has presented the procedures used in this study to code utterances doing questioning. Two records of questions found in the data have been included in order to exemplify many of the coded fields which have been described.

## 3.3. Conclusion

The structure of this work emerged from the process of coding the data, *i.e.*, a number of morphosyntactic patterns became apparent. Subsequent analysis revealed that these patterns correlated closely with specific communicative functions. I did not hypothesize that certain morphosyntactic patterns correlated with certain communicative functions and then go about testing the validity of such an hypothesis. Instead, the process of coding for a broad range of interactional, semantic, morphosyntactic and informational factors revealed these correlations. Because the data are so rich, I believe that any rigorous examination of conversation will reveal significant facts of language usage.

# Chapter 4

# Declarative Questions: Morphosyntactic Patterns

## 4.1. The Problem of Declarative Questions

In this chapter, I will examine the relation between morphosyntactic form and the communicative function *doing questioning* by describing those functional questions which are realized by a declarative clause. The problematic issues which relate to questions in any form are:

(1) How recipients recognize interrogative clauses, declarative clauses and particles, words, or phrases as questions and
(2) How speakers decide which syntactic form to use in each instance to accomplish their interactional goals.

Sinclair and Coulthard (1975) express the problem from the perspective of the recipient in conversation as follows.

> How, for example, does a hearer know when a declarative structure has the function of a question, and how does he know that a clause asks or does not ask a question depending on where it occurs in a sequence of clauses (p. 2)?

Interrogatives are typical question forms (Pike 1975, Quirk *et al.* 1985); therefore, from the perspective of morphosyntactic form, declarative forms typically are not expected to do questioning. In contrast to interrogative forms, declarative forms normally have no *wh*-word as an argument of the verb (but see example 20) and exhibit unmarked word order in which the subject precedes the verb. Recipients in conversation, however, have no trouble interpreting certain declarative forms as doing questioning. It is this fact which needs to be explained. Intonation, gesture, accessibility of information and sequential position in the talk along with morphosyntactic form are relevant factors in the interpretation of any utterance. While each of these factors will be considered, this chapter will focus on the role of morphosyntax in the interpretation of declarative questions.

In order to understand how their morphosyntactic form contributes to interpretation, the following will be discussed:

(1) Questions which have a declarative form;
(2) Various morphosyntactic types of declarative questions;
(3) Interpretive procedures relative to the morphosyntax used to interpret each type as doing questioning (the social action);
(4) The role of intonation and gesture with regard to declarative questions;
(5) How these forms are distributed in the data.

## 4.2. Data

The database is comprised of 14 conversations examined according to the principles and procedures underlying the analytical approach described in Chapter 2. Utterances identified as questions on the basis of their function in the talk are included in the data, although the morphosyntactic form of the utterance, in itself, is not a criterion in this identification process. Utterances identified as doing questioning are classified by form as follows:

- interrogative forms;
- Declarative forms; and
- Nonclausal forms, *i.e.*, those which are realized by particles, words, phrases (see Chapter 2 for explicit definitions of these syntactic types).

From this set of utterances which function to do questioning in the talk, those which have a declarative form were extracted. These utterances comprise the set of declarative questions.

The following example exhibits a declarative form utterance which introduces a topic by doing questioning:

```
(17)  N    What's doing,
            (.)
      H    Ah:, noth [i: n:,        ]
      N             [Y' didn't g ]o meet "Grahame?=     ⇐
      H    =*pt *hhhhhahh Well, I got ho::me,
      N    =u-hu:h?
            (.)
            a::::n he hadn't called yet
            an there weren't any messages or anythi[n:g    ]e- ]
                                                   [Uh  h ]u ]:h
```

>       H       a:n hh then I kind of got on the pho:ne
>               an I heard a couple of clicks
>               an hhhhhhh *hh I don't know if he was trying to call =
>               =but I'm too tired to go all the way back to Westwood
>               anyw[ay,   ]
>       N            [Ye : ]:ah,
>
>                                                           HGII 1:17

In this example, the subject *you* precedes the verb phrase *didn't go meet Grahame*, thus exhibiting unmarked declarative clause word order.

### 4.3. Morphosyntactic Patterns of Declarative Questions

While some syntactically declarative forms used by speakers to ask questions show no explicit marking suggestive of question function, others have lexical elements in the clause which play a role in their functional interpretation. Others have lexical or morphosyntactic elements immediately preceding or immediately following in the talk. Following is an example of those declarative utterances which have no elements to support their interpretation as questions. I have classified these utterances as *declarative questions with no associated marker*.

Although a full discussion of the interpretation of this type of declarative question will be deferred until later in the chapter, I feel that this disjunction will enable the reader to contrast this type with those which follow. The focus on the morphosyntactic patterns of declarative questions is not meant to imply that intonation and gesture play no role in interpretation. These topics will be further discussed in connection with the interpretation of declarative questions with no associated marker. As discussed earlier, however, there is no such thing, in general, as unambiguous question intonation, *viz.*, rising terminal intonation.

#### 4.3.1. Declarative Questions with No Associated Marker

Questioning can be done with a declarative form which, in no lexical or morphosyntactic way[1] suggests it is doing questioning:

>       (18)    S       I don't know  have you been studying  lately,
>                       (0.2)
>               M       No eh not at aw- not at all:
>                       I have to study this whole week, every night *hh
>                       and then I've got something planned on Sunday with
>                       Laura,
>                       (0.4)

```
M    She she wa- she and I are gonna go out and get drunk at
     four o'clock in the afternoon.
S    Uh huh *hhh
M    It's a religious
     (0.5)
     thing we're gonna have.
     (0.5)
     I don't know why. (but
     I don't know why but um
     (0.2)
     no her ex boyfriend's getting married
     and she:'s (-)gonna be  depressed s:o
     (1.1)
S    She    [wasn't invited to the "wedding?          ⇐
M           [ (I'm gonna take her out.)
     (1.0)
     She's  [ oh no. hell no.
            [(hell no)
S           [hardly.
R    h(h)m /*hm hm
     (.1)
M    She's trying to stay away from the wedding.      SN4 10:5
```

This utterance exemplifies the interpretive problem of how recipients know a declarative clause is a question and not a statement because morphosyntactically, this clause type is associated with making a statement. There is no such thing as an unambiguous question intonation (Chapter 1); therefore, we cannot appeal to intonation to solve the interpretation problem — and declarative clauses with rising intonation do not always function as questions in conversation (Bolinger 1957:13, Bolinger 1989:145, Couper-Kuhlen 1986:156). How do recipients correctly interpret such utterances as doing questioning? These interpretive procedures will be discussed after the types of marked declarative questions are presented.

*4.3.2. Marked Declarative Questions*

Because language is a temporal phenomenon which is produced and interpreted bit-by-bit in real time, the ways in which speakers mark declarative questions can be categorized in terms of real-time production. Because an utterance is produced in time, its constituent elements occur in a certain order; and participants use this order to project the syntactic form of the utterance being produced. This fact is relevant for explaining the turn-taking system in conversation.

To what extent do participants project the function of an utterance during the course of its production? In other words, do speakers mark declarative questions so that recipients can use morphosyntactic resources to project the question function of the utterance? To answer these questions, lexical elements within the declarative clause will be considered in terms of how soon into the turn they are produced; and elements not within the clause will be considered in terms of when they are produced (before or after the declarative clause which functions to do questioning). Note: some declarative questions exhibit more than one type of marking which supports an interpretation of question function.

In regard to marked declarative questions, then, I will distinguish between:

(1) Those utterances which have lexical elements within the clause which are suggestive of question function;

(2) Those utterances with some prior discourse marking which plays a role in the interpretation of the utterance as doing a question; and

(3) Those utterances with some subsequent discourse marking which plays a role in the interpretation of the utterance as doing a question.

### 4.3.2.1 Marking which Occurs within the Declarative Clause

*Lexical Elements*

Some lexical elements are supportive of an interpretation of question function solely by virtue of their meaning. These lexical elements appear within the declarative clause, *i.e.*, they are integrated into the clause structure. (Discourse markers which appear before or after the clause will be discussed separately. The second-person pronoun subject *you* will also be discussed separately.)

Bolinger (1957) classifies lexical markers of declarative questions as "tentations" or "imputations." Tentations are markers which underscore the assumptiveness of the assertion. Typical tentations are:

- Hypothetical verbs (*I suppose, assume, imagine, hope, believe, guess, bet, say*),
- Hearsay verbs (*I understand, am told, am informed, hear*),
- Inferential adverbs (*then, so, therefore*),
- Potential adverbs (*perhaps, probably, maybe, possibly*),
- Adverbs of assurance (*doubtless, no doubt, undoubtedly, of course, surely*) and
- Impersonal expressions (*it must be that, it is certain that, it is to be supposed, it is to be hoped, it is to be expected*) (p. 61).

Imputations are markers that involve presumptions. Typical imputations are:

- Verbs that imply convictions (*tell, claim, think, ask, believe, imagine*) (p. 62, see also Geluykens 1987).

Bolinger notes that the category "person" is one of the factors which determines how effective an imputation is *as a Q-marker*. He states that "(t)he pronoun *you* marks an area that includes more (questions) than (nonquestions)" (p. 62). (See also Geluykens 1987.)

In her study of questions and responses in English conversation, Stenström (1984: 153-154) observes that questions in declarative form generally contain a lexical indicator of question function. Of the various types of lexical markers she lists, the following appear within the clause structure itself:

- Tentative expressions which introduce a declarative complement (*I don't think/suppose*) and
- Modal verbs (*might, would, ought*).

Note: Stenström includes the second-person subject *you* among lexical markers.

In these data, lexical marking of question function within a clause is accomplished by the use of certain verbs and adverbs. In the following example, the speaker M visits R and S in their dorm room:

```
(19)    M     How're you guys.
              ((door slams))
              (0.3)
        R     Just fi:ne.
              (0.4)
        S     U::h tired
              (0.4)
        M     Tired,
              I hear you're getting "married.     ←
              (0.6)
        ( )   °((sniff))
              (0.3)
        S     Uh:: you hear right.
        M     Uh sh- I hear right.=                      SN1:12
```

The matrix verb *hear* means something like: "people have been telling me this." What people have been telling the speaker is disclosed in the complement clause which follows. The matrix clause appears early in the turn and before the clause that presents the information to be confirmed. The lexical element *hear* is interpretable as suggesting the speaker has reason to believe the information to be presented in the complement clause is true or accurate. The recipient is implicitly invited to confirm it.

*Wh-word*

Marking within the clause is also realized by a *wh*-word. The occurrence of a *wh*-word within a clause does not necessarily indicate it is an interrogative form. Interrogative forms have a *wh*-word in subject position with subject-verb word order or have subject-verb inversion (Chapter 1) in conjunction with a *wh*-word in another grammatical role.

The following example from a dinner table conversation includes a declarative clause with a *wh*-word. In the prior conversation, the participants had been discussing foods which contained oxalic acid. M reintroduces the subject when he thinks of another food containing the acid. The participants are eating spinach soup which B refers to in her last turn:

(20)  M   Sorrel.
          (.)
          Sorrel has a lot of oxalic acid too.
          (0.1)
      L   heh  [heh heh
               [((laughter))
      ( )      [(Sorrel? )
      B        [Sorrel has a lot of "what?    ←
      M   Sorrel. yes.
      T   What's (.) what's that?
      M   That's a sort of green, clover-like grass.
      (B)  mm hmm
      B   has a lot of what?=
      M   =( ) tastes like[spinach.]
                          [acid?   ] which acid?
          Oxalic.
      B   Oxalic. Yeah.
          Yeah, this has a lot of oxalic acid,
          yeah, but I cook it
          and I throw away the water carefully, you see.
                                              Shapley/Fer 6:155

B produces the NTRI *sorrel has a lot of what* after the trouble-source turn. The *wh*-word substitutes for (and thus targets) that portion of the prior utterance which is the source of the trouble.

Marking within the clause can be accomplished by a "gap." Following, the participants had been discussing the difference between the Hebrew of the Ashkenazy and the Sephardic Jews. They are looking at a book and discussing the writing system for Hebrew:

(21)   B    The dots distinguish the vee sound,
            There's a letter.
            I ca- (.)
            Say how you pronounce that in Sephardic, I can't remember
            it.
            How do you pronounce beyt in Sephardic, I can't remember.
            How do you pronounce beyt in Sephardic?
       A    Beyt?
       B    Beth or something like that.
            Beth I guess you say.
            *hhh uh but tha      [-
       L                         [(I know that.)
       B    Pardón.
       A    [bɛ] [bɛ]=
       L    =([bɛ])
            Is our book Sephardic, or not.
       B    (Oh, I'll try)
            This this is an Israel- it's a book about the la- the Israel
            language.
       A    Ye [ah.
       B        [Yeah.
       L    which is shall we say Sephardic.
            **And "they call it?**              ⬅
       A    [bɛ]                                    Shapley/Sha 18:11

The speaker produces a declarative clause in which the final element projected by the form is missing from the discourse — and this missing element is the information queried. The recipient of the question subsequently produces the element which completes the declarative form. In effect, two speakers cooperate to construct a declarative clause. Ochs (1976, p. 12) notes that the sequential expression of propositions is observed in both child-and-adult discourse and child-child discourse (Bloom 1973, Keenan and Schieffelin 1976, Scollon 1976, Atkinson 1979, Lerner 1987, 1989, 1991).

*4.3.2.2 Marking which Occurs before the Production of the Declarative Clause*

*Prior Declarative Clause*

In the data there are several cases in which a declarative question is preceded by an utterance containing a lexical element suggestive of question function. The example below contains the verb phrase *don't know*. The participants are discussing a play they are going to see that evening. H is referring to a review of the play in that day's newspaper:

(22)  H    Yeh but I don't want you to read it.
             (.)
       N    [O  ]kay,  ]
       H    [Plea]se don't. ]
             *hh
             b [ecause- ]
       N    [See "I do]n't know what it's a [bout yer n]ot
             gonna                                          ←
       H                                           [Yeah,  ]  ←
       N    "tell  [me?]
       H           [*p*]
             becau:se there's one point in there
             where it gives away s:something th[at- ]
       N                                        [Oh:] rea [lly:?   ]
       H                                                  [i-is a sho ]:cker=
             =and I don't want y[ou to kno:w,]
       N                        [Okay I wo ]:n['t,
       H                                       [Cause it'll affect you more
             [when you see it.]
       N    [I'll read it a: f ]ter,                    HGII 9:15

*I don't know what it's about* expresses a gap in the recipient's knowledge. The complement clause is the embedded question, *what it's about*, realized by a *wh-*word. The entire utterance sets the stage for the following declarative question *you're not gonna tell me*. This question does not receive an answer. H simply goes on; N redoes the question and then gets an answer, as shown in the following extended example:

(23)  H    Yeh but I don't want you to read it.
             (.)
       N    [O  ]kay,  ]
       H    [Plea]se don't. ]
             *hh
             b [ecause- ]
       N    [See "I do]n't know what it's a [bout yer n]ot
             gonna                                          ←
       H                                           [Yeah,  ]  ←
       N    "tell  [me?]
       H           [*p*]
             becau:se there's one point in there
             where it gives away s:something th[at- ]
       N                                        [Oh:] rea [lly:?   ]
       H                                                  [i-is a sho ]:cker=

|   |   |
|---|---|
| H | =and I don't want y[ou to kno:w,] |
| N | [Okay I wo ]:n ['t, |
| H | [Cause it'll affect you more    [when you see it.] |
| N | [I'll read it a: f  ]ter, |
| H | =*khhh Yeah. |
|   | But anyway so the review is pretty goo:d |
|   | an so I go |
|   | oh if it's this goo:d you know= |
|   | [ I'd really [like     [to     [see it. ] |
| N | [Ye:ah.    [Might as [well  [cha:nc]e it, |
|   | (.) |
|   | That sounds goo:d, |
|   | (.) |
| H | Yea:h.= |
| N | =Kind of looking forward to it. What u:m, |
|   | (1.0) |
|   | **Can you tell me what it's "abou:t?=**  ⇐ |
| H | =*khhhhhh   [Yeah. It take-  ] |
| N |             [O:r would it-uh-]   ⇐ |
|   | (.) |
|   | [(I don't know,)] |
| H | [No. It takes  ] pla:ce, i:n, *t |
|   | (0.2) |
|   | u-ni:neteen thirties in Oklahoma, ((etc. on the plot)) |

HGII 9:15

N redoes her original request to be told what the play is about with an interrogative form; thus, she demonstrates that her original utterance was intended to function as a question. Because the second-pair part was not produced, N redoes the first-pair part and this utterance does get an answer.

*Prior Interrogative Forms*

There is a type of declarative question realized by a *wh*-word or an interrogative clause and a candidate response. This example is from a dinner table conversation. The speaker N, who is L's mother, responds to a nonverbal facial gesture made by her daughter. The dinner was cooked by N, and L's gesture related to the food:

|   |   |   |   |
|---|---|---|---|
| (24) | N | "What. Ya don't "like it,  ⇐ |   |
|      | L | ( ) It's te::rrible. | Weber 6:85 |

In this type of question, the first part of the utterance is a *wh*-word which is doing questioning — and the second part of the utterance is also doing questioning.

In this type of question, the first part of the utterance is a *wh*-word which is doing questioning — and the second part of the utterance is also doing questioning. Utterances of this type are produced without any pause between the *wh*-word or clause and the candidate response. They are interpretable as one question immediately following another. This is, in a sense, a general question followed by a more specific one. The declarative form is taking a guess at an answer and asking for confirmation of the guess.

Below, the speaker B responds to E's prior revelation that a school-aged classmate who had run away from home to live with her boyfriend has decided to return home:

(25)   B   What "happened, It didn't work "out?   ⇐
       E   I don't kno:w, I didn't get the detai:ls.            Weber 3:24

The initial interrogative clause projects question function which carries over to the completion of the candidate response. This strategy is also used with nonclausal forms (Chapter 6). In these cases, the *wh*-word or interrogative clause sets up the function of doing questioning. The declarative clause which follows is interpretable as being in the domain of that function. This strategy may be compared to the referent-proposition constructions of Keenan and Schieffelen (1976) or left dislocation utterances (Duranti and Ochs 1979, Geluykens 1992). (This strategy will be discussed more fully in Chapter 9).

*Prior Self-Repaired Interrogative Forms*

Some declarative forms which function to do questioning in the data are immediately preceded by a self-repaired utterance which is produced as an interrogative clause (see Chapter 2 for a discussion of repair phenomena). Schegloff (1979) shows that the occurrence of repair in an utterance has consequences on syntactic form. He states:

...the occurrence of repair in a sentence can have consequences for the shape
of the sentence and for the ordering of its elements beyond the consequences
embodied by sheer inclusion of the repair elements... (p. 263).

An utterance which a speaker repairs may undergo a change in syntactic form. The following example demonstrates that an utterance begun as an interrogative form can be redone as a declarative form (Schegloff 1979: 264). J and L are husband and wife:

(26)   J:   We saw Midnight Cowboy yesterday-
            or [Suh-Friday
       E:   [Ch?

L: Didju s- you saw that, it's really good. ←

JS:II:61

The utterance starts with an interrogative clause which is aborted; a declarative clause is then constructed and goes to completion. Schegloff (1979) states that repairs leave interactional effects. Even in the most simple case of repair in which one word is substituted for another, "the replacement cannot excise all traces of the word that was initially said or starting to be said" (p. 263; Jefferson 1975). Similarly, when an utterance is begun, aborted and then completed with a syntactically different form, the initial form of the utterance may not be excised from the recipient's perception. Schegloff (1979) presents evidence which suggests that recipients do, in fact, attend to talk which has been "edited out."

Edited-out talk may be relevant for the interpretation of declarative questions. When an utterance is begun with an interrogative form, the possible completion point of the interrogative is projected (this is a projection of form). Because of the projected interpretation of its function, the interrogative-in-progress also projects a range of possible next turns (an answer). When a speaker aborts an interrogative clause and then starts a declarative clause, a different possible completion point for the utterance is then projected. As the declarative form is produced, it gets interpreted with regard to its function on the basis of its position in the talk. With regard to both form and function, the projection of the prior-repaired interrogative is part of the prior talk. As such, it is relevant for the ongoing interpretation of the declarative form which is in the process of being constructed.

The repaired utterance and its projections may not be disregarded by the recipient. The repaired interrogative may project question function for a declarative clause in the same way a prior *wh*-word/clause does. Here is an example of a declarative question immediately following a self-repaired interrogative question. The declarative is also marked by a second-person subject and the discourse particle *oh* which indicates some shift in orientation to information ( Heritage 1984, Schiffrin 1987). The speaker E introduces a new topic with an interrogative which she then aborts:

(27)    E    **Did I tell y- Oh, "yo:u heard it.**    ←
        L    Yeh, [a]bout K___?
        E    [( )]
            No:, about (1.2) A___.                Weber 2:4

After the aborted form, the speaker continues by producing a declarative clause which goes to completion. The recipient responds with a confirmation. The response itself demonstrates that the declarative form utterance was interpreted as making a confirmation relevant. The prior self-repaired interrogative in conjunction with both the discourse particle *oh* and the second-person subject may play a role in the recipient's interpretation of the declarative form doing questioning insofar as it makes a confirmation relevant.

## Prior Discourse Marker

There are declarative questions in the data which are preceded by conjunctions, adverbs and discourse particles (*but, then, well, oh,* etc.) In her analysis of these discourse markers, Schiffrin (1987) views them as "indicators of the location of utterances within the emerging structures, meanings and actions of discourse" (p. 24). Although usually appearing with other elements which support the interpretation of the clause as doing questioning, these discourse markers may appear as the sole marker of a declarative question and may be relevant to the interpretation of a declarative clause as doing questioning. Below, the participants have been discussing the origin of the split between Ashkenazy and Sephardic Jews:

```
(28)    B    The separation occurred (.) when the: uh Ashkenazies
             moved west (.) across Europe. (.)
             moved EAST across Europe.
        L    (and) that's why they call (them) western.
        B    u:h n [o
        M         [because they 'came from the "west?      ⟵
        B    They're called western because right now (.) the word
             west refers not to direction,
             but to western culture.                Shapley/Sha 9:19
```

B is explaining how the separation originated. L then offers a candidate explanation for why Ashkenazy Jews are called western which he has inferred from the prior turn. M adds to that candidate explanation with a declarative question introduced by the discourse marker *because*. This utterance is interpretable as asking whether the Ashkenazy Jews are called western *because* they came from the west. In this utterance, *because they came from the west* explicitly articulates, via questioning, the causal relation between B's description and L's inference.

In the following, the declarative clause is marked by the discourse particle *well* and the conjunction *if* (see Chapter 2 for a justification of this classification). While the *if*-clause is not an independent clause according to strict grammatical criteria, such subordinate forms do appear in conversation (Ford forthcoming). In the following example from a telephone conversation, B and V, brother and sister, are discussing B's imminent trip from San Francisco to Los Angeles. It had previously been arranged that he would stay with his sister:

```
(29)    B    I c[an (either ) stay with you or with Sco:tt.
               [   (just   )
        V      [Ye-
             No that's fine
             stay he:re.
             *hh U:mm::
             (.)
```

|   |   |
|---|---|
|   | (0.2) |
| V | We:ll un-nuh-u:h it's fine.= |
|   | The only thing is to just realize |
|   | that if I have to study at times:, |
|   | (0.4) |
|   | actually I have to study alo:t. |
|   | Just do-= |
| B | Both of you do I know.= |
|   | =Well I'm (.) down there (.) not to be part of you |
|   | c(hh)utting into uh |
| V | uh (h)huh, |
| B | uh t(h)o (h) his research (.) |
|   | bu:t you know (company) |
|   | and things like that. |
| V | uh hh [huh] |
| B | [( )] |
|   | (.) |
| V | And you have you ca:r |
|   | so that'll make it quite easy. |
| B | Yeah. |
| V | *hhh Oka:y |
|   | is there any kind of food you want me to g(h)e:t? |
|   | (0.9) |
| **B** | **Ah-ha well if you "do:n't want me to co:me** ⇐ |
|   | **Vane:ss.** ⇐ |
| V | Wu-[of course- I no of course I actually ] |
| B | [hhhh hhh! huh hhh nuh huh huh] |
| V | you know what [I'm doing] right now for you= |
| B | [*hhh ] |
| V | =[tomorrow ] is |
| B | [hhh ] |
| V | I'm vacuuming right now. |
|   | (0.2) |
| B | Oh is it for me:. |
| V | Yea: [h ] and I washed some [sheets. ] |
| B | [hhh] [( ) live] there. |
|   | *hhh |
| V | No no it's only for y-hhh huh! huh! huh!-ou hhh! |
|   | And I'm also washing some sheets. |
|   | (0.2) |
| B | Okay. Lazaraton 2:54 |

B responds to V's question *Okay is there any kind of food you want me to g(h)e:t?* with the utterance *Ah-ha well if you do:n't want me to co:me Vane:ss.* B

B responds to V's question *Okay is there any kind of food you want me to g(h)e:t?* with the utterance *Ah-ha well if you do:n't want me to co:me Vane:ss.* B prefaces his response with *well*. Schiffrin (1987: 107) notes that *well* "is used when respondents diverge from the options for coherence offered them by a prior question."

Rather than addressing the question posed concerning his food preferences, B responds with the utterance *Ah-ha well if you do:n't want me to co:me Vane:ss.* Marked explicitly by the subordinating conjunction *if*, the clause projects a subsequent *then* clause. Although not produced, the projected clause is inferable as "then I won't." By using the *if* clause, B ascribes to the recipient the attitude of not wanting him to visit her. This imputation makes a confirmation or disconfirmation relevant. This form is interpretable as implicitly asking the recipient if she wants B to come and stay with her.

*4.3.2.3. Marking which Occurs Subsequent to the Production of the Declarative Clause.* There are several types of declarative questions which are formed by adding a particle or a word at the end of a clause. Quirk *et al.* (1985: 814) call these invariant tags because they have the same form regardless of the form of the declarative clause. I will refer to these types as *particle tags* or *word tags*. Example 30 is produced with a particle tag, and examples 31 and 32 are produced with word tags.

Below, the speaker K had been describing how a guest lecture which she gave before a women's studies class was very poorly received. She concludes her description as follows:

(30)  K     It went on from there. Down hill.
            ((laughter))
      C     ( ) They didn't "like it, "huh?              ⟵
      K     I'm afraid this elegant (.) heh heh theoretical
            exposition (.) just went  (.) ha
            went (.) um [t$^s$] (.) by them (apparently).
      ( )   heh heh                            Shapley/Nel 3:12

C responds to K's story with an appreciative uptake done as a declarative clause plus a particle.

Previously, the participants in the following example had been discussing M's sign language class; B begins to quiz M:

(31)  B     What's thi:s. ((signs)) *hhh ha  ha
      L     That's She knows what that [is.
      M                               [That?
            they taught me the other night.
            It's, it's (.) you know,
            this is (.) your mother, ((signs))

|   |   |   |
|---|---|---|
| | B | Must be Italian. |
| | | ((laughter)) |
| | M | That's a joke. Actually it's not. |
| | L | **The mother and grandmother are "right,"** ⇐ |
| | | **right?** ⇐ |
| | M | Yeah.                    Shapley/Boys 16:550 |

The speaker of the declarative question requests confirmation that two of the three previously produced signs were done correctly and not as a joke. The addition of the word tag *right* in conjunction with rising intonation unambiguously signals that the clause is doing questioning.

Below, the participants were discussing a message K had received from her daughter that someone named X (surname) had called; but K did not recognize the name. In fact, the caller C had given her maiden name, and K did not connect that name with C when she received the message:

|   |   |   |
|---|---|---|
| (32) | C | (No, ) I changed it several years ago |
| | | but she (.) , you know, |
| | | I don't I (.) don- I don't describe myself ( ) |
| | D | (.) she didn't know |
| | M | did you send out announcements. hh |
| | C | No, I didn't. |
| | L | **(If) she had said "C__ called,** ⇐ |
| | | **(it'd) be no "trouble, "right?** ⇐ |
| | K | Right.                   Shapley/Nel 1:6 |

This example has both an hypothetical clause and a conditional clause. The speaker is confirming that if the message had been given with a first name reference, K would not have had any trouble recognizing the caller. Again, the *right* with rising intonation signals question function.

Grammarians have described some declarative questions as tag questions. The form of these tags varies depending on the prior assertion and may be affirmative or negative (Quirk *et al.* 1985: 810-814). Both variant and invariant tags share the basic structure: declarative clause + tag.

In the following example, V is relating how she feels when she discusses her father's recent knee surgery with her mother. C responds with a clarification done as a declarative clause plus a clause tag:

|   |   |   |
|---|---|---|
| (33) | V | But do you know what I wanna do when I see her, |
| | | I wanna say I talked to the nurse, |
| | | tonight I asked the nurse-I asked her two times, |
| | | (0.4) |
| | V | I said are you s(h)ur:e this is gonna make him more |
| | | comfortable. |

```
V    I said are you s(h)ur:e this is gonna make him more
     comfortable.
     I mean what[is the- ]
C              [What? ]
     (0.2)
V    The surgery.=
C    =But it's already "done anyway, ("isn't it)?    ⇐
V    Oh it's done but I- I[   ] was so-[up         ]set I w-
C                         [Oh.]        [Yeah uh huh ]
                                                      Ford 10:299
```

Here, the declarative question is marked by the discourse marker *but* and a clause tag *isn't it*. The *it* refers to the surgery.

## 4.4. The Interpretation of Declarative Questions with No Associated Marker

Earlier, a declarative question with no associated lexical or morphosyntactic marking suggestive of question function was discussed. The issue of how such forms get interpreted as questions was deferred at that time until after marked declarative questions were presented. Following are some factors which are relevant to the interpretation of declarative questions without lexical or morphosyntactic marking.

### 4.4.1. *Intonation and Declarative Questions with No Associated Marker*

In English, intonation contour does not unambiguously signal "this is a question" vs. "this is not a question." If this in fact were the case, there would be no problem associated with the interpretation of declarative forms as questions — those forms with question intonation would be interpretable as questions, while those without question intonation would be interpretable as statements.

Cruttenden (1986) states that the intonation of *yes/no* questions which have no co-occurring syntactic marking (*i.e.*, declarative questions), "is almost invariably reported as having either a 'terminal rise' or in some way a higher pitch than the corresponding statement pattern" (p. 162). He cites Bolinger's (1978) survey of 36 non-tone languages in which all but four languages had a rise or a higher pitch for questions. Ultan reports (1978) from a survey of 53 languages that only three had a fall only for questions. Two of these were tone languages, leaving only one reported case of a non-tone language which did not have a terminal rise for questions. Swadesh (1946) reported this for Chitimacha on the basis of the only surviving speaker of the language.

The fact that *yes/no* questions in numerous non-tone languages are reported to have rising intonation is only half the story. Cruttenden raises the following important point:

> Although a very large number of intonation languages (*i.e.*, non-tone languages) are reported as having a final rise for yes/no questions, what remains uncertain is just how many of these languages have a fall as an alternative, since descriptions very rarely mention alternative intonations for a particular sentence-type (p. 163).

Cruttenden cites the fact that pedagogic textbooks on English describe *yes/no* questions as having only a rising intonation, although that is clearly not the case. It is, however, the generally held naive view of intonation as it relates to question function.

Discussions of rising terminal intonation in English often fail to make critical distinctions. Bolinger (1972:27) discusses the differentiation between the simple rise and the rise-fall-rise. He states that the latter type of pitch movement is extremely limited in questions. Bolinger (1989:100) suggests that overall intonation contour, rather than terminal direction, is relevant to understanding restrictions on intonation with respect to *yes/no* questions (see also Geluykens 1988, 1989b). Cruttenden (1986:105-111) notes that while the meaning of the high-rise contour is fairly consistent (echo or repeat question) (p. 108), the meaning of the low rise varies depending upon whether or not there is a preceding high-pitch accent (p. 105-6). Thus, not only is there variation between rising and falling intonation in declarative utterances which do questioning, but all patterns of rising intonation are not necessarily associated with question function.

Many linguists have noted that there is variation between rising and falling terminal intonation for declarative forms which do questioning in English. Stenström (1984:154) examined the relation between rising and falling intonation and declarative form questions. She found that falling intonation is more common than rising intonation (174 vs. 52 occurrences in her database), and lexical markers of question function in declarative forms appear as frequently with rising-terminal intonation as with falling intonation. She points out that such markers are equally common with rising intonation. These facts belie the common-sense view that rising intonation signals question function and that lexical markers signal question function when there is falling terminal intonation. Stenström hypothesizes that variation in intonation for forms which do questioning reflects the speaker's degree of certainty (p. 151, Couper-Kuhlen 1986).

Bolinger (1972) makes the point that rising intonation is associated with signaling a more general function than question function. He notes a simple rise in intonation is associated with all forms of incompleteness (p. 27); and while incompleteness includes interrogation, it is not limited to it. Geluykens (1988) suggests that rising intonation serves as a marker of nonfinality associated with the turn taking system, *i.e.*, as a cue the speaker has not finished his/her turn (p. 483).

Literature on the relevance of intonation to declarative questions suggests that variation between rising and falling terminal intonation characterizes declarative questions. Thus, it cannot be claimed that rising intonation associated with declarative forms, in itself, signals question function.

### 4.4.2. Gesture and Declarative Questions with No Associated Marker

Gesture may be a relevant factor in the interpretation of declarative questions (Chapter 1). Telephone conversations or face-to-face interaction in which the speaker's face is invisible exclude this dimension to some extent. Facial gesture can be "heard" in some cases (when the speaker is smiling, holding pins in the mouth, etc.). Because all but one of the conversations upon which this study is based are audiotaped rather than videotaped, the role of gesture in the interpretation of question function has not been considered.

### 4.4.3. Accessibility of Information and Declarative Questions with No Associated Marker

The accessibility of information associated with a clause has been proposed as a relevant factor in the interpretation of declarative questions. Labov and Fanshel (1977:100) have discussed declarative questions in terms of a rule of confirmation. There are cases where the response of the listener indicates that a declarative clause was heard as a request. Listeners respond with an affirmative or negative answer, thus implying a *yes/no* question. According to the authors, the interpretation of a declarative clause as a question is the result of applying a rule of confirmation. This rule depends on the classification of statements according to the shared knowledge of the participants.

The following classification system is proposed with regard to *social* facts involved in an interaction between two individuals, A and B (p. 100). Social facts are "generally agreed upon categorizations shared by all those present" (p. 100):

| | |
|---|---|
| A-events: | Known to A, but not to B |
| B-events: | Known to B, but not to A |
| AB-events: | Known to both A and B |
| O-events: | Known to everyone present |
| D-events: | Known to be disputable |

A-events typically involve states and events which concern individual A, (his or her emotions, daily experiences, likes and dislikes and elements of his or her personal history). The rule of confirmation is stated as follows:

If A makes a statement about B-events, then it is heard as a request for confirmation (p. 100).

Labov and Fanshel's rule of confirmation is exemplified below. This is a case in which a declarative question with no associated marker is used to introduce a topic by questioning:

```
(34)   N    What's doing,
            (.)
       H    Ah:, noth    [i: n:,       ]
       N                 [Y' didn't g  ]o meet "Grahame?=  ⇐
       H    =*pt *hhhhhahh Well, I got ho::me,
       N    =u-hu:h?
            (.)
            a:::n he hadn't called yet
            an there weren't any messages or anythi[n:g    ]e- ]
                                                   [Uh  h ]u ]:h
       H    a:n hh then I kind of got on the pho:ne
            an I heard a couple of clicks
            an hhhhhhh *hh I don't know if he was trying to call =
            =but I'm too tired to go all the way back to Westwood
            anyw[ay,  ]
       N        [Ye :]:ah,
                                                        HGII 1:17
```

N had some prior expectation that H was going to meet Grahame that day. When H responds to N's request for news with *Ah, nothin,* rather than a report of her meeting with Grahame, N makes the inference that the meeting did not take place. Because there was an expectation that a meeting was to have taken place, H's failure to report it as news becomes mentionable to N. She constructs the declarative question with a negative verb, thus exhibiting a bias for a negative answer (Chapter 2). Whether or not H went to meet Grahame is a B-event, *i.e.,* known to H but not to N.

Below is an extended turn in which the speaker M is describing his plans for the weekend:

```
(35)   S    I don't know  have you been studying lately,
            (0.2)
       M    No eh not at aw- not at all:
            I have to study this  whole week, every night *hh
            and then I've got something planned on Sunday with
            Laura,
            (0.4)
```

### 4.5. Next-Turn Repair Initiators and Declarative Questions with No Associated Marker

```
M    She she wa- she and I are gonna go out and get drunk at
     four o'clock in the afternoon.
S    Uh huh *hhh
M    It's a religious
     (0.5)
     thing we're gonna have.
     (0.5)
     I don't know why. (but)
     I don't know why but um
     (0.2)
     no her ex boyfriend's getting married
     and she:'s (-)gonna be  depressed s:o
     (1.1)
S    She [wasn't invited to the "wedding?     ←
M        [ (I'm gonna take her out.)
     (1.0)
     She's  [ oh no. hell no.
            [(hell no)
S             [hardly.
R    h(h)m /*hm hm
     (.1)
M    She's trying to stay away from the wedding.
                                           SN4 10:5
```

S had an expectation that Laura's relation with her former boyfriend meant she would have been or should have been invited to his wedding. Because M's talk makes clear that Laura will be with him at the time of the wedding, the issue of the invitation becomes mentionable for S. S constructs the utterance with a negative verb, demonstrating that she anticipates a negative answer (Chapter 2). Whether or not Laura was invited to her former boyfriend's wedding is a B-event, (known to M but not to S, since he is describing the relevant events).

### 4.5. Next-Turn Repair Initiators and Declarative Questions with No Associated Marker

In Chapter 2, I have discussed how participants in conversation manage to effect repair (address problems in speaking, hearing and understanding). When repair is initiated by a participant other than the speaker, the repair occupies "one main position: the turn just subsequent to the trouble source turn" (Schegloff, Jefferson, and Sacks 1977:367). These repair initiators are next-turn repair initiators (NTRI's).

Declarative clauses which are NTRI's are interpretable by virtue of a number of factors: next-turn position with regard to the prior utterance, their repetitive elements, *wh*-words, the discourse marker *you mean* and in some cases, rising terminal intonation (Garvey 1979). The example below exhibits an NTRI. N repeats L's prior declarative form utterance, thereby signaling some trouble in understanding:

(36)    E     Wasn't she gonna go to UCLA that (.) thing=
          N     =It's at UC[LA
          L               [Pass the milk.
          B     Yeah, ok.
          N     Pass the salad,
          L     She can still go.
          N     **She can "s-till go?**           ⇐
          L     Maybe she's going,           Weber 9:134

N is displaying some trouble in understanding the prior utterance by repeating it verbatim. This type of NTRI, a repetition of an entire declarative clause, is rare in my data. (This example will be further discussed in Chapter 5.)

Below, the declarative question is an NTRI marked by *you mean*. Not interpretable as *do you mean*, this is a discourse marker. Schiffrin (1987) notes that *you mean* "allows a speaker to propose a modification of another's talk" (p. 299). In this example, M is demonstrating some signs which she has learned at a sign-language class:

(37)    M     Husband i:s ((signs))
                 (1.0)
          L     Like a hat.
          M     This is ma:n. ((signs))
                 It's sort of (.)
          L     Like that.
          M     assume a hat.
                 And this is woman, which they say you assume is the strings of a bonnet.
          L     ( )
          M     So a man (0.1) and a (.) woman (0.1)
                 a man (.) and a woman are married,
                 and a husband is a man who is married.
          L     this is married.
                 (0.5)
          M     I think.
                 This is all pantomime.
                 You sort of get used to that.
          P     Hm.
                 **You mean somebody just "stands up (.) there,**     ⇐
                 **and (.) "talks (.) that way,**                    ⇐

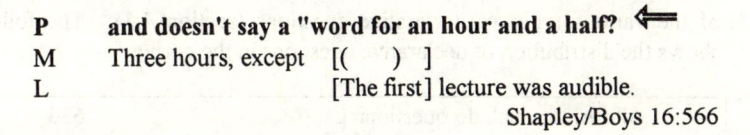

```
P    and doesn't say a "word for an hour and a half?  ⇐
M    Three hours, except  [(   )  ]
L                          [The first] lecture was audible.
                                              Shapley/Boys 16:566
```

P produces the NTRI *you mean somebody just stands up there and talks that way and doesn't say a word for an hour and a half* after M explains that all the instruction took place in sign language. By producing the discourse marker *you mean* plus a declarative clause, P is clarifying his concern about whether any spoken language was used in the class.

The discourse marker *you mean* can also appear after the declarative clause. Below, the participants are discussing C's college student daughter M:

```
(38)   K    (.) I guess I did talk to M__ a little bit about u:h (.) her
            women's study course,
            (.) which I gave a lecture to.
            Did   [she ever talk to you about that?
       C         [Oh did you?
            No: she never really told me about (much) about the
            course, °you know.
       M    What did you lecture about women's studies.
       K    We:ll (.) they put together this women's studies course.
            U:h
       C    (yeah) she was in some subset.
            What was that.
       K    lets see (.) I'm [trying to think.
       C                     [third world women or something.
       L                     [( )
            Oh That's like "black studies, °you "mean?     ⇐
       ( )  ( )
       C    Yeah right right right.             Shapley/Nel 2:15
```

L produces the NTRI *Oh that's like black studies, you mean* to clarify his understanding of the prior turn in which C relates the course to third-world women. Declarative clauses are interpretable as questions insofar as they are interpretable as initiating repair. Next-turn position, repetitive elements, *wh*-words, *you mean* and rising intonation, in some instances, are factors relevant for interpreting a declarative clause as initiating repair.

### 4.6. Distributive Facts

In this section, I will examine the distribution of declarative questions vs. other syntactic types of questions in the corpus. I will also examine the distribution of the various types of declarative questions (section 4.3). The following table shows the distribution of declarative questions in the corpus:

| All forms which do questioning | 636 | 100% |
| All declarative forms which do questioning | 108 | 17% |

**Table 4.1.**
**Distribution of Declarative Questions**

This table demonstrates that declarative clauses constitute 17% of all forms doing questioning in this data, confirming that speakers regularly use declarative clauses to ask questions. The problem of how such forms get interpreted as questions is not a trivial one. The production of declarative clauses to do questioning and their interpretation, as questions, is a fact of language use.

The following table exhibits the distribution of lexically or morphosyntactically marked declarative questions vs. declarative questions with no associated lexical or morphosyntactic marker in the data:

| Marked | 82 | 76% |
| No associated marker | 26 | 24% |
| **Total** | **108** | **100%** |

**Table 4.2.**
**Marked Declarative Questions**
**vs.**
**Declarative Questions with No Associated Marker**

Three out of four declarative questions are marked by lexical or morpho-syntactic elements.

### 4.6.1. Marked Declarative Questions

The following table presents the distribution of marking in declarative questions described in section 4.3. The types of marking have been distinguished according to temporal criteria as follows: Section I — marking which occurs within the declarative clause; Section II — marking which occurs prior to the declarative clause; Section III — marking which occurs subsequent to the declarative clause. Note: some utterances have more than one type of marking (which is why the total number of instances is more than the total number of marked forms):

| | | |
|---|---|---|
| **I: Within the Clause** | | |
| Lexical meaning of verb/adverb | 13 | |
| Wh-word addition/substitution | 2 | |
| Gap | 1 | 14% |
| **II: Prior to the Clause** | | |
| Prior lexical element | 1 | |
| Prior clause with lexical element | 3 | |
| Prior wh-word/clause | 6 | |
| Prior self-repair | 2 | |
| Prior discourse marker | 37 | 43% |
| **III: Subsequent to the Clause** | | |
| Subsequent interrogative clause | 3 | |
| Subsequent discourse marker | 2 | |
| Particle tag | 10 | |
| Word tag | 10 | |
| Clause tag | 22 | |
| Alternative tag | 2 | 43% |
| **Total** | **114** | **100%** |

Table 4.3.
Instances of Marking in Declarative Questions

Within-clause marking constitutes 14% of all instances; marking before the clause, 43%; and marking subsequent to the clause, 43%. While marking before and after the declarative clause appear equal, marking within the clause is less common. From this temporal perspective, the distribution of these markers only takes the total number of occurrences of each type into account; it does not consider how these markers co-occur in particular forms.

Before we can understand how these markers get used by speakers in real time, we must examine their distribution in individual clauses. The following table exhibits the distribution of markers by number per clause:

| | | |
|---|---|---|
| 1 marker | 57 | 70% |
| 2 markers | 19 | 23% |
| 3 markers | 5 | 6% |
| 4 markers | 1 | 1% |
| **Total** | **82** | **100%** |

Table 4.4. Number of Markers per Clause

Among the declarative clauses that have a lexical or morphosyntactic marker suggesting question function, 70% have a single marker. Two markers occur in 23% of all declarative forms, and three markers occur in 6%. There is a single instance of a form with four markers. We can conclude, then, that if a form has a marker, more than two out of three times it will get only one.

The distribution of one-to-a-form markers according to temporal criteria is shown in the following table:

| | | |
|---|---|---|
| Within the clause | 13 | 23% |
| Prior to the clause | 15 | 26% |
| Subsequent to the clause | 29 | 51% |
| **Total** | **57** | **100%** |

Table 4.5.
**Distribution of Single Markers Per Clause**

When there is a single marker per form suggesting question function, over half of the time it is subsequent to the declarative clause. When there are two markers per form, one is always a prior marker (except in one case, in which there were two subsequent markers). Of these two-to-a-form markers with prior markers, all but two contain at least one discourse marker. (The two exceptions are marked by a prior *wh*-word and a prior interrogative clause.)

The two markers per form distribute as follows according to temporal criteria:

| | | | |
|---|---|---|---|
| Prior marker + within the clause | 2 | 10.5%} | |
| Prior marker + subsequent marker | 10 | 52.6%} | 63% |
| Prior marker + prior marker | 6 | 31.5% | |
| Subsequent marker + subsequent marker | 1 | 5.0% | |
| **Total** | **19** | **100%** | |

Table 4.6.
**Distribution of Two Markers Per Clause**

When there are two markers per form, they belong to different temporal domains in 63% of all cases of marked forms. In 31.5% of the cases, there are two prior markers; in one case (5%) there are two subsequent markers. This distribution is quite interesting. With only one exception, all forms with multiple markers have a prior marker.

A marker suggestive of question function precedes the declarative utterance in time, signaling, at the least, the possibility of the question function of the utterance to follow. With multiple markers, the declarative form gets marked before and after its production over 50% of the time. The initial marker is reinforced by a second which serves to frame the declarative with respect to its question function.

Because this is not the only possible pattern available to speakers, we may ask why they prefer this one rather than, for example, piling up markers suggestive of question function before or after the declarative clause. (The temporal marking patterns of declarative clauses will be discussed more fully in Chapter 9).

There are five cases in the data with three markers. In the following example, the declarative clause is marked by the prior discourse marker *but*, the word tag *right* and the clause tag *wasn't he*. The speaker V is telling how her mother caused her to doubt the necessity of her father's knee surgery:

(39)  V   But then when I talked to my Mom
          and she was all hysterical,
          then I started getting hys [teri   ]cal.
      C                              [Yeah. ]
          (0.2)
      V   Like oh my Go:d all this for nothing,
          my D  [ad   ] was okay:,
      C         [Yeah ]
      K   O:h(h)
      V   he could ski,
          he could wa:lk,
          why's he going through this pai:n=
      C   =But you knew he was in pain          ⇐
          "before. "right?                      ⇐
          "wasn't h[e:                          ⇐
      V           [He didn't complain about it.
                                        Ford 7: 209

In this case, the clause tag is not the one predicted by grammars of English, which would be *didn't you*. It addresses the complement clause, *he was in pain*.

Below, the declarative clause is a repair of an interrogative. The repair itself begins as an interrogative, is aborted and then redone as a declarative marked by *right*. The recipient of the question, D, had been talking about a bad case of dysentery. The speaker H inquires about his weight:

(40)  H   So are you gaining "weight?          ⇐
          I mean (.) di- you lost a lot of "weight,  ⇐
          ["right?=                            ⇐
      D   [(hh) Yeah, I'm well
          I think I am.
          (0.2)
          It's hard to tell.
          (0.5)
          I feel I mean I feel like I'm ea:ting fu:ll meals.
                                    Riggenbach 10:263

In this example, *so* is resumptive and does not mean "result." The prior markers of question function involve prior clauses — an interrogative clause which goes to completion and a self-repaired interrogative. These clauses are different from discourse markers because they have semantic meaning and are interpretable in their own right independently of the following declarative question. Prior marking which involves repair is different in kind from prior lexical or morphosyntactic marking. The final declarative question is itself marked by a word tag.

There is one case in which a form has four markers. Though fluent in English, the speaker of this declarative question is not a native speaker. This fact may or may not be relevant with regard to this unique case. During a dinner table conversation, the participants are being served spinach soup:

(41)   T          [You know, in the old da:ys]
        M     Spinach [ spinach has this      ] huge
               negative ion (.) iron (.) ance, because it it chelates the iron (.) in the rest of your foods=
        B      =Oh it does not have (.)
               it is not a good source of iron.=
        M     =It extracts iron.
        ()     ()
        B      Really?
               hh
        L      what does it do with it.
        B      Why this myth [then
        M               [it chelates it into some absorbable form.
        B      why this myth for so for so long
        L      Does it build up?
        M     Most  [of the myths are that children    ]
        T            [the myths were started by the=   ]
        M     =the myths among children are that spinach is terrible and that it tastes bad.
               *hh
        B      Yes.
        M     so the other myths are an attempt by the adults [to
        B                                       [I see.
        M     = compensate for it.
        B      ()
               But "I thought,     ⇐
               that every- everything that was dark "green was  ⇐
               uh (.)   ⇐
               no everything "red is high in iron. Or "what.  ⇐
               "what is it.  ⇐
               what is the "truth.  ⇐
               ()    uh

M    There is no truth.                              Shapley/Fer 2:25.1

The declarative is marked by a prior discourse marker *but*, an alternative tag and two subsequent interrogative clauses. The multiple marking accumulates after the production of the declarative clause. The final two interrogative clause markers are syntactically independent of the declarative clause. The pronoun *it* is interpretable in terms of the repaired declarative form which contains two hypotheses about which vegetables are high in iron.

*4.6.2. Declarative Questions with No Associated Lexical or Morphosyntactic Marker*

Table 4.2. demonstrates that 24% of all cases of declarative questions have no lexical or syntactic marking suggestive of question function. Stenström (1984) describes these "plain" declarative clause questions as the prototypical declarative questions which are often cited when the form/function problem is discussed. The problematic issue is how such forms get interpreted.

The following table presents the plain declarative questions in the data by the categories which have been outlined above, *i.e.*, NTRI's and requests for confirmation inferable from the accessibility of information:

| | | |
|---|---|---|
| NTRI | 3 | 12% |
| Requests for Confirmation | 23 | 88% |
| Total | 26 | 100% |

Table 4.7.
Distribution of Declarative Questions
with No Associated Marker by NTRI's and Rule of Confirmation

One hundred percent of all declarative questions with no associated marker are in these two categories. Note: these categories are not *ad hoc*; they are well established in the literature as devices used by participants in conversation.

*NTRI's*

Conversation analysts regard NTRI's to be a highly organized and effective conversational device (Chapter 2). In regard to the discussion of declarative questions, the relevant NTRI's are those which are repeats or partial repeats with or without a *wh*-word. In terms of the temporal aspects of their interpretation, NTRI's relate to the prior discourse because they are only interpretable as repetitions in terms of a prior utterance which they target as a source of some trouble. In that sense, then, they are interpretable as NTRI first-pair parts doing questioning by reference to a prior utterance. In my data, only three declarative questions with no

86    VARIETIES OF QUESTIONS IN ENGLISH CONVERSATION

associated marker are NTRI's. In all instances of NTRI's involving repetition, most are not declarative clauses, rather, partial repeats which are less than a complete clause. (As such, they will be discussed in relation to nonclausal questions in Chapter 6.)

*Labov and Fanshel's Rule of Confirmation*

According to Labov and Fanshel's rule of confirmation, all the declarative questions with no associated marker which are not NTRI's involve a request for confirmation based on the distinction between A- and B-events. In other words, the declarative questions involve B-events. An examination of these utterances reveals that over one-third of all cases have second-person subjects (*you*) as shown below:

| | | |
|---|---|---|
| Second-person subjects | 10 | 38% |
| Third-person subjects | 13 | 62% |
| **Total** | **23** | **100%** |

Table 4.8.
**Subjects of Declarative Questions with No Associated Marker
(excluding NTRI's)
Interpretable in Terms of Labov & Fanshel's Rule of Confirmation**

In a way, the second-person pronoun *you* is a lexical marker of question function (Bolinger 1957, Stenström 1984). Second-person subjects appear far less frequently in discourse than first- and third-person subjects (Chafe 1982; Thompson and Mulac, 1992). The second-person pronoun refers to a participant in the interaction (unless it is a generic or "impersonal" *you*). If an utterance includes a referential *you*, it refers to the recipient of that utterance. These utterances appear most often in interrogative forms which do questioning and are, therefore, associated with question function in both interrogative and declarative forms.

The following example is a declarative question with a second-person subject without any other marker of question function. The recipient of the question, M, has come to S and R's dorm room:

(42)    M    I came to talk to Ruthie about borrowing her (0.1)
              notes () from (0.1) econ.
        R    Oh ( ).
        S    **You didn't come to talk to "Karen?**    ⬅
              (0.5)
        M    No
              (0.2)
              Karen: (0.3) Karen and I are having a fight.

SN 4 4:2

# DECLARATIVE QUESTIONS: MORPHOSYNTACTIC PATTERNS

The second-person subject *you* was not initially classified as a lexical marker of question function because inclusion in that category was limited by a strictly semantic criterion. It is not the meaning of the second-person pronoun which makes it suggestive of question function; it is the fact that it refers to the recipient in an interaction. If *you* is considered to be a lexical marker suggestive of question function in declarative forms, then the number of marked forms vs. forms with no associated marker presented in Table 4.2. increases. This amended distribution is presented below:

| | | | |
|---|---|---|---|
| Marked | 92 | (82 + 10 *you* subjects) | 85% |
| No Associated Marker | 16 | | 15% |
| **Total** | **108** | | **100%** |

Table 4.9.
**Amended Marked Declarative Questions
vs.
Declarative Questions with No Associated Marker**
(includes *you* as a lexical marker)

In this amended table, 85% of all declarative questions are marked. If *you* were considered to be a lexical marker suggestive of question function in declarative forms, the number of marked declarative questions with one marker would decrease. The following table exhibits this amended distribution:

| | | |
|---|---|---|
| 1 marker | 50 | 54% |
| 2 markers | 29 | 32% |
| 3 markers | 10 | 11% |
| 4 markers | 3 | 3% |
| **Total** | **92** | **100%** |

Table 4.10.
**Amended Number of Markers per Clause**
(includes *you* as a lexical marker)

More than half of all marked declarative questions have a single marker. In other words, not quite half of marked declarative questions have multiple markers.

There are only 16 cases of declarative questions in Table 4.9 which have no associated marker — three NTRI's and 13 declaratives with third-person subjects. The three NTRI's are interpretable as repetitions with a rising terminal intonation and are marked sequentially, being repetitions. Of the 13 remaining declaratives with no associated marker, three appear within the context of a narrative. The speaker uses the declarative form to question the narrator with regard to some aspect of the story he/she is telling. There is no ambiguity about who has access to the information. Seven of the declarative questions with no associated marker occur during the course of an exposition/description of a subject by an expert on that topic. These subjects are not part of common knowledge subjects, *e.g.*, Hebrew writing symbols, Russian words, Indian mythical figures.

There are two cases of declarative questions in which the participants are involved in making arrangements. Below, the participants are discussing a play they are going to see that evening. (*So* here is resumptive; it does not mean "result"):

```
(43)   H    Ye:s I cried hysterically=
            =at the mov[ie. I don't know if I'm]=
       N             [Oh: guy              ]
       H    =gon[na cry::,          ]
       N        [Can you imagine] how=
            =[its gonna] be in per [son?    ]=
       H     [*hhhhh   ]           [e-hheh ]=
            =I don't kno, how its gonna b [e:, ]=
       N                                  [oh: ]=
       H    =fer the pla ]: [:y.  ]
       N    =wo::w,      ]  [So it ]=
            = 'starts at eight "thir [ty?]             ⟵
       H                             [*hh] Yeah.
            So, if I- k- pick you up li:ke by eight o'clo::  [ck,
       N                                                     [Yeah,
                                                                HGII 13:23
```

Because H has invited N to the play and made all the arrangements including reserving the tickets, there is no ambiguity as to which of the two participants is in the position of being the authority on the curtain time.

Here is another case in which the declarative question is doing a joke:

```
(44)   (0.1)
       M    Who are you going to hear tonight?
       B    Stravinsky? [ Stravinsky
       P                [Stravinski's going to show "up?        ⟵
       B    No:. he:'s dead. ( )                  Shapley/Boys 12:21
```

P produces a declarative question which is interpretable as a joke because it is common knowledge among the participants that Stravinski is a composer, not a performer, and he is deceased. The speaker of the question, however, treats the possibility of Stravinski's appearance as a performer as a B-event.

## 4.7. Summary of Distributive Facts

The distributive facts reveal that 85% of all declarative questions are marked either lexically (including *you* subjects) or morphosyntactically. The remaining 15% consist of NTRI's and third-person subject clauses. The NTRI's are repetitions of a prior utterance; they exhibit a distinguishing high-rise intonation contour and are interpretable by position and intonation in that position. Cruttenden (1986) notes that the high-rise intonation contour has a fairly consistent meaning across all clause types. He states that "(t)his meaning is basically that of 'echo or repeat question'... sometimes also called 'contingent queries' or 'pardon questions'" (p. 108). The repetition combined with the rising intonation is, in a sense, an overt marker of the function of the utterance. It is lexical because all or most of the lexical elements of the utterance which is the source of the trouble are repeated.

Of the 13 third-person subject clauses, three question something in an ongoing narrative. Because the recipient of the story produces them, there is no ambiguity about these clauses being requests for confirmation. (It is clear that the narrator has access to the information.) Similarly, seven questions asked of experts leave no doubt as to who has access to the information queried. There are two declarative questions which involve making arrangements. Again, these declarative questions are not ambiguous; it is clear who "owns" the information. The final declarative question is a joke which plays off the common knowledge of the information queried.

In summary, an examination of the morphosyntactic patterns of declarative questions demonstrates that they either:

(1) Have lexical or morphosyntactic marking;
(2) Are NTRI's; or
(3) Are interpretable in terms of Labov and Fanshel's rule of confirmation.

This does not imply that interpretation is made solely on the basis of the morphosyntax. Sequential position or intonation or their interaction may be a crucial factor in determining question function in any particular instance. The morphosyntactic facts described in this chapter, however, must be considered in any investigation of why participants in conversation do not have problems interpreting declarative questions.

The same morphosyntactic marking, of course, may not indicate question function when combined with differences in pitch prominence, direction of terminal intonation and other sequential contexts (see Chapter 8). When approached from a semiotic perspective, however, morphosyntactic form exhibits patterns amenable to interpretation in conjunction with intonation and sequential position. These patterns are relevant when considering the fact that declarative questions do not present a real interpretive problem to participants in conversation.

# Chapter 5

# Declarative Questions: Function

## 5.1. Multiple Functions of Declarative Questions

All the declarative forms in the data, of course, are functioning to do questioning, because this was the criterion by which all forms to be included in the data were identified. Although "doing questioning" is a broad categorization of discourse function, it is not a trivial one. If a participant in conversation is asked a question, a response is made conditionally relevant and will be noticeably absent if not produced. Question forms in their social context, however, may exhibit functions which can be described in ways other than doing questioning. In fact, a form may realize multiple functions which accomplish a speaker's goals in interaction.

## 5.2. Functional Distribution of Declarative Questions

The declarative questions in the data have been categorized functionally as follows:

(1) Next-turn repair initiators (NTRI's),
(2) Requests for confirmation interpretable in terms of A- and B-events,
(3) Instances of other functions, and
(4) Instances of *you're kidding*.

The function of repair in conversation has been described by Schegloff, Jefferson and Sacks (1977) (Chapter 2). Labov and Fanshel (1977) have described the interpretation of declarative questions by a proposed rule of confirmation based on the notion of A- and B-events (Chapter 4). The functional category "other" includes topic solicitations, candidate understandings, expressions of ignorance and story uptakes. There are also a number of instances of *you're kidding* in the data which receipt new or interesting information. The 108 clauses in the data distribute as follows:

| | | |
|---|---|---|
| NTRI's | 10 | 9% |
| Requests for Confirmation (in terms of A- and B-events) | 68 | 63% |
| Other Functions | 25 | 23% |
| You're kidding | 5 | 5% |
| **Total** | 108 | 100% |

Table 5.1.
**Distribution of Declarative Clauses by Function**

This table shows that declarative clauses produced as NTRI's (9% of all cases of declarative questions) are rare in the data, while requests for confirmation in terms of A- and B-events constitute 63% of the cases. Other functions constitute 23%, and instances of *you're kidding* constitute 5% of all cases.

### 5.3. Next-Turn Repair Initiators (NTRI's)

Ten declarative questions in the data function as NTRI's and, as such, display some trouble with hearing or understanding the prior utterance (Chapter 2). Eight of these 10 declarative NTRI's function specifically to check the understanding of the prior turn rather than to demonstrate some trouble with hearing or with a reference. Understanding checks are accomplished via full or partial repeats or the use of the discourse particle *you mean* plus a candidate understanding of the prior turn.

In the following example, N produces a complete repetition of the entire prior utterance with terminally rising intonation. Previously, N had started telling a story about her friend's daughter J who had run away from home. J is a friend of N's daughter L. Note: L produces the utterance *she can still go* three times:

```
(45)   J     Did she go to (. ) boarding school.
       N     No. She wouldn't go to boarding school.
             So they (might) have her at Fernald.
       J     hmm
       L     They what?
       N     Fernald's the only school that would take her now.
       L     She can still go.
       N     She tried to get into other private schools.
       L     She can still go to Fernald.
       J     Is that?[Where is that.
       E             [Wasn't she gonna to go to UCLA that (. ) thing=
       N     =It's at UC[LA,
       L                [Pass the milk.
```

## DECLARATIVE QUESTIONS: FUNCTION

    J    Yeah, ok.
    N    °Pass the salad,
    L    She can still go.
    **N**    **She can "still go? (.)**    ⇐
    L    Maybe she's going,
    N    Yeah. I don't kno:w,
    (1. 0)    Weber 9:134

In answer to a question, N offers the information that the referent refused to go to boarding school; and consequently, the only school that would admit her is a local private school, Fernald (probably because the school year had already begun). In response, L produces *she can still go*.

    The use of *still* indicates that the temporal dimension was interpreted as being significant. The stress is on *still* and seems to be denying that she could no longer go to any other school. N interprets this turn as meaning the referent can still go other places, because in her next turn, she gives background information explaining *why* the referent cannot go other places. This turn denies that the referent can still go other places.

    L redoes *she can still go* with the addition of the prepositional phrase *to Fernald*. This is a correction of the prior turn and suggests how L had intended her prior production (*she can still go*) to be interpreted initially, viz., the referent can still go to Fernald.

    This turn may be an example of the Sack's substitution principle in which a repetition is fuller or more explicit than the original. If L's first production of *she can still go* were intended to be interpreted as *she can still go to Fernald*, it meant, "she is not going to Fernald yet, but still has the option to go." In any event, L's first production of *she can still go* seems to indicate that she misinterpreted what was said. After two NTRI's and some food talk, L produces *she can still go* a third time.

    This persistence is fascinating and directs us to ask again what the turn was doing in the first and second productions. Generally, repetitions mean "I am saying now what I said before." N produces an NTRI which repeats the prior declarative clause with a different intonation contour and a break in rhythm on the *s* of *still*. This full repetition is checking the understanding of the information presented about the referent. L responds to the repetition as if it were projecting some disagreement with the prior turn. In response to the repetition, L's next turn appears to be a stepping up of her assertion that *she can still go*. L states that maybe the referent has actualized her option to go and is, in fact, going to Fernald. N responds with an affirmative token and concedes that she does not know.

    This example is a rare case of a full-repetition declarative clause NTRI. The exchange involves misunderstandings which continue over several turns. The NTRI is not interpreted merely as a problem in understanding, but as a challenge to the assertion, and the response upgrades that assertion. Note: NTRI's will be more fully discussed in Chapter 6 in relation to nonclausal forms.

## 5.4. Requests for Confirmation

One factor involved in the interpretation of declarative forms with no associated marker is Labov and Fanshel's rule of confirmation (Chapter 4): if A makes a statement about a B-event, it is interpreted as a request for confirmation. B-events are typically known to B but not to A, *e.g.*, his or her emotions, daily experiences, likes and dislikes, etc. The confirming function of declarative questions has been frequently noted in the literature.

Bolinger (1957) refers to declarative questions as plain assertive *yes/no* questions. He notes that "(a)ny utterance that may serve as an assertion may also serve as a Q, provided no markers are present which exclude Q's;" and that functionally in assertive Q's, "a fact is assumed, pending confirmation" (p. 59). An assumption is possible in any situation where there is "no strong reason for doubt or curiosity" (p. 60).

Chafe (1970: 333-335) also notes the confirmative function of declarative questions. Stenström (1984) classifies declarative questions lexico-grammatically as declarative, declarative plus tag and declarative plus prompter (p. 152). She states that these forms function to either confirm or acknowledge information (pp. 156-58). Quirk *et al.* (1985: 814) state that declarative questions "invite the hearer's verification." An analysis of the data in this study supports the claims of the above authors with respect to the confirmative function of declarative questions, illustrated in the following table.

Table 5.2 presents the distribution of declarative questions in the data as marked forms vs. forms with no associated marker according to their interpretability of A- and B-events.[1] Although many of the declarative questions are interpretable in terms of A- and B-events, some are not. Those which are not interpretable in these terms constitute the category "other." Declarative-form NTRI's have been excluded from this table (10 instances) because they are interpretable as first-pair part repair initiators, by virtue of their position, repetitive elements and intonation. The instances of *you're kidding* which are interpretable as news receipts because of the semantics of their elements and function are also excluded. The total number of forms considered is 93:

|  | Marked | No Associated Marker | Total |
|---|---|---|---|
| Interpretable in terms of A & B-Events | 45  48% | 23  25% | 73% |
| *Not* Interpretable in terms of A & B-events | 25  27% | 0 | 27% |
| Total | 70  75% | 23  25% | 100% |

Table 5.2.
Declaratives Interpretable as Requests for Confirmation
in Terms of A-Events and B-Events
by Marked Forms vs. Forms with No Associated Marker

Declarative questions which are interpretable in terms of A- and B-events as requests for confirmation are marked in 48% of these cases, and ones with no associated marker constitute 25% of the cases. When declarative questions both with and without an associated marker are considered, 73% of all declarative question forms are interpretable in terms of A- and B-events as requests for confirmation — while the remaining 27% are *not* interpretable *in terms of A- and B-events* as requests for confirmation. All of these cases have some associated marker. (The fact that there are zero instances with no associated marker will be discussed in section 5.5.).

If requests for confirmation in terms of A- and B-events with second-person subjects were included in the category marked, there would be only 13 cases of requests for confirmation with no associated marker (instances of marking are limited to lexical or morphosyntactic elements). A lexical element suggestive of question function is entirely dependent upon its meaning. Because there is nothing in the meaning of the second-person subject which is suggestive of question function, *you* was not initially considered a lexical marker. As we have seen in Chapter 4, however, there are other reasons for considering *you* a marker suggestive of question function. The following table includes second-person subjects in the category marked:

|  | Marked |  | No Associated Marker |  | Total |
|---|---|---|---|---|---|
| Interpretable in terms of A & B-Events | 55 | 59% | 13 | 14% | 73% |
| *Not* Interpretable in terms of A & B-events | 25 | 27% | 0 |  | 27% |
| Total | 80 | 86% | 13 | 14% | 100% |

Table 5.3.
**Declaratives Interpretable as Requests for Confirmation
in Terms of A-Events and B-Events
by Marked Forms vs. Forms with No Associated Marker
(includes *you* subjects as marked)**

This amended table illustrates that marked declarative questions interpretable in terms of A- and B-events constitute 59% of all declarative questions which are neither NTRI's nor instances of *you're kidding*. In the following sections, I will first discuss those forms interpretable in terms of A- and B-events which are marked.

### 5.4.1. Marked Requests for Confirmation in terms of A-events and B-events

As we have seen in Table 5.3., most requests for confirmation interpretable in terms of A- and B-events are marked either lexically, morphosyntactically or with second-person subjects. The following table presents the distribution of subjects of marked requests for confirmation by subject number:

| 1P | 2 | 4% |
|---|---|---|
| 2P | 32 | 58% |
| 3P | 21 | 38% |
| Total | 55 | 100% |

Table 5.4.
**Distribution of Subjects in Marked Requests for Confirmation**

In only 4% of the cases do requests for confirmation interpretable in terms of A- and B-events have first-person subjects (examples 19 and 74). This low percentage is expected, because situations in which the speaker asks for confirmation is relatively restricted for first-person subjects (Sadock 1984). There apparently are few situations in which a speaker asks a recipient to confirm something *about himself/herself* by using a declarative question. First-person subject requests for confirmation in this data occur with hearsay verbs, hypothetical verbs and verbs of cognition (*hear, imagine, know*) (Bolinger 1957). The request for confirmation involves information expressed in a complement clause; and it is the information in this complement clause that is interpretable as a B-event.

Table 5.4. also indicates that 58% of subjects of marked requests for confirmation interpretable in terms of A- and B-events are second-person subjects. These instances are prototypical cases of requests for confirmation because they explicitly mention the participant who owns the information (*you*).

The following examples contain a lexical or syntactic marker suggestive of question function in addition to the second-person subject. The next example is taken from a telephone conversation:

```
(46)  R    So you took the (. ) job, huh?
      A    Well I'm working daytimes,
      R    yeah?=
      A    =a:nd um (0. 2) for (. ) wha:t I what I did was
           I asked them if I could work like from one to seven,
           (0.3)
           for this week and next week,
           [(0. 3) ]
           [*hhh  ] so that still gives me: (. ) the mornings,
      R    "Oh,                                                    ⇐
           so you're still doing the "part time thing,              ⇐
           you're not doing the "full time th  [ing,                ⇐
      A                                        [No: and then
           (. ) what they really want me: is uh to start full time on the
           twenty first.
           (1.0)
      R    *Um hm:                                      Mannon 1:17
```

In this example, R asks about A's employment status, and R begins his answer with the discourse marker *well* and then responds with his work schedule. Schiffrin (1987:106) notes that *well* often precedes responses to *yes/no* questions when "neither option offered by the question provides sufficient basis from which to choose an answer" (see also Schegloff, Sacks and Jefferson 1977, Labov and Fanshel 1977, Svartvik 1980, Owen 1983, Pomerantz 1984). A simple affirmative or negative response will not suffice to encompass A's employment situation. R infers from A's response that he is not yet working full time; confirmation is requested in the declarative question *so you're still doing the part time thing, you're not doing the full time thing*.

In the following, the participants had been discussing the meaning of *ergodic*, *ergotic* and *argosy*. This example is one of two simultaneous conversations (the other one has not been included):

(47) L   Ergodic means something palliatory.
    N   Is this [ a ( )
    M          [Ergot is a fungus of wheat.
    N   yeah.
        **you take "it,** ⇐
        **↑"don't you,** ⇐
        **"do you,** ⇐
        **for your "headaches.** ⇐
    M   No. (0.3) I take aspirin now.
        It works like a charm.
        It took me thirty years to discover this fact.
    N   How many aspirin.
    M   Four.
    N   Four?
    M   mm hmm.
    N   I tried that once.
        I tried six.
        it didn't help.                    Shapley/Fer 14: 351

N requests confirmation of her assumption that M takes ergot for medicinal reasons.

The following two examples are requests for confirmation in which the only marker suggesting question function is the second-person subject; there are no other lexical or morphosyntactic markers. This is taken from a telephone conversation between B and V, brother and sister. V, who lives in Los Angeles, is expecting B to arrive for a visit the next day:

(48) B   I was just getting ready to leave right now.
    V   Where are you going,
    B   I'm going down to Los Angeles.
    V   **You're leaving "toni:g(h)t?**                    ⇐
    B   I'm leaving right now. Mmhmm?          Lazaraton 1:8

B states he is getting ready to leave immediately for Los Angeles; this plan of action is unanticipated by V. The declarative question *You're leaving tonight* expresses the fact that his statement runs counter to her expectations.

In the next example, L produces a declarative question to clarify the topic of conversation:

(49) Na  I think the split came when they they were (. ) kicked out of
        Rome, basically,
        and some went east and some went west.
    L   **you're talking about the (. ) [("Jewish split,)**   ⇐
    No                                      [(diaspora)

Na   Yeah.
The Sephardic and the Ashkenazy.          Shapley/Sha 17:8

At the time, two simultaneous conversations were in progress about the differences between Sephardic and Ashkenazy Jews. Na interjects *I think the split came when they they were kicked out of Rome, basically, and some went east and some went west* into L and No's ongoing conversation. L makes an inference about the content of Na's talk and requests confirmation.

The previous table (5.4.) illustrated that third-person subjects are 38% of all subjects in marked requests for confirmation interpretable in terms of A- and B- events. Some third-person subjects involve questions asked during the course of a story by a recipient, as in the following example. The speaker offers a candidate explanation for why the participant in the story, a young woman who had run off with her boyfriend, returned home to her parents:

(50)  E    Did I tell y- Oh, yo:u heard it.
      L    Yeh, [a ]bout K___ ?
      E         [( )]
           No:, about (1. 2) A___.
      L    A___ who?
      E    is coming home,
      B    Oh [the one who left to go to ] Italy?
      N       [Oh yeah, I remember her ]
      L       [( )                      ]
      E    She called and wants to come [home, ]=
      L                                 [Same  ]=
           =[same terms ] as J.
      B    [Hallelujah! ]
      N    [(is she gonna get-)
      L    [NO CAR.
      N    O::h
      B    °Oh this eggplant is [so::( ).
      N                         [Good, I should have made mo:re.
           Then running away is running away,
           no matter what country you go to, h [uh?
      L                                        [huhuhu [hu
      E                                                [hehehe [he
      N                                                        [Down the
           corner,
           or if you go to Rome,=
      B    =What "happened, it didn't work "out?          ⇐
      E    I don't kno:w, I didn't get the detai:ls.
      L    She didn't like her, (. ) boyfriend?           Weber 3:24

The speaker requests confirmation that her candidate explanation *It didn't work out* is correct. This is a very general formulation, however, and actually serves to solicit more details of the story from the narrator.

The example below is marked by a word tag. No has been explaining to L about the historical origin of the split between Ashkenazy and Sephardic Jews. L synthesizes the prior information in terms of the following proposal. (No has been the expert in the prior talk relating to Jewish history and Hebrew):

(51)  L    I like my (. ) MY distinction then,
           to use the words Moslem/Christian to distinguish the two
           types.
           ((laughter))
      Na   That's right
           ((laughter))
           right, [right.
      L           [doesn't that really describe it.
      Na   that's it, [you're abs- he's right.
      L              **[and after "all, if you go "far      ⇐
                     enough back, the "Moslem world was 'the   ⇐
                     'cultured (. ) 'world.                ⇐
                     Right?**                              ⇐
           They preserved the culture in Spain, and where else
      No   Yeah
      L    around the world, and invented algebra, and everything
           else.
      No   Except the cleavage occurred after the Moslem
           ascendancy, I think.                    Shapley/Sha 15:26

The speaker does not leave room for a response immediately after the tag *right*. Although the recipient No responds affirmatively, this declarative question seems to be asking more for acknowledgment than for confirmation (Stenström 1984:156).

Below, the example is marked by a prior interrogative clause and a clause tag. The narrator jokingly produces a declarative question in order to underscore the risqué nature of the story he is about to tell:

(52)  M    Have you heard about the orgy we had the other night?
           that's how I got this black eye:
           You like the black eye:?
           ( )
      R    Oh it's lovely.
           (. 2)
      M    great
           (0. 1)
           *hhh anyway (0. 1) *hh um (-)we were having this orgy,

| | | |
|---|---|---|
| M | is this okay to talk "abou:t ? | ⇐ |
| | this doesn't "offend you. does "it? | ⇐ |
| | (0. 2) | |
| S | No= | |
| R | =no= | |
| M | =oh. | SN 4: 5:15 |

In this example, confirmation is equivalent to permission to continue the story.

In the following example (marked by a clause tag), an expert is discoursing on Hebrew (an esoteric topic: Hebrew writing symbols). The participants are discussing the way modern Hebrew is written with regard to the representation of vowels:

| | | |
|---|---|---|
| (53) | No | (But when they) |
| | | Like like what, what the Israelis have done (. ) |
| | | when they write |
| | | when they use regular Hebrew for, u:h u:h you know as as a national language, |
| | | *hh when they teach kids, |
| | | when they teach the people how to read Hebrew. |
| | | and in particular children, |
| | | they put the dots in. |
| | | But then for example ordinary I- Israeli newspapers |
| | | they write without the dots. |
| | L | It's like training wheels. |
| | No | *hh |
| | Na | or like accents in Russian. |
| | (M) | hmm |
| | ( ) | [heh heh |
| | No | [yeah and    [I u:h u:h |
| | Na | [They don't exist [but ( ) |
| | No | [No (it's i-) It's just the way the Israelis have of keeping people, you know uh, uh of making it harder to a-a-a-a-acclimatize, and things like that. °you know. *hh |
| | M | Do they have any (. ) scientific literature in Hebrew? |
| | No | yeah. |
| | M | They have. = |
| | | = [They certainly would use ]dots for "that?   ⇐ |
| | No | = [( )                           ] |
| | M | wouldn't they.                           ⇐ |
| | No | I don't think so. |
| | | It's all fake anyway. |
| | | When whenever they, there's a (. ) journal, |
| | | I think A___ showed me one one time. |

M        But they but they always put in English translations,
         s:o so in case anybody wants to read it.
                                              Shapley/Sha 35:22

M infers that even readers of scientific Hebrew need help to decipher texts, and that scientific journals provide the additional clues (dots). Confirmation of this inference is requested by the declarative question *They certainly would use dots for that wouldn't they*.

In summary, most third-person subjects of requests for confirmation (interpretable in terms of A- and B-events) occur during the course of a story or a description/exposition of an esoteric subject. They are produced most often by recipients. Two are requests by narrators which check on recipients' knowledge or sensibilities.

### 5.4.2  Requests for Confirmation Which Have No Associated Marker

The following table presents the numeric distribution of subjects of requests for confirmation (interpretable in terms of A- and B-events) which have no associated marker. (Because second-person subjects have been considered markers suggestive of question function, none are included in the following table.)

|       |     |       |
|-------|-----|-------|
| 1P    | 0   | 0%    |
| 3P    | 13  | 100%  |
| Total | 13  | 100%  |

**Table 5.5.**
**Distribution of Subjects of Requests for Confirmation**
**Which Have No Associated Marker**

There are zero first-person subjects of requests for confirmation (interpretable in terms of A- and B-events) which have no associated markers. Previously, it was noted that first-person subject requests for confirmation in the data appear with hearsay verbs, hypothetical verbs and verbs of cognition. These verb types are all lexical markers of question function. They all take a complement clause which codes information interpretable as a B-event. Normally, the request for confirmation does not involve information concerning the speaker. It is unlikely (although imaginable) that during the course of ordinary conversation, a speaker would request confirmation of some information about *himself/herself* interpretable as a B-event because this would necessitate that a recipient knows a fact about the speaker of which the speaker is unaware.[2]

Third-person subjects constitute 100% of all subjects of requests for confirmation (interpretable in terms of A- and B-events) which have no associated marker. In the following example from a dinner-table conversation, there are two, separate, simultaneous conversations. I have included both below because the participants interact in both conversations. M's initial declarative question is motivated by the presence of a Colonel Sanders' chicken box on the table. L joins in and becomes a co-teller of the story of Colonel Sanders:

(54) M [It doesn't]
 ( ) [        ]
 M [It doesn't tell the (. ) uh the later part of the story of=
 B [It's without onions.
 M = Colonel Sanders, does it.
 B It's a Swiss dish ramekin.
 ( ) (What story. )
 M of his unsuccessful suit to get them to stop using his name and picture (. ) you know.
 L and letting him have his own restaurant.
 B May I give you a piece of [ramekin?
 M                          [yes. ( )
 B Do you like cheese.
 T **He's no longer in 'charge of this "thing?** ⇐
 B I mean my father did not like cheese. So ( )
 L No (at least now ) most recently since the the lawsuits, they've got him the commercials again.
 M uh huh
 L so he must be on the payroll.

Shapley/Fer 10:250

As a result of M's utterance that the Colonel had sued to have his name and picture removed from the company's advertising, a recipient T makes an inference about Colonel Sanders' relation to the company which bears his name. L, as co-teller, responds to the question.

Below, several questions with no associated markers are asked during the course of a description by an expert on the subject. The participants had been discussing plants containing oxalic acid. They are trying to determine whether the plant L is describing is oxalis. Previously, they agreed that oxalis ejected seeds or beans:

(55) L It was very lo-
 the stuff I was thinking about was very low.
 M mmhmm
 N ( )
 L It's a it's a sort of a [ survives lawnmowers.
 M                        [yeah,
 right.
 It's like clover.

```
        M    [It has ] three leaves.
        L    [(yeah,)]
             but somewhere in there it's got these little,
        M    (b()-) Right. That's the ones.
        L    And these 'beans are oxalic "acid?                    ⇐
        M    N(h)o bu- but the leaves have it.
             I guess the whole plant has it.
             I don't know if anyone has ever cooked the seeds.
                                                    Shapley/Fer 10:236
```

L requests confirmation that oxalic acid is contained in the plant's beans.

Whether they appear with or without an associated marker in requests for confirmation (interpretable in terms of A- and B-events), third-person subjects tend to appear in stories or in the course of an exposition on an esoteric topic. They are produced by the recipient and elicit a relevant response from the narrator. Clearly, the narrator "owns" the information, and the declarative form is understandable as a request for confirmation.

There are several instances of declarative questions which do not occur during a narrative or exposition by an expert. In the next example, *so* is resumptive. The participants are involved in making arrangements to see a play, and they are discussing the plot:

```
   (56)  H     Ye:s I cried hysterically=
               =at the mov[ie. I don't know if I'm]=
         N              [Oh: guy              ]
         H     =gon[na cry::,        ]
         N        [Can you imagine] how=
               =[its gonna] be in per [son?   ]=
         H     [*hhhhh   ]            [e-hheh ]=
               =I don't kno, how its gonna b [e:, ]=
         N                                   [oh: ]=
         H     =fer the pla ]: [:y.   ]
         N     =wo::w,      ] [So it ]=
               = 'starts at eight "thir [ty?]              ⇐
         H                              [*hh] Yeah.
               So, if I- k- pick you up li:ke by eight o'clo::  [ck,
         N                                                      [Yeah,
                                                    HGII 13:23
```

Because H has invited N to the play and made all the arrangements (including the reservations) there is no ambiguity as to who has access to the relevant information. N is requesting confirmation of the time of the play. This utterance is beginning a new sequence which is doing making arrangements.

Below is a joke done as a request for confirmation with no associated marker:

(57) (0. 1)
    M    Who are you going to hear tonight?
    B    Stravinsky?    [Stravinsky and
    P                 [**Stravinski's going to show "up?**  ⇐
    B    No:. he:'s dead. ( )            Shapley/Boys 12:21

The request for confirmation is patently playful; it plays off the potentially ambiguous meaning of *going to hear*. This phrase is interpretable in terms of *who* is actually performing as well as *whose music* is being performed. The phrase is treated as ambiguous; however, it is not ambiguous because these participants all know (presumably) that Stravinsky is the deceased composer, not the performer. The fact that Stravinsky is deceased is an O-event, *i.e.*, known to all the participants. It is treated by the speaker, however, as a B-event.

There are several cases in the data in which the speaker of the question sets up the prior discourse creating the context for the production of the declarative question. Below, V resumes a previous topic concerning the fact that B would soon leave San Francisco to begin his trip down the coast to Los Angeles where he will stay with V, his sister:

(58)    V    And-uh-okay uh:
                so you're gonna "leave,
                **and it's gonna take you about 'five hours to get to**  ⇐
                **"Betsy?**  ⇐
                (0. 5)
    B    yes.
    V    Uh h:uh,
    B    So: I'll- I'll probably leave there at the latest ten
           so I'll probably be there at the latest () midnight.
    V    Yea:h. (0. 2) Shyoo!
           *hhh Okay well if I go to bed I'm gonna leave the door open.
    B    Oh okay.                                Lazaraton 4:114

In this example, the speaker produces the resumptive *so* and then *you're gonna leave*. Although not done as a question, the utterance has a second-person subject. It is a restatement of information already known. Previous talk has established: (1) B was about to leave and (2) B was going to stop at Santa Barbara and have dinner with Betsy:

(59)    B    I was just getting ready to leave right now.
        V    Where are you going,
        B    I'm going down to Los Angeles.

```
V    You're leaving "toni:g(h)t?              ⇐
B    I'm leaving right now.  Mmhmm?
V    You a:re. = When are you coming in then,
B    Uh,                                      ⇐
     well I'm gonna stop at Santa "Barbara,   ⇐
     and have dinner with uh "Betsy.          ⇐
V    uh hu:h,
B    A:nd so: it'll probably be later. (. ) in the evening.
V    Uh hu:h.  (. ) Oh it's tonigh-
     Oh I was preparing for you tomorrow.         Lazaraton 1:8
```

Following *you're gonna leave*, V produces the declarative question *and it's gonna take you about five hours to get to Betsy*. This turn evokes the prior sequence in which V first tried to establish when B would arrive at her house (example 48). *You're gonna leave* restates B's answer *I'm leaving right now*. And *it's gonna take you about five hours to get to Betsy* incorporates the information in B's answer *Uh, well I'm gonna stop at Santa Barbara and have dinner with uh Betsy* by giving a candidate estimate of the time it will take B to drive from San Francisco to Santa Barbara.

In this section, declarative questions with no associated marker have been discussed. These questions are all interpretable as requests for confirmation in terms of Labov and Fanshel's rule of confirmation understood in terms of A- and B-events. In section 5.4, we noted that 73% of all declarative questions are requests for confirmation interpretable in terms of A- and B-events and 86% are marked. The remaining 27% of declarative questions which are not requests for confirmation interpretable in terms of A- and B-events will be covered in the next section.

### 5.5. Declarative Questions Not Interpretable in Terms of A-Events and B-Events

In this section, I will discuss the 25 declarative questions in the data which are *not* interpretable as requests for confirmation in terms of A- and B-events (Table 5.3.). *All* the declarative questions which are not interpretable in terms of A-events and B-events *are marked*. Although some of these declarative questions may be considered requests for confirmation, they differ in terms of A- and B-events.

In the discourse, these declarative questions serve a variety of functions, *e.g.*, to do jokes, to make evaluations and to solicit topics or sequences. The fact that all the declarative questions not interpretable in terms of A- and B-events are marked suggests that they would not be interpretable *as questions* without explicit marking. Because recipients of this type of question cannot utilize information accessibility to interpret these utterances as questions, morphosyntactic marking appears to be necessary.

As exemplified below, speakers use this type of declarative question in order to perform a variety of functions. By constructing them as declarative questions, speakers are correlating this form with requests for confirmation interpretable in terms of A- and B-events. As a result, speakers in many instances are making assertions in a non-assertive way.

## 5.5.1. Topic/Sequence Solicitations

Below, seven people are sitting in the living room of one of the participants after seeing a movie together. The speaker comments on the action of another participant who takes some of the food made available by the hostess:

(60)        (3. 0)
     W      "Could'nt resist, "huh:.                    ⇐
     D      No
            (0. 6)
     W      The pull: of food.
            (0. 4)
     D      The pull of crackers. The lure of crackers. =
     W      =(Do) people sit around eating in Nepal?
            (0. 2)
     D      All the time that's all they do          Riggenbach 3:63
            ((etc. on this topic/sequence))

W produced this example after a three-second silence in the conversation. It functions as an evaluation of a participant's behavior. This gets a response, and W expands the sequence with another comment on the effect of having food readily available. D responds to this. W then asks a question done as an interrogative clause which solicits the development of a topic by D.

Although this question is an evaluation, it is done as a, it is not serious. If it were, it would be "doing criticism" and would make a defense conditionally relevant; however, D produces only a minimal negative response. Videotapes would undoubtedly show the lighthearted nature of this exchange reflected by the participants' facial expressions. The absence of an explicit *you* subject probably suggests that this is not done as a serious evaluation.

In the next example, there are two, separate, simultaneous conversations around the dinner table. M's declarative question is motivated by the presence of a Colonel Sanders' chicken box. M and L are guests; and the food, including the chicken, has been provided by the host and hostess, T and B. This sequence begins after the end of another topic/sequence and a 10-second silence:

(61) M   [It doesn't]
    ()   [        ]
    M    [It doesn't tell the (. ) uh the later part of the story of=
    B    [It's without onions.
    M    = Colonel Sanders, does it.
    B    It's a Swiss dish ramekin.
    ()   (What story. )
    M     of his unsuccessful suit to get them to stop using his
         name and picture (. ) you know.
    L    and letting him have his own restaurant.
    B    May I give you a piece of [ramekin?
    M                              [yes. ( )
    B    Do you like cheese.
    T    **He's no longer in 'charge of this "thing?**    ⇐
    B    I mean my father did not like cheese. So ( )
    L    No (at least now ) most recently since the the lawsuits,
         they've got him the commercials again.
    M    uh huh
    L    so he must be on the payroll.

                                              Shapley/Fer 10:250

M makes an assumption about what information is contained in the public-relations story about Colonel Sanders printed on the box. This declarative question serves to open a topic/sequence. M's friend L joins in and becomes a co-teller of the story of Colonel Sanders.

### 5.5.2. *Request for a Reason*

The following is a request for information — specifically, a reason. The declarative question has the structure *how about* plus a declarative clause (see Chapter 2, 2.1.1. for justification of this utterance as a declarative question). V has been describing how her mother was reacting to her father's knee surgery:

(62) C   Your parents are just too normal, Ken.
         You don't understand what its like to have weird parents.
     K   Oh I have a grandmother
         [that makes me understand  [Vick  ]ie's Mom  ] a lot so,
     C                              [Oh             ]
     V   [He has a grandmother that's like my Mom.    ]
     C   Uh huh *hh
     V   He does.
     C   I mean that- the-

| | |
|---|---|
| C | but ya know ya don't understand how Vickie could be so affected. I think about my D [ad ya know ] |
| K | [( ) ] [I understand.] |
| V | [I get ] sucked in. |
| K | I understand. |
| C | Yeah? |
| K | But I- I don't unde[rstand- |
| V | [cause his Mom gets sucked i[n. |
| C | [O::h. |
| V | Doesn't she? |
| K | Yeah. |
| | (0. 2) |
| C | [It's so easy wss ] |
| K | [I mean I under ]stand but it- but it see- ya know but it [still seems like ]= |
| C | [It's still frustrating ] |
| K | =ya oughta be able to say no- |
| | (0. 3) |
| | Ya knew before, |
| | **How come**                                                        ⇐ |
| | (0. 2) |
| | **you're letting**                                                  ⇐ |
| | **this "cra[zy ] person change your mind**=   ⇐ |
| V | [Right.] |
| K | =ya [know.]                                                         ⇐ |
| V | [We ]ll s- it's like she made me believe that yeah you know the doctors are you know horrible an yes this is ridiculous an *hh gu- I gue[ss |
| C | [Why do you think yo- your Mom is probably just |
| V | jealous |
| K | eh heh |
| C | Well I mean pr- maybe that too but she just can't handle |
| | (0. 2) |
| V | Reality. |
| C | People close to her being in pain you know she wants to |
| K | it- it seems weirder than that. |

K    More insidious or something.
     cause
C    really?
K    All the stuff that Vickie's told me
     that she - that she pulls
     an that-
     you know wanting to claim all the misery in the family
     [for  ] herself=
C    [yeah]
K    =an stuff like that?                                    Ford 9: 256

The declarative question is asking for a reason, not requesting confirmation. K is asking V why she lets her mother raise doubts about the appropriateness of her father's operation. Earlier, K had begun the topic/sequence in which the above example appears with the following.

(63) K    It was like the other day uh
          (0. 2)
          Vickie was talking on the phone to her Mom?
     C    Mm hm.
     K    An uh she got off the phone
          and she was incredibly upset?
     C    Mm hm
     K    She was going
          God do you think they're performing unnecessary surgery
          on my Dad
          or som'm like that?                                Ford 1:1

In producing the declarative question in (62), K implicitly criticizes V's response to her mother, whom he refers to as *this crazy person*. This utterance is interpretable as criticism because it implies that V is irrational for letting a crazy person change her mind. K's prior utterance *you knew before* suggests that previously, V knew her Mother was a "crazy person." Further, it suggests that V also knew her father's surgery was appropriate. In this example then, the utterance is implicitly criticizing both V and her mother.

## 5.5.3. Uptakes

Below, the speaker produces an uptake of a news announcement. An uptake is an utterance which confirms that the recipient got the point of the prior announcement or story (see Labov and Fanshel 1977:109 for a discussion of listener's evaluations of narratives). The sequence begins with a pre-announcement by E, followed by a number of NTRI's:

(64) E   Did I tell y- Oh, yo:u heard it.
    L   Yeh, [a ]bout K__?
    E        [( )]
        No:, about (1. 2) A__.
    L   A__ who?
    E   is coming home,
    B   Oh [the one who left to go to ] Italy?
    N      [Oh yeah, I remember her  ]
    L      [( )                      ]
    E   She called and wants to come [home, ]=
    L                                [Same  ]=
        =[same terms ] as J.
    B   [Hallelujah! ]
    N   [(is she gonna get-)
    L   [NO CAR.
    N   O::h
    B   °Oh this eggplant is [so::( ).
    N                        [Good, I should have made mo:re.
        **Then "running "away is "running "away,**  ⬅
        **no matter what country you go to, h [uh?**  ⬅
    L                                          [huhuhu
    E                                          [hehehe
    L   [hu
    E   [he
    N   **["Down the corner, or if you go to "Rome,=**  ⬅
    B   =What happened, it didn't work out?
    E   I don't kno:w, I didn't get the detai:ls.
    L   She didn't like her, (. ) boyfriend?                Weber 3:22

After the series of NTRI's, E announces the news that A had *called and wants to come home*. L then expands the sequence by adding more news, *viz.*, the conditions her parents had set for her (*no car*). This additional information is receipted by N. B then does a compliment which addresses the food. This is responded to by N, the hostess, with an appreciation (*good*) and a self-deprecation (*I should have made more*). N takes more turn which serves as an uptake of the announcement produced collaboratively by E and L, both classmates of the young woman who had run away from home.

N begins her turn with the discourse marker *then*. This functions to code what follows as a conclusion of sorts (Schiffrin 1987:246). Though it is a request for confirmation, it is not interpretable in terms of A- and B-events – N's utterance is functioning as an evaluation. It is revealed in subsequent conversation that the boyfriend is Italian, and A had run away to Rome with him. These are rather exciting details. N's utterance places the episode, however, squarely in the category it belongs, from a mother's perspective. Even though the circumstances of this particular episode might be glamorous, it is the same as running away with a local boy to an apartment at *the corner*. The consequences are also the same – no car, among other probable punishments. The two teen-aged girls respond to this question with laughter.

In the next example, C is talking about her college-student daughter. D tells how he has just misunderstood something that was said. This is one of two simultaneous conversations; the other has not been included in the transcript of this example:

(65)    M    What is she majoring in?
        C    Latin (. ) American studies,
        M    Really, at Yale
        D    I thought she was pre-med
        C    well she is pre-med,
            but that's not a=
        D    Latin American - Oh pre-med is not a major
        C    no
       La    No people major in biology
        M    oh I see
        L    but she's in ( Latin American)
        D    ( )
            That's amazing(. ) how I misread that,
            despite the fact that I (. ) despite the misheard it.
            Despite the fact that I know exactly what she's doing.
            You said Latin (. ) and American studies.
        C    Oh (yeah) What a strange combination. heh heh
        D    Right. and what is
            What is really puzzling is that it immediately translates
            though I know exactly what she's doing.
            Latin American studies.
        C    Some sort of combination of classics and English.
        D    And all of a sudden I forgot totally who we are talking
            about
            except that I know she was going to be pre-med.
        C    How very interesting.
            **Well She'll know all those "words,** ⇐
            **when she gets to "medical school,** ⇐
            **"won't she.** ⇐
            all those Latin words.
            (0. 2)
            she's in Panama.                          Shapley/Nel 5:6

M asks C her daughter's major. She answers Latin and American studies. D misinterprets this as Latin American studies. C's first response to D's narration of his experience acknowledges the plausibility of his misinterpretation by evaluating that the correct interpretation is a *strange combination*. C's next response expands on the type of combination involved — *Some sort of combination of classics and English*. C's third response evaluates D's experience — *How very interesting*. C continues by producing the declarative question — *Well She'll know all those words when she gets to medical school, won't she.*

With this declarative question, C connects her daughter's strange combination major to medical school. This is not a request for confirmation because the fact that C's daughter will benefit in medical school from her knowledge of Latin is not a B-event, *i.e.*, a fact known only to D. This question does an uptake of D's description of his experience by making his previous remark — *I know she was going to be pre-med* — relevant to her daughter's unusual major.

### 5.5.4. Knowledge Gaps

In the following example, the speaker expresses a gap in his knowledge. He wonders what the word *postulate* means. This is followed by an interrogative clause.

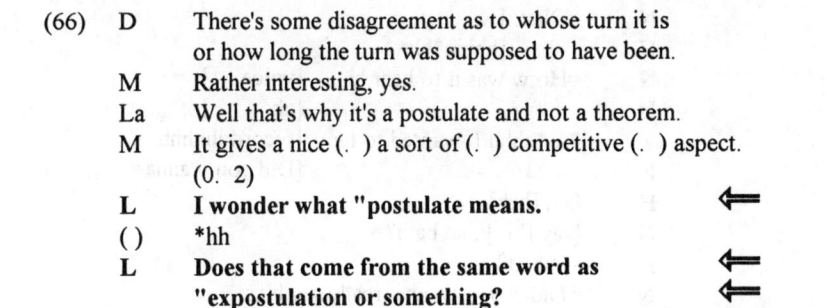

(66)  D    There's some disagreement as to whose turn it is
            or how long the turn was supposed to have been.
       M    Rather interesting, yes.
       La   Well that's why it's a postulate and not a theorem.
       M    It gives a nice (. ) a sort of (. ) competitive (. ) aspect.
            (0. 2)
       L    **I wonder what "postulate means.**          ⇐
       ( )  *hh
       L    **Does that come from the same word as**      ⇐
            **"expostulation or something?**              ⇐
       K    I don't know.                        Shapley/Nel 12:11

The gap in the speaker's knowledge is revealed with the lexical marker *I wonder*. This clause takes an embedded question as its complement. This utterance is followed by a guess at the derivation of "postulate."

Below, the speaker expresses her uncertainty as to whether or not she will get charged for a long distance call:

(67)  N    You called Richard,=
       ( )  =hh-hh=
       H    = y(h)Yea(h)h

```
H    and I h(h)ung up
     wh(h)en he ans[wer
N                   [Oh: Hyla why::::[::,
H                                    [*hhh
     well first of all
     I wasn't about to spend seventy five cents
     for three mi[nutes *uh] *eh=
N                 [Yea:h,  ]
     =That's true,=
H    =*hihhhh that's a lot of money
     plus (.) uh then it's twenty five cents for extra minute
     a [fter that.]=
N      [Yeah,   ]=
H    =* hh y[ou know,   ]
N           [How do you] know
     he [answered could you tell his voi:ce?]
H       [so for four minutes its a bu:ck.  ]
     (0.2)
     Hu:h?
     (.)
N    Could you tell his vo[i:ce,]
H                         [Yea ]h I knew his voice,=
N    =Oha:::[w,
H           [hhhih*hh=
N    =Ho:w was it to hear his   [voice,  ]
H                               [ah:    ]::,
     *u-*ehhh I  wanted to tape [record ihhhhh
N                               [Did you wanna=
H    heh [heh]
N    [say [hi ]:, so ba:d?=
H    =Wha:t?=
N    =Didn't you wanna  really say hi:,=
H    =Ye:s, but as soon as he said hello I hung up.=
N    [°Oh ::::::::,                                 ]
H    [So 'I don't know if I'll get char ]ged the seventy-   ⇐
     five "c(hh)ents(h ) or not,=                            ⇐
N    =No I don't think you will but- (.) (you ) might get charged
     something,
     (0.3)
H    ↓Oh:.                                         HG II 24:9
```

The declarative question expresses the speaker's uncertainty about the phone company's procedure at a particularly emotionally difficult point in the talk. The utterance appears to be trying to change the direction of the talk to a less painful subject.

## 5.5.5. Candidate Understandings

In a candidate understanding, a speaker offers a recipient a characteristic description of an aspect of the recipient's experience. In the following example from a dinner-table conversation, the speaker does a candidate understanding of her mother's cooking techniques.

```
(68)    L    I thought I was eating all the same thing you been eating,
             Like last night, (. ) the green beans and the (0. 2)
             [( ) very weird lately Mom?
        E    [hehehe.
        N    What do you mean?
        L    mixing things u:p↑
        N    Oh↑ I know I'm la::zy
             (0. 4)
             I put everything in the same pot,
             (0. 2)
        L    °Just throw 'together a "little something (uh?)=    ⇐
        N    =mmhm                                          Weber 5:64
```

L is criticizing her mother's cooking in a teasing manner. She offers a candidate restatement of the prior turn *I put everything in the same pot* with the declarative question *Just throw together a little something (uh?)*. Note that the subject pronoun *you* is not produced (see example 4), perhaps suggesting the non-serious nature of the criticism.

This declarative question is not a request for confirmation interpretable in terms of A- and B-events. The fact is that N puts everything in the same pot (already established in the prior turn). The declarative question is not a request for confirmation of this fact; rather, through its lexical elements, it creates a characterization of this practice.

In the following example from a telephone conversation, R has been discussing the possibility of a new project being approved. If this approval happens, his job will be secure for quite a while to come:

```
(69)    R    Wuh- we're wai:ting for Arthur to make a *de[cision.
        A                                                [hhh
             whhe hhh
             but i(h)ts it's (. )
             what I'm rea:lly enjoy:ing is: (. ) uhm:: getting a pa:y check.
             heh ha [h hhh heh ha hhh              ]
```

116    VARIETIES OF QUESTIONS IN ENGLISH CONVERSATION

```
          R        [Ya "know? (0. 4) it's it's (.)]          ⇐
                   it's [uhm "surpri:s(h)ing(h)ly gra:tifying.=    ⇐
          A        [hhh
          R        [isn't" it? ]=                            ⇐
          A        [wu-      ]=
                   =Yeah en: uh you know I-
                   (0. 5)
                   And I also gotta check from a cable fee that (. ) uh in
                   New En:gland,
                   you know,
                   I let them show sewing woman once.
                                                      Mannon 11:217
```

The speaker R offers a candidate understanding in response to A's expression of pleasure at getting a regular paycheck. In doing so, he is demonstrating that he appreciates how A feels. This declarative question is not a request for confirmation interpretable in terms of A- and B-events because the fact that getting a paycheck is surprisingly gratifying is not a B-event, *i.e.*, a fact known only to B.

### 5.5.6. Arrangements

Following, the speaker is using a marked declarative question to complete and confirm arrangements for attending a play that evening:

```
          (70)  H     =*hh maybe we can go for a drink tonight.
                      (. )
                N     Ye::ah. That soun-
                      Yeah I owe you a dri:nk.
                      (. )
                      I wanna buy you a dri:n [k.
                H                             [Aow. alri [:ght, ]
                N                                        ["Oka: ]y?    ⇐
                      so we "will fer sure. =
                H     =Alri [ght. ]
                N           [Af  ]ter, (. ) the play,
                                                         HG II 38:18
```

N offers to buy H a drink in response to H's suggestion that they go for a drink after the theater. H accepts this offer. N then confirms this date with the declarative question — *Oka:y? so we will fer sure.* This question is not a request for confirmation in terms of A- and B-events. Whether H and N do in fact go for a drink after the theater is not a B-event, *i.e.*, a fact known only to B. Both parties must confirm the date. In producing this declarative question, the speaker is *both* simultaneously confirming and requesting confirmation.

### 5.5.7. Narrator Checks

There are two examples classified as narrator checks on their recipients:

    (71)   A    And I got a check from a cable fee that (. ) uh
                    in New England you know,
                    I let them show sewing woman once.
                    [(0. 4)]
                    [hhh   ] and that was four hundred do:llars the:re,
                    (0. 3)
                    **(and was) "that easy money 'too, righ[t ?=**   ⇐
           R                                   [Uh↑huh
           A    = I just send them a ma:ster and they *sh- air it over cable,
                    **and I get this check. ri:ght?=**   ⇐
           R    =ye:ah                                                Mannon 11:226

This declarative question is not a request for confirmation in terms of A- and B-events. A is not asking R to confirm the fact that his residual check is easy money, rather he is requesting acknowledgment that the recipient appreciates the significance of receiving residuals.

### 5.5.8. Criticism

There is one example in the data which is an explicit criticism. B and V are brother and sister; B is coming from San Francisco to Los Angeles. The *she* in the first utterance refers to their mother:

    (72)   V    [so you're er- she] said
              B    [hhh hhh       ]
              V    is he coming for vacation or for um (0. 4) tsk! *hhh work.
                    And I said I:: do::n't kno::w.
              B    VaNE:ssa:.
              V    I said [both.
              B          [**You're a lot of "ba:ckup, aren't "you? "for**  ⇐
                    **me.**  ⇐
              V    I know, I said-no I said both.
                    It's both.
                    (0. 4)
              V    °Both. See? I defended you.          Lazaraton 4:105

B's declarative question *you're a lot of backup aren't you for me* is done ironically. It is interpretable as meaning that she did not back him up in response to their mother's query about the purpose of his visit. In this example the tag is embedded.

### 5.5.9. Topic Continuation

There is one example in the data which is continuing a topic/sequence in progress:

    (73)    M    That's about it
                            hell I haven't been doing anything but (0. 2) ts (0. 2)
                            well like (0. 2)
                            going out [actually.
            K             [mmm*
            M    I have to start studying now:
                            (0. 7)
            K     yeah I s[hould (too)*
            M         [and I've gotta pap*er to write after
                          (0. 7)
                          have to wait until Friday
                          (0. 3)
                          see the last films
                          (0. 7)
            K     You'd ne[ver know         ⇐
            M         [In that film class ( )
            K     I had a paper due "Wednesday, "would you.   ⇐
                          (0. 4)
            M    N(h)o hhh                              SN 4 22:15

M states that he has to start studying, and K echoes the sentiment. M then mentions the paper he has to write. K, in turn, produces the declarative question *You'd never know I had a paper due would you* which continues the litany of what needs to be done. M responds with a negative token. This question exhibits an impersonal form of *you* ; it is interpretable as meaning "people in general."

### 5.5.10. Reported Questions

There are several instances of reported questions in the data. In the following example, the speaker is telling a story:

    (74)    C    Ro:n uh::, Ron's family moved,
                          into (Serrano Park) where we live right near Mount ( ).

I met his sister one day
and I said
**I hear you have a 'brother that goes to "Lehigh.** ⬅
(0. 9)
and she said yeah.                                    Clacia 13:7

The speaker is reporting direct speech which is a declarative question.

In the following example, the question of a third party is reported:

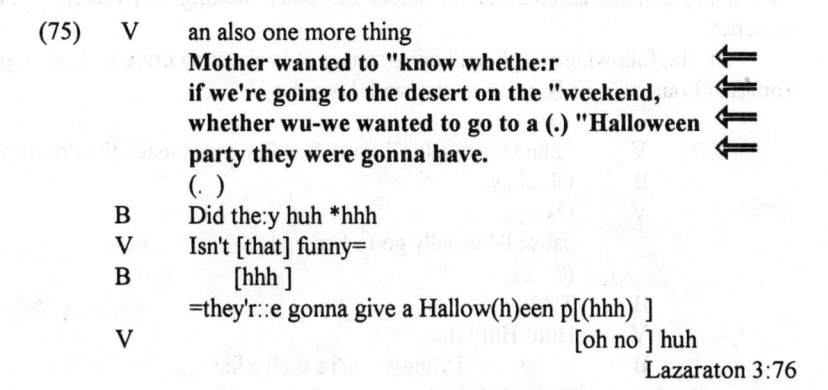

(75)   V    an also one more thing
            **Mother wanted to "know whethe:r** ⬅
            **if we're going to the desert on the "weekend,** ⬅
            **whether wu-we wanted to go to a (.) "Halloween** ⬅
            **party they were gonna have.** ⬅
            (. )
       B    Did the:y huh *hhh
       V    Isn't [that] funny=
       B         [hhh ]
            =they'r::e gonna give a Hallow(h)een p[(hhh) ]
       V                                         [oh no ] huh
                                                        Lazaraton 3:76

A third person's question is reported as indirect speech with a declarative clause.

In this section all the declarative questions not interpretable in terms of A- and B-events are marked; and the various functions these questions serve in the talk have been described.

### 5.6.   You're Kidding

Several instances of *you're kidding* are found in the data. These utterances show receipt or appreciation of interesting newsworthy information; thus, it is not always clear that these forms are doing questioning. It may be argued that they are question-like in that some forms receive literal *yes/no* answers. Bolinger (1957:84) states, however, that these forms "have become fossilized signals for yes-no answers" and that "...they rarely appear as (questions) except with high or rising terminal pitch...."

Instances of *you're kidding* share some characteristics with NTRI's (*e.g.*, position). At times, they may indicate some problem with the prior turn, even if that problem is simply surprise. In the next example, the speaker A had been discussing a possible large television project on which he might work. The final decision regarding network funding was imminent:

(76)  A    So: uh: if it's ye:s,
             *hh (*) I could be employed until nineteen-eighty ei:ght,
             an if it's a no:,
             (*) then everybody goes home that day:. t(hhh) (hhh)
             (hhh).
       R    "You're:: 'ki::d[ding.]    ⇐
             [*hhh] (hh) N(h)O:(h):: (hh) (hh).
                                                            Gee 7:173

This example demonstrates that instances of *you're kidding* can receive a literal response.

In the following telephone conversation, B is about to drive to Los Angeles from San Francisco; he is going to stay with his sister V:

(77)  V    *hhh Okay well if I go to bed I'm gonna leave the door open.
       B    Oh okay.
       V    Oka:y,
             cause I-I usually go to bed early.
             (0. 2)
       B    Tsk!!
       V    Huh! Huh! [hhh
       B              [Vaness you're such a liar
             I can't believe it.
       V    No I do actually I go to bed at ten thirty every night now.
       B    you're "kidding,    ⇐
             you're the one that used to read until three in the morning
             every day.
       V    (0. 2)
             Mmm. That has changed for the past five years.
                                                            Lazaraton 5:132

The speaker produces more turn immediately after the news receipt *you're kidding* (he does not allow time for a response); and V responds to the part of the turn produced after *you're kidding*.

## 5.7.  Conclusion

In Chapter 1, I discussed literature which maintains that interrogatives always are the syntactic-clause type most frequently associated with question function. In fact, interrogatives constitute 59% of all questions in the data. In Chapter 4, we have seen that declarative questions constitute 17% of all question forms in the data. These declarative questions are used to request confirmation of

B-events 73% of the time. We can say, therefore, that they are typically used to do this.

Speakers also use declarative questions to accomplish interactional goals other than requesting confirmation of B-events. These functions include soliciting new topics, making jokes, doing evaluations and doing both serious and nonserious criticism. In some cases, these declarative questions capitalize on the correlation between declarative questions and requests for confirmation of B-events in order to make assertions in a nonassertive diplomatic manner.

# Chapter 6

# Nonclausal Questions: Morphosyntactic Patterns

## 6.1. The Problem of Nonclausal Questions

In this chapter, I will address the form/function problem by examining those functional questions which are realized by particles, words or phrases, (forms which do not constitute a syntactic clause). In the literature, these forms are referred to as fragmentary sentences, "lacking constituents that are normally obligatory" (Quirk *et al.* 1985:838).

Omission of grammatical elements is known as *ellipsis*. The ellipted elements may be recoverable from either the linguistic form of the utterance or from prior discourse. According to Quirk *et al.* (1985:838), not all fragmentary utterances are elliptical, and such forms cannot confidently be analyzed in terms of clause structure. These fragments are referred to as *nonsentences*.

In this study, I will not refer to utterances as either full/complete utterances or fragmentary/elliptical utterances. *From the point of view of production*, these terms in themselves suggest that utterances which exhibit syntax at the clause level are in some way primary, basic or nonderivative, while utterances which do not exhibit such syntax are broken, incomplete or derivative. From the point of view of discourse strategies utilized by speakers, however, clause structure is basic. An examination of language-in-use reveals a preferred argument structure which reflects principles of information management (Du Bois 1985; 1987a, b, Ochs 1988). Below, Hopper (1988) discusses the role of the clause in relation to discourse and grammar:

> The relation between text and grammar is mediated by preferred ways of formulating clauses in specific discourse contexts. Clauses both respond structurally to textuality and are central to the ongoing process of constructing textuality. Like other linguistic units, therefore, clauses cannot be described in isolated, autonomous terms "first" (*i.e.*, *a priori*) and then fitted into a discourse framework; instead, the clause must always be seen as having a particular role in the construction of the text, and is form understood, however imperfectly, from that perspective alone (p. 109).

While there is no "pre-existing ideal (invariant) form" for clauses in discourse, there are clause types preferred for building texts (Hopper: 109).

Utterances which do not exhibit clause structure (words and phrases) are often interpretable, though not always, in terms of clauses in the prior discourse. Because clause structure is fundamental to the organization of discourse, those kinds of forms which do not exhibit clausal syntax will be referred to as *nonclausal forms* rather than particles, words or phrases. These forms are not uncommon in ordinary conversation; and participants have no problem either producing or interpreting them. In fact, communication can consist of turns in which the participants utter only single words and yet "understand each other perfectly" (Rommetveit 1974:29).

In the linguistics' literature, nonclausal forms are not associated with any particular functional type (in the way declarative forms are associated with statements, and interrogative forms are associated with questions). Quirk *et al.* (1985:850-1) state that nonclausal forms can function to give commands, ask questions, make assertions or serve as exclamations.

Nonclausal questions, therefore, present a different kind of form/function problem from that discussed in Chapter 4 with regard to declarative questions. In the case of declarative-clause questions, the problematic issue is: *how do recipients know that the utterance is functioning as a question rather than as a statement*?

Because nonclausal forms are not associated in the literature with a typical function, the issue for these forms is simply how recipients interpret them with regard to their function, *i.e.*, as statements, questions, etc. Nonclausal forms which are doing questioning in these data, however, *are* associated with the function of doing repair in conversation; specifically, many function as next-turn-repair initiators (Chapter 2). The functions of nonclausal question forms will be discussed in Chapter 7.

In order to understand how morphosyntactic form contributes to their interpretation, I will focus on the description of those questions in the data which are accomplished with a nonclausal form. I will first discuss the data and give a brief description of the various morphosyntactic types of nonclausal questions. Then I will consider what interpretive procedures relative to the morphosyntax may be used to interpret each type as doing questioning (the social action). Although in some instances, intonation and sequential position in the discourse will be considered, this chapter will focus on the role of morphosyntax in interpretation. Finally, I will consider how these forms are distributed in the data.

## 6.2. Data

All utterances in the data were identified as doing questioning on the basis of their function in the talk. (Syntactic form was not a criterion of this identification process.) From this set of data, those utterances with a nonclausal form were extracted and thereby, comprise the set of nonclausal questions.

The following is a nonclausal question. It is realized by a noun phrase. The participants are discussing a former date of H's:

(78)  N   What's his last name,
      H   Uh:: Freedla:nd. *hh[hh
      N                      [Oh[:,
      H                          [('r) Freedlind.=
      N   =Nice Jewish "bo:y?            ⟵
      (.)
      H   O:f cou:rse,=
      N   ='v [cou:rse, ]
      H       [hh-hh-hh] hnh *hhhhh=           HG II 25: 21

N is doing questioning with a noun phrase. This utterance is in response to the referent's name and constitutes a candidate characterization of his religion/ethnicity. This utterance is a request for confirmation.

Syntactic forms which are not realized by a subject and a complete verb phrase are classified as *nonclausal*. These forms include particles, nouns, adverbs, noun phrases, prepositional phrases, gerundive phrases, forms with a subject and an auxiliary verb (but no main verb) and forms with a main verb (but no subject and no auxiliary verb). Note: forms which are realized by a complete verb phrase but have a phonologically reduced subject or zero subject have not been classified as nonclausal forms, rather as declarative clauses.

### 6.3. Morphosyntactic Patterns of Nonclausal Questions

Nonclausal utterances which are used by speakers to ask questions exhibit a variety of forms:

- No explicit marking suggestive of question function;
- Particles, *wh*-words and tags;
- Lexical elements as part of their constituent form which play a role in their functional interpretation and/or
- Lexical or morphosyntactic elements immediately preceding/following in the discourse.

An example follows of those nonclausal utterances which have no elements which support their interpretation as questions — *nonclausal questions with no associated marker*. (This disjunction needs to be presented in order to enable the reader to contrast this type with those which follow.) A description also follows of those nonclausal utterances which have some elements which support their interpretation as questions: *marked nonclausal questions*.

The focus on the morphosyntactic patterns of nonclausal questions is not meant to imply that intonation and gesture play no role in interpretation; however, there is no such thing — in general — as unambiguous question intonation, *viz.*, rising terminal intonation. There are instances, however, in which intonation *can* be the crucial factor in determining the function of an utterance (Couper-Kuhlen 1986:209, McLemore 1991).

### 6.3.1. Nonclausal Questions with No Associated Marker

Questioning can be accomplished with a nonclausal form which suggests it is doing questioning (but not in a lexical or morphosyntactic way). In the following example, D is describing a type of drink found in Nepal. H, who has also lived in Nepal, produces a prepositional phrase doing questioning. This is a request for confirmation:

```
(79)   D     It's not like wi- I mean it's it's not like wi:ne.
             It doesn't taste like wine
             but it's
       W     fermented.=
       D     =white and milky
             but it's [fermented
       H            ["oh yeah?                              ⇐
             (0.3)
             in "bo:wls?                                    ⇐
       W     O' that [sounds disgusting
       D             [Y-yeah well it's in these big
             (.)
             va[:ses,[you know.    [Huge. ]
       W        [vats.
       H              [yeah.       [yeah. ]      Riggenbach 6:141
```

With the utterance *in bowls*, the speaker is doing questioning with a prepositional phrase. Given the prior discourse *but it's fermented*, this phrase can be interpreted as *It's fermented in bowls?* This inferable utterance, in turn, is asking for confirmation that the drink is fermented in bowls.

Labov and Fanshel's rule of confirmation is applicable here. The nonclausal question is produced during the course of an extended turn by D in which he is describing the drink that had made him sick. In Labov and Fanshel's terms, he has access to the relevant information.

## 6.3.2. Marked Nonclausal Questions

The marking of nonclausal forms will be categorized in terms of real-time production (as in the case of declarative clause questions). In these data, nonclausal forms are realized by a wide range of forms (particles, nouns, noun phrases, prepositional phrases, verb phrases, adverbs, etc.).

Lexical or morphosyntactic marking suggestive of question function is categorized as:

- Occurring within the nonclausal form when it constitutes the utterance, e.g., a *wh*-word or an element within the constituent structure of the form.
- Occurring before or after the production of the nonclausal form in relation to the particular constituent structure of each form.

This categorization is quite straightforward. Prior markers consist of discourse particles, *wh*-words and lexical items which are clearly not part of the constituent structure. Intonation clearly distinguishes the *wh*-words and lexical items from the constituent structure of the nonclausal form (see example 89 and Chapter 8 for further discussion).

Subsequent markers consist of discourse particles; conjunctions; and particle, word or clause tags — all unambiguously distinguishable from the constituent structure of the nonclausal form. (There are two instances of an alternative choice (example 97).)

### 6.3.2.1. Marking which Occurs within the Constituent Structure of the Nonclausal Form.

*Lexical Marking*

There are cases in which the word *really* constitutes a turn. This form is a receipt marker of news. In the data, it sometimes functions as a question which makes a response relevant. In the following example, the speaker, K, is discussing turn-taking behaviors:

(80)  K  Even infants and mothers take turns.
         They well,
         Children learn that the first thing.
      M  "Really?"   ←
      K  Oh, yes.                              Shapley/Nel 9:49

M responds to K's statements with *really*, registering them as news. K then produces an affirmative token, confirming that, in fact, her previous statements were accurate.

There are two cases in the data in which the word *pardón* functions to do questioning. In the following example from a dinner-table conversation, the speaker L is referring to some food on her plate:

```
(81)  L   What's the da:rk green thing.
          (0.4)
      N   Pardón?= ((French))                                    ←
      E   =he=
      L   =What's this?
      N   That's Japanese eggplant.                      Weber 5:48
```

N's production of *pardón* displays some trouble with hearing or understanding. L redoes her original question in response to this next-turn repair initiator (NTRI).

*Subject/Verb Inversion*

In the data, there are three cases in which the verb consists only of a form of the auxiliary *do*. In this example, the speaker V is telling about her father's weak knees and how this problem runs in his family:

```
(82)  V   An:d the family has weak knees,
          his Mom had very weak knees,
          same problem.
          (0.2)
          [Only         ]
      C   [Does your] "brother?                                  ←
          (0.6)
      V   Not yet.                                       Ford 2: 51
```

C does questioning via a subject and a form of the auxiliary *do*. Given the prior discourse, the utterance is interpretable as "Does your brother have weak knees?" — an interrogative marked by subject/verb inversion. It is not a request for confirmation.

*Particles*

There are particles in the data which do questioning, *e.g., huh, hm*. Below, the speaker C is telling a story about trying to dismiss a talkative visitor while preparing for a luncheon the following day:

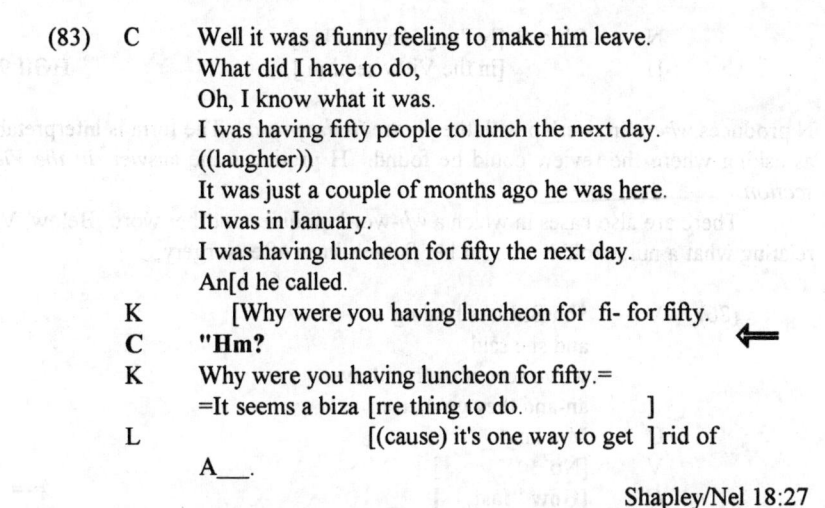

(83)  C   Well it was a funny feeling to make him leave.
          What did I have to do,
          Oh, I know what it was.
          I was having fifty people to lunch the next day.
          ((laughter))
          It was just a couple of months ago he was here.
          It was in January.
          I was having luncheon for fifty the next day.
          An[d he called.
      K      [Why were you having luncheon for fi- for fifty.
      C   "Hm?   ⟵
      K   Why were you having luncheon for fifty.=
          =It seems a biza [rre thing to do.            ]
      L                    [(cause) it's one way to get ] rid of
          A___.
                                                 Shapley/Nel 18:27

*Hm* functions as a next-turn repair initiator (NTRI) by indicating some trouble in the talk with hearing or understanding. This form, which is minimal, targets the entire prior utterance as the trouble source. When it constitutes a turn, this form, along with *huh*, unambiguously does questioning when combined with rising terminal intonation. Intonation appears to be crucially relevant for the interpretation of these particles as NTRI's.

In the following example taken from a telephone conversation, the speaker produces the particle *huh*, an NTRI.

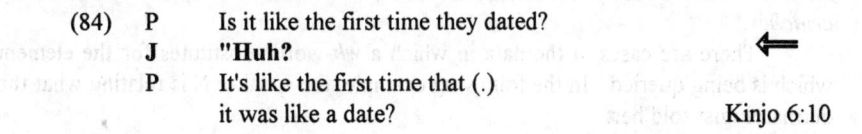

(84)  P   Is it like the first time they dated?
      J   "Huh?   ⟵
      P   It's like the first time that (.)
          it was like a date?
                                                 Kinjo 6:10

This example shows that *huh* with rising intonation is interpretable as showing some trouble with hearing or understanding the prior utterance.

*Interrogative Words*

There are cases in the data in which a single *wh*-word does questioning. Below, H is talking about a play which she and N are going to see:

(85)  H   *hh Toda:y there was a who::le (.) review on it in
          [the paper. ]
      N   [u-"where.]   ⟵
          (.)

>       N    Oh real [ly I'm gonna loo:k, ]
>       H            [in the View section.]                    HGII 9:3

N produces *where* in overlap with the phrase *in the paper*. The form is interpretable as asking where the review could be found. H produces the answer: *in the View section*.

There are also cases in which a *wh*-word modifies another word. Below, V is relating what a nurse told her about her father's knee after surgery:

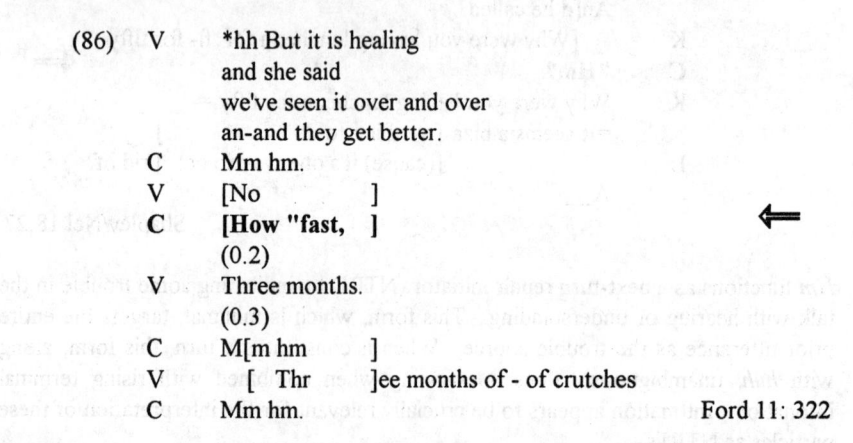

>   (86) V    *hh But it is healing
>             and she said
>             we've seen it over and over
>             an-and they get better.
>        C    Mm hm.
>        V    [No       ]
>        C    [How "fast, ]                                    ←
>             (0.2)
>        V    Three months.
>             (0.3)
>        C    M[m hm    ]
>        V     [  Thr   ]ee months of - of crutches
>        C    Mm hm.                                    Ford 11: 322

*How fast* is interpretable by virtue of the prior discourse as meaning "How fast will it (your father's knee) get better." V answers this question with the phrase *three months*. After a receipt marker by C, V expands the answer — *three months of crutches*.

There are cases in the data in which a *wh*-word substitutes for the element which is being queried. In the following example, the speaker N is relating what the dermatologist told her:

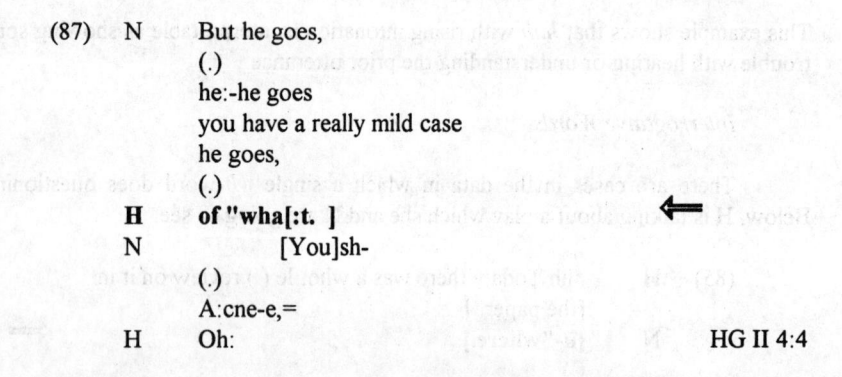

>   (87) N    But he goes,
>             (.)
>             he:-he goes
>             you have a really mild case
>             he goes,
>             (.)
>        H    of "wha[:t. ]                                    ←
>        N         [You]sh-
>             (.)
>             A:cne-e,=
>        H    Oh:                                        HG II 4:4

H produces a next-turn repair initiator (NTRI) with the prepositional phrase *of what*. This is interpretable as: "He goes, you have a really mild case of what." The *what* is produced in the place of the element whose identity is being queried. N produces the answer *acne*. This answer is receipted with the particle *oh*.

Below, the participants are college students who live in a dorm, and M is talking about two young women who are friends of his:

(88)  M   There's a rumor going around (Spilly now) like crazy.
          (0.2)
          *h people on their floor think that we are having an affair
          the (.) three of us.
          (0.2)
      S   Who.
          (0.5)
      M   Th- These three guys on the- on their floor
          on the tenth floor.
          (0.5)
          I'd know who they are [but* that's who.
      S                         [The three of "who though.   ⟵
          (0.4)
      M   Uh the two girls and I.
          (0.1)
      S   Oh                                                SN 4 15:27

S produces the next-turn repair initiator *who* indicating she is having some trouble with reference. M responds with the referents of the noun *people*. S then produces the noun phrase *the three of who* plus the conjunction *though*. This phrase is a third-position repair which is demonstrating that M did not satisfactorily clarify the reference which was the source of the trouble.

This next-turn repair initiator indicates that the speaker cannot identify the referents for *the three of us*. M subsequently produces the reference *the two girls and I*, which S receipts with the particle *oh*. The question *the three of who, though*, redoes the phrase *the three of us* with one difference — the *wh*-word *who* replaces the pronoun *us*.

6.3.2.2. *Marking which Occurs before the Nonclausal Form.* In each case, marking which occurs before a nonclausal form is dependent on the constituent structure of the nonclausal form.

*Prior Interrogative Words*

There are cases when the speaker produces a *wh*-word and offers a candidate response to the *wh*-word. The following utterance is analyzed as a noun phrase with a prior interrogative form which is a next-turn repair initiator soliciting a confirmation. This form also appears with declaratives (see example 24). Following, the speaker is discussing her visit to the dermatologist's:

>     (89)  N    So he gave me these pills to ta:ke?=
>           H    ="What. "Tetracycline?
>                (.)
>           N    *PT NO:
>                cuz I used to take that
>                and it didn't he:lp
>                so he gave me something else.=
>           H    =Hm:.                                    HG II 4:17

H produces the *wh*-word *what* followed by a candidate guess of the prescribed medication, and the *wh*-word projects question function to the guess. Note: the intonation distinguishes this utterance from one in which the *wh*-word modifies the noun (see example 93). N answers the question with a negative token *no* followed by the reason why tetracycline was not prescribed.

Below, the participants are looking at a book about Indian mythology. As before, the speaker produces a *wh*-word and offers a candidate response to the *wh*-word. The utterance is a noun phrase with a prior interrogative form:

>     (90)  Na   Oh he's blue.
>           (M)  *hh
>           Na   He's got to be something special.
>           M    Yeah. He's a god.
>                Some sort of [god with blue skin.
>           Na              [°Yeah
>                I forget his name.
>                Do you remember
>           L    "Who. "Ganesh?
>           M    No it isn't Ganesh,
>                cause he has a man's head.
>                because he has a man's head.          Shapley/Sha 7:126

L produces the *wh*-word *who* and a candidate name of the god M and Na were discussing. The interrogative pronoun *who* projects question function to the subsequently produced candidate name.

In the following example from a telephone conversation, the participants are kidding about a mutual friend who is P's roommate:

>     (91)  P    I'm not going to beat up Euclid=
>                why would I want to beat up Euclid=
>                he's one of the best roommates I've ever ha::d.

### NONCLAUSAL QUESTIONS: MORPHOSYNTACTIC PATTERNS 133

> J     "Oh, "compared to what. (.) to "Daryl?    ←
>         Yeah, I'm sure he is.
> P     No::: compared to all the other ones too=
>         =he's one he's one of the best.           Kinjo 3:4

In this example, the speaker produces a verb phrase containing a *wh*-word and offers a candidate standard of comparison. The *wh*-word stands in the place of an individual to whom Euclid should be compared. This suggests that Euclid is one of the best roommates when compared to one of the worst, *i.e.*, when measured against a very low standard.

### *Prior Lexical Element*

There are cases in which a prior lexical element is suggestive of question function. Below, the participants are talking about the possibility of meeting an eligible male at the play they are planning to see that night. They have previously discussed the characters in the play, including one "Jewish guy" character.

> (92)   N    So I'll see you about- ei:ghtish,
>               (0.2)
>               O [kay? ]
>       H      [\*e-\*a]a::::, ei[ghtish,      ]
>       N                     [What are you] gonna wea:r,
>               (0.9)
>               Just nice pants or so[mething,
>       H                     [Yeah. I'm[not gonna ]=
>       N                             [Okay,        ]
>       H      =get dressed uh=
>               =cause it's supposed to rai:n tonight=
>               =too[:.
>       N        [Oh that's ri[:ght.      ]
>       H                   [Least the ]re's a chance of it.=
>       N      =Oka::y then I'll just wear pant[s
>       H                                  [cause I don't wanna mess up
>               my [clo:thes,]
>       N        [hhhhhh ]
>               ka::y,
>               (.)
>       H      You know who do I have to look nice for.
>               (.)
>               hh    [h-hh-hhh    ]
>       N         [Well you nev]er know who's gonna be in the play
>               I mean we are si [tting close to the stage.           ]

```
         H              [khh-*hh- h-hhh-hh-hh (eh heh)]
                 eh eh e=
         N       =*hhe:hh=
         H       *hhh  [Maybe the "Jewish [gu:]y, hunh        ⇐
         N             [He'll look out an   [ go,]
                 He'll go, Juliet, Juliet- Nancy. Hyla.          HG II 45:21
```

H does questioning with the utterance *Maybe the Jewish guy*. The *hunh* after the utterance is a laugh token and not a particle. This form is analyzed as a noun phrase preceded by the lexical element *maybe*. This utterance is interpretable as raising the possibility that the actor who plays "the Jewish guy" will notice them. A confirmation or disconfirmation is made relevant. Note: this form is overlapped by an utterance referring to the actor who will be playing the character of "the Jewish guy." N redoes part of her utterance which was overlapped.

*6.3.2.3. Marking which Occurs Subsequent to the Nonclausal Form.* The identification of marking which occurs subsequent to a nonclausal form is dependent in each case on the constituent structure of the nonclausal form.

*Subsequent Discourse Marker/Conjunction*

In the following, participants are discussing whether or not spinach is a good source of iron:

```
    (93)    T          [You know, in the old da:ys]
            M     Spinach [ spinach has this      ] huge negative
                  ion (.) iron (.) balance,
                  because it it chelates the iron (.) in the rest of your foods
            B     Oh it does not have (.)
                  it is not a good source of iron.
            M     It extracts iron.
            ()    ( )
            B     Really?
                  hh
            L     what does it do with it.
            B     Why this "myth [then.                              ⇐
            M                    [it chelates it into some absorbable form.
            B     why this "myth for so for so long.
            L     Does it build up?
            M     Most  [of the myths are that children  ]
            T           [the myths were started by the=]
            M     =the myths among children are that spinach is terrible and
                  that it tastes bad.
                  *hh
```

```
         B     Yes.
         M     so the other myths are an attempt
               by the adults   [to compensate for it.
         B                     [I see.( )
               But I thought
               that every- everything that was dark green was uh (.) no
               everything red is high in iron. Or what.
               what is it.
               what is the truth.
         ( )   uh
         M     There is no truth.                            Shapley/Fer 1:15.1
```

B is referring to the myth that spinach is a good source of iron. The question *why this myth then* is interpretable as asking why is there such a myth since the facts do not support it. The discourse marker *then* implies a false connection between the fact and the myth.

*Particle Tag*

There are cases in which a particle tag is added to a nonclausal form, as in this telephone conversation:

```
  (94)   R     Hello?
         A     Hello Richard?
               (0.2)
         R     O:hh Arthur
               How are you:.
         A     O:h pretty good
               how are you?
         R     *hhh (*) a::hhh (0.2)
               off an on?
               What's up.
               (0.2)
         A     Off an "on:? uhh [h           ]*hhh            ⇐
         R                      [Ye:ah(hh)? ]                 Gee 1:8
```

A questions R's response to *How are you* and solicits more talk on R's state of being. The particle *uh* with rising intonation is a signal of question function.

*Word Tags*

Word tags are also used by speakers to do questioning with nonclausal forms. Below, V is talking about her father's medical problem with his knees:

(95)  V   Okay
          This is what t-the problem is,
          my Dad's knee- leg was very bow-legged.
          It was like thirt[een degrees    ]
      C                  [All his "life. ] (.) "right?   ←
      V   Well: more in old age(h).=
      C   uh huh.                                          Ford 2: 37

C does questioning with the utterance *all his life, right* which is analyzed as a noun phrase followed by a word tag. The nonclausal form is produced in overlap (the tag *right* is in the clear — it is not produced simultaneously with another's talk). The tag's rising terminal intonation is a signal that the noun phrase is functioning as a question.

*Clause Tags*

Questioning can be done with a clause tag. Below, the participants are college students talking about S's upcoming wedding. The transcript reflects two possible hearings for M's first turn (*well* vs. *what*) and final turn (for the word *mean*):

(96)  M   *h So (well )have you called any other hotels or anything?
                 (what)
          (0.3)
      S   Yeah
          I called the Ambassador n stuff.
          I've got so much work that I don't believe it
          so I'm just not thinking about that.=
      M   =In 'school you "mea[n.]                         ←
                              mea: [n?]
      S   Yeah                                             SN 4 3: 30

M does questioning with a prepositional phrase plus the clause tag *you mean* which is a discourse particle even though it has clause structure (see Chapter 4, example 37 & 38). This utterance is an NTRI. The tag unambiguously signals that the prepositional phrase is doing questioning.

*Alternate Choice*

In the following example, M reintroduces the subject of oxalic acid which had been previously discussed. The participants are eating spinach soup which B, the hostess/cook, refers to by *this*:

(97) M   Sorrel.
     (.)
     Sorrel has a lot of oxalic acid too.
     (0.1)
L   heh  [heh heh
           [((laughter))
( )       [(Sorrel? )
B       [Sorrel has a lot of what?
M   Sorrel. yes.
T   What's (.) what's that?
M   That's a sort of green, clover-like grass.
(B)     mm hmm
B   has a lot of what?=
M   =( ) tastes like [spinach. ]
                [acid?  ]which acid?
B   Oxalic.
M   Oxalic. Yeah.
B   Yeah, this has a lot of oxalic acid,
     yeah, but I cook it
     and I throw away the water carefully, you see.
     Unlike people who always tell you
     ah but you are throwing all the vitamins away.
N   Why why must you throw away ( )?
B   Well, we've been always [(s )=
L   [For spinach you have to get rid of the sand.
B   =Well, my mother even throws away the water several times
N   Is there something (.) bad about    [it?
B                                      [For the oxalic acid.
M                                      [Probably.
B   (yeah) rheumatism and things like this.
M   Gout.
N   **from oxalic "acid?=**                   ⇐
M   =Well now it can't [be both insolu     ]able
N               **[or spinach "water? ]**    ⇐
M   and bad for you, can it.
     (1.0)
L   Why not.
B   Why not.
M   I suppose it could. (.)
     You absorb a little bit.
     It's quite poi  [sonous.
N                [I see.
B   yeah.                              Shapley/Fer 7:172

N asks whether rheumatism and things like that are caused by oxalic acid or spinach water. The speaker offers two alternatives making a choice between them relevant.

### 6.4. The Interpretation of Nonclausal Questions with No Associated Marker

Some nonclausal forms have no lexical or morphosyntactic markings suggestive of question function. As with declarative questions, other factors are relevant to the interpretation of these forms as questions. Some nonclausal questions, for example, are interpretable by virtue of being next-turn repair initiators.

#### 6.4.1. Next-Turn Repair Initiators and Nonclausal Questions

Next-turn repair initiators (NTRI's) indicate some trouble with hearing or understanding in the talk. Schegloff, Jefferson and Sacks (1977) have described the variety of morphosyntactic forms used to effect repair in talk. The speaker of the NTRI must construct the utterance so the recipient can identify the source of the trouble (necessary if the trouble is to be remedied). As discussed in Chapter 2, NTRI's may be declarative clauses. Particles (example 83), words (example 81) or phrases (examples 87, 88 & 96) may also serve to initiate next-turn repair.

#### 6.4.2. Accessibility of Information and Nonclausal Questions

Chapter 4 discussed declarative questions with no associated marker which may be interpretable as requests for confirmation (Labov and Fanshel's rule of confirmation). The same interpretive procedures also facilitate the interpretation of nonclausal questions with no associated marker (examples 78 & 79).

### 6.5. Distributive Facts

The distribution of nonclausal questions vs. other syntactic types of questions in the corpus and the distribution of the various types of nonclausal forms are discussed in this section. Table 6.1. represents the distribution of questions in the corpus by their syntactic form:

| | | |
|---|---|---|
| All forms which do questioning | 636 | 100% |
| All declarative forms which do questioning | 108 | 17% |
| All nonclausal forms which do questioning | 153 | 24% |

Table 6.1.
Distribution of All Questions by Syntactic Form

This table demonstrates that speakers in these data use nonclausal forms to do questioning more frequently than declarative questions. From a distributional point of view, the problem of how nonclausal questions are interpreted is as significant as how declarative questions get interpreted.

The following table exhibits the distribution of lexically or morphosyntactically marked nonclausal questions vs. nonclausal questions with no associated marker in the data:

|  |  |  |
|---|---|---|
| Marked | 96 | 63% |
| No Associated Marker | 57 | 37% |
| Total | 153 | 100% |

Table 6.2.
**Marked Nonclausal Questions
vs.
Nonclausal Questions with No Associated Marker**

This table shows that more than 60% of all nonclausal questions are marked lexically or morphosyntactically.

### 6.5.1. Marked Nonclausal Questions

The following table exhibits the distribution of the types of marking in the nonclausal questions described above. As with declarative clause questions, the types of marking have been distinguished according to temporal criteria as follows: Section 1 — marking within the constituent structure of each particular form; Section 2 — marking prior to the constituent structure of each particular form; Section 3 — marking subsequent to the constituent structure of each particular form. *Note: since several forms have more than one instance of marking, the number of instances is more than the total number of forms.*

| | | | |
|---|---|---|---|
| **I: Within the Constituent Structure** | | | |
| Lexical | 17 | 16% | |
| Particle | 11 | 10% | |
| wh-word | 45 | 42% | |
| Subject/verb inversion | 3 | 3% | 71% |
| **II: Prior to the Constituent Structure** | | | |
| Prior particle | 1 | 1% | |
| Prior wh-word | 3 | 3% | |
| Prior lexical element | 2 | 2% | |
| Prior discourse marker | 11 | 10% | 16% |
| **III: Subsequent to the Constituent Structure** | | | |
| Subsequent discourse marker | 4 | 4% | |
| Particle tag | 3 | 3% | |
| Word tag | 2 | 2% | |
| Clause tag | 2 | 2% | |
| Alternative choice | 2 | 2% | 13% |
| **Total** | **106** | **100%** | |

Table 6.3.
Distribution of Instances of Marking by Temporal Criteria

This table shows that 71% of all instances of marking suggestive of question function appear within the constituent structure of the nonclausal form. Within this category, wh-words and particles constitute 52% of all instances. The meaning of these forms in conjunction with intonation unambiguously signals question function. Marking which occurs prior to the nonclausal form constitutes 16% of all instances, and marking which occurs subsequent to the nonclausal form in 13% of all cases.

To understand how speakers actually use marking associated with nonclausal questions, the following table examines their distribution in individual nonclausal forms:

| | | |
|---|---|---|
| 1 marker | 86 | 90% |
| 2 markers | 10 | 10% |
| **Total** | **96** | **100%** |

Table 6.4.
Number of Markers per Clause

Nonclausal forms which have a lexical or morphosyntactic marker suggestive of question function overwhelmingly have only one such marker per form (two markers occur in only 10% of all cases).

Previous example 88 is repeated below as an example with two markers — a *wh*-word and subsequent discourse marker:

(98)  M    There's a rumor going around ( Spilly  now ) like crazy.
           (0.2)
           *h people on their floor think that we are having an affair
           the (.) three of us.
           (0.2)
      S    Who.
           (0.5)
      M    Th- These three guys on the- on their floor
           on the tenth floor.
           (0.5)
           I'd know who they are [but* that's who.
      S              [The three of "who though.  ⇐
           (0.4)
      M    Uh the two girls and I.
           (0.1)
      S    Oh                                     SN 4 15:27

This example is a third-position repair. Third-position repairs are produced by the speaker of the trouble source turn. With this utterance, the speaker is repairing her original NTRI *who*. M's response to *who* shows that he misunderstood the reference about which S was unclear. The phrase *the three of us* is repeated with a *wh*-word in place of the pronoun *us*. The entire nonclausal phrase is followed by the conjunction *though*. *Though* demonstrates that the prior turn did not identify the original trouble source, the referent of *us*. (This utterance is also functioning as an NTRI.)

The following example in which the participants are discussing a former date of H's also exhibits two markers — a prior-discourse marker and *wh*-word:

(99)  N    I guess, I guess- (0.6) he'll write you,
           (.)
      H    ishhhhh [ ih-uh
      N             [Next wee(.)k=
      H    =*hhhh  Sure.
           (.)
           [Sure
      N    [Give it another week.
           (.)

142  VARIETIES OF QUESTIONS IN ENGLISH CONVERSATION

      H    [And "then w]ha[t.                      ⇐
      N    [And the:n,   ]   [send him a thank you   [no(h)te, hh
      H                                                                  [hehh ( )
                                                                                                                                HG II 32: 19

The participants produce *and then* in overlap. The particle *then* is often used in narrating events. When used with *what* in doing questioning, it suggests a gap in the knowledge of what will occur next.

     There are several cases, as in example 100, in which the particle *oh* occurs with another marker. This particle signals some shift of orientation to information (Heritage 1984, Schiffrin 1987). Schiffrin (1987:86) states that only those questions which are evoked by the reception of information are prefaced by *oh*:

    (100)  N     Anything else to report,
                     (0.3)
           H     Uh:::::::m:::::,
                     (0.4)
                   Getting my hair cut tomorrow,=
           N     Oh "really?                            ⇐
                   (.)
           H     Yea: ::::h,                                          HG II 16:4

N produces the particle *oh* and the word *really*. This utterance is a receipt of news which shows some characteristics of NTRI's, *e.g.*, position. The *oh* signals the speaker's shift of orientation to the information in H's announcement while the word *really* registers the utterance as news. The utterance is interpretable as requesting confirmation that the statement is true as it stands.

### 6.5.2. Nonclausal Questions with No Associated Marker

     Table 6.2. indicated that 37% of all nonclausal questions have no lexical or morphosyntactic marking suggestive of question function. These forms, then, are relevant to the typical formulation of the characterization of the form/function problem. The issue is how these forms are interpreted. The role of rising terminal intonation is crucial for their interpretation as questions (see Chapter 8).

     The following table presents the distribution of nonclausal questions by the interpretive factors outlined previously (NTRI's and Labov and Fanshel's rule of confirmation):

| | | |
|---|---|---|
| NTRI | 35 | 62% |
| Rule of Confirmation | 7 | 12% |
| Other | 15 | 26% |
| Total | 57 | 100% |

Table 6.5.
**Distribution of Nonclausal Questions with No Associated Marker
by
Interpretive Factors**

Of all nonclausal questions with no associated marker, 61% are interpretable as NTRI's, 12% as requests for confirmation while 26% fall into the category "other."

Although not marked morphosyntactically, forms which are NTRI's and requests for confirmation (according to Labov and Fanchel's rule of confirmation) are amenable to well documented interpretive procedures. NTRI's are interpretable by virtue of their position, intonation and/or repeated lexical elements (Chapter 2). Requests for confirmation are interpretable in terms of A- and B-events, *i.e.*, in terms of who has access to the relevant information (Chapter 4). When these factors are taken into account, Table 6.2. can be amended as follows.

| | | | |
|---|---|---|---|
| Lexically/Morphosyntactically Marked | 96 | 63% | |
| NTRI's | 35 | 23% | |
| Requests for Confirmation | 7 | 4% | }90% |
| Others with No Associated Marker | 15 | 10% | |
| Total | 153 | 100% | |

Table 6.6.
**Amended Distribution of Marked Nonclausal Questions
and Nonclausal Questions with No Associated Marker**

When NTRI's and requests for confirmation are combined with morphosyntactically marked forms, Table 6.6 shows fully 90% of nonclausal questions are amenable to well documented interpretive procedures. Those cases which have no associated marker and are neither NTRI's nor requests for confirmation account for 10% of all nonclausal questions; however, they are, nevertheless, unambiguously interpretable as doing questioning. I will now discuss the 15 forms which fall into the category "others with no associated marker."

During dinner, there are seven cases in which the speaker uses nonclausal questions to make offers of food:

(101)  M  more "corn,  ⇐
            more "salad,  ⇐
            more "bread,  ⇐

more "meat,  ←
(.)
anything for "anybody?  ←

Shapley/Boys 13:22.1

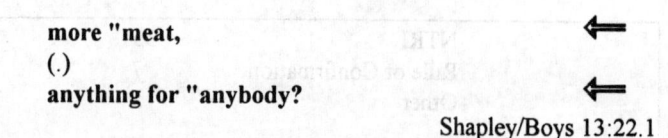

The speaker, who is the hostess/cook, asks the participants if they would like more of the various items which were served. She accomplishes this by producing *more* plus the food item. Each of these forms is interpretable as a question simply because the speaker is in a position to offer more food. These utterances serve as offers, or perhaps more accurately, permission to take a second helping. The final utterance *anything for anybody* is interpretable as "does anybody want anything" or "can I get anything for anybody." (These nonclausal questions are expected of hostesses.)

There are three cases in which the nonclausal question with no associated marker is a second-pair part — a response to a question which is itself a question. These are all "try questions" or informed guesses. Following, participants are discussing the space shuttle vehicles:

(102) M   Where are these things going to be on display.
      B   at "Edwards?  ←
      L   at Edwards Air Force Base.           Shapley/Boys 4: 14.2

There is one case in which a nonclausal question with no associated marker is used to do a candidate understanding during a story. Below, K is telling a story about a lecture she gave:

(103) C   Yes I think
          M___ thought of it as a (.) stand for women.
          (So ) she (was) (.) she [(thought it ) was=
      ( )                         [( )
      C   =the only thing to do.
      K   Yeah
          I never really (.) talked to uh
          I guess
          I did talk to M___ a little about uh her women's studies
          course.
          which I gave a lecture to.
          Did [she ever tell you about that?
      C       [Oh did you?
          No:, she never really told me about (much) much about the
          course.
      M   What did you lecture about women's studies?
      K   Well, they put together this women's studies course.
          A:h
      C   Yeah she was in some subset.

|   | What was tha[t. |
|---|---|
| K | [Let's see (.) |
|   | I'm try [ing to think |
| C | [third world [women? or something], |
| L | [( ) ] |
|   | Oh that's like black studies, you mean? |
| C | Yeah righ[t. |
| K | [I'm trying to think how they (.) |
|   | characterized it. Um |
| ( ) | he he |
| D | It (.) It hasn't gone that far ( ) |
| K | Um, I guess |
|   | it was just called women's studies. |
|   | but uh I was trying to, (.) |
|   | I was talking on sex differences |
|   | and trying to put together a very sophisticated |
|   | developmental argument, |
| C | ((laughing)) |
|   | ( you know ) so that they could use on the barricades, |
| K | Right, exactly, you know I had I (.) |
|   | [I you know |
| C | [a slogan or tw[o |
| K | [actually it was one of my most uh animated |
|   | lectures. |
|   | I mean I was really all= |
| C | =scholarly, though huh? |
| K | It wa:s: (.) a bit (.) |
|   | you know |
|   | it wasn't exactly schol[arly. |
| L | ["sparkling with footnotes, ⇐ |
|   | "[j]uh? ⇐ |
| D | ( ) |
|   | [((laughter)) ] |
| K | [No, no. but it was, it was, you know it ] |
|   | there was there was a certain coherence to it, |
|   | I mean [you [know |
| ( ) | [((laughter)) |
| L | [Oh |
| K | [ha ha ha there was a ha ha ha = ] |
| ( ) | [((laughter)) ] |
| K | [a theoretical idea behind it. ] |
| ( ) | [((laughter)) ] |
| K | And uh I saw these glazed faces ((laughs)) |
|   | and uh as soon as I got through, |

```
K       uh, you know I didn't get through
        I you know (just) came to the end
        and said
        how about some questions,
        and the first question I got was (0.2)
        why do you keep talking about mothers.
        (0.8)
                [laughs)) in- in- instead of parents.    ]
( )             [((laughter))                            ]
L       parent persons?
( )     ((laughter))
D       [(  )person ((laughs))
( )     [((laughter))
K       well uh you know sorry about that.
        But uh=
L       (P) P (person ) parents.
K       =um mothers are [(.)                ]generally the people
L                       [that's a question. ]
K       we generally see in the laboratory with the (.) babies.
        and  and uh *hh in the in  in the   [ ( ) (pres-)  ] present
        day society=
C                                           [sexist        ]
K       =they (. ) are the most likely people to be taking care of
        (.) babies.
        It went on from there.
        D [own hil   [l.=
( )       [((laughter))
C                    [down.
( )       [((laughter))      ]
        [They didn't like it, huh?]
K       I'm afraid this elegant ha ha theoretical exposition just
        [went ha ha (.) ]
( )     [((laughter))   ]
        went uh (.) ( [t^s])by them apparently.
C       ( )
K       [It turned out to be entirely a class of ( ).
( )     [((laughter))
        I mean it was a (.)
        It's orientation was:  sli:ghtly to the radical side of where
        I was,
        where  (.) I had always found myself rather comfortable.
                                                    Shapley/Nel 3:4
```

L produces the candidate understanding *parent persons*. With this utterance, L displays an understanding of K's point regarding the position of the undergraduates on nonsexist terminology. The utterance *parent persons* suggests the absurdity of the linguistic elimination of sex differences in certain cases. Neutral terminology is appropriate where the sex difference ought not to make a difference. In parenting, the distinction between the mother and the father is, and ought to be, relevant. (It is certainly relevant in terms of the reality of child rearing in this society. Mothers still raise the children most often.)

There is one case in which a nonclausal question with no associated marker is pointing out an object:

(104)　　　　(3.0)
　　Na　　S-see that plant (.)hanging(.)in　　　　⇐
　　　　　　the dining room, N___.　　　　　　　　⇐
　　　　　　In the "white pot　　　　　　　　　　　⇐
　　　　　　From the "ceiling.
　　No　　Yes.
　　Na　　Now that's a Boston fern.
　　No　　Yeah　　　　　　　　　　　　Shapley/Sha 3:61

This example is interpretable as "do you see." The subject and the auxiliary verb are recoverable from the form rather than from the prior discourse (Quirk 1985:838). By asking if No can see the plant, the speaker is pointing it out to him; and she adds prepositional phrases for direction as he tries to locate it.

Here is one case which is a request for an evaluation. The recipient of the question, L, has just tasted Na's banana cake which he mistakenly thinks is carrot cake:

(105)　Na　　"Like it?　　　　　　　　　　　　　　⇐
　　　　L　　I don't taste the carrots.
　　　　Na　　I don't think there are any in here.
　　　　　　But you can't taste any carrots in the carrot cake I make either.
　　　　　　((laughter))　　　　　　　　Shapley/Sha 2:30

The utterance is interpretable as the interrogative form "Do you like it." The subject and the auxiliary verb are recoverable from the form rather than from the prior discourse.

Below, the speaker N begins a new topic/sequence:

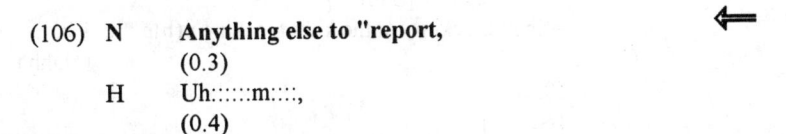

(106)　N　　Anything else to "report,　　　　　　⇐
　　　　　　(0.3)
　　　　H　　Uh::::::m::::,
　　　　　　(0.4)

|   | H | Getting my hair cut tomorrow,= |
|---|---|---|
|   | N | Oh really? |
|   |   | (.) |
|   | H | Yea:[:::h,       HG II 15:24 |

The utterance *Anything else to report* is interpretable as the interrogative form, "Do you have anything else to report." As in the previous examples, the subject and the verb are recoverable from the form rather than from the prior discourse.

Here is a case which is a repeat of a prior question which had been misheard when it was first produced. This example is the continuation of example 106. The transcript reflects two possible hearings for N's third turn (*so soo:[d]* = *so soon* vs. *for food*):

```
(107)   N     Anything else to report,
              (0.3)
        H     Uh:::::::m::::,
              (0.4)
              Getting my hair cut tomorrow,=
        N     Oh really?
              (.)
        H     Yea: [:::h,
        N          [Oh ( so soo:[d]?)
                        (for foo:d?)
              (0.4)
        H     Wha:t?
              (0.2)
        N     Cause member
              you said
              you w[ere gonna m    ]ake an appo [intment n, ]
        H          [°whhhhhhhoo ]              [Oh:    y ]eah.*=
              =*a-* Yihknow what I thought you sai:d *hh=
        N     [°What, ]
        H     [for f    ]oo:d, hhhhh [hhhhhhh    ]
        N                            [e-f(hh)or] f(h)oo(h)d
              (.)
        H     *ihhhhh=
        N     =Oh for foo:d? ehh he    [ heh *i     ]h]
        H     (so I says)   [wha::t.]=
        N                              [*hhehh-*e-     ]h] hhuh
                             [Su:re.  ]=
              =She's cracking up the kid's cracking u(h)p *u:::[:.
        H                                                     [*hihhh
              (0.2)
              [No:,  ]
```

```
N    [No:    ] for- (.) so "soo:[[d]?hhhh]                    ←
H              [so soo  ]n. Yes. *hh
      Yeah at (.) eleven fiftee:n,
      (.)
N     Mmmm.=
H     =then I('ve) gotta go to Robinson's and return *uhh*
      birthday gift my brother (.) bought me,=           HG II 17:2
```

The speaker N repeats her original question *so soon* without the particle *oh*. H repeats this utterance and produces an affirmative token *yes*, confirming that she understands that the original utterance was (*so soon*). She then answers the question by producing *Yeah* and giving the time of the haircut appointment *at eleven fifteen*.

In this section, I have discussed nonclausal questions with no associated marker. Chapter 4 discusses all declarative questions with no associated marker which are interpretable in terms of two factors: they are either NTRI's or requests for confirmation (according to Labov and Fanshel's rule of confirmation). These two factors are also relevant to the interpretation of 74% of all nonclausal questions with no associated marker (Table 6.5.).

How recipients interpret the remaining 26% of nonclausal questions with no associated marker deserves further examination. The relevant forms function as offers of food which occur at dinner, try questions, candidate understandings, requests for action and evaluation, topic/sequence solicitations and a repeat of a prior form which was misheard.

Schiffrin (1987:85) notes that questions are rarely totally disconnected from their environment. The offers which involve food are all related to items present in the recipient's immediate physical environment. The question which is a request for an evaluation also involves a physically present food item; in fact, the recipient has just tasted it. The request for action involves an object present in the physical environment; thus, nine of the 15 nonclausal questions without an associated marker make reference to physically present entities.

The three try questions in the data are themselves second-pair parts; they are interpretable in terms of the prior questions to which they themselves respond. The candidate understanding occurs during the course of a narrative and is interpretable in terms of the immediately prior turn and makes reference to the story. The instance of the repeat of the prior question is making explicit that the recipient's initial interpretation of the utterance was incorrect. This question is interpretable as a repeat/correction which makes reference to the original utterance.

The topic/sequence solicitation is the only question which is interpretable neither in terms of an entity in the physical environment nor in the semantic/informational content of the prior discourse. Because the solicitation appears immediately after the opening sequence of a telephone conversation, it is interpretable in terms of its sequential position in the talk as a request for news (Button and Casey 1984).

## 6.6. Summary of Distributive Facts

Nonclausal questions exhibit a wide variety of morphosyntactic forms ranging from minimal particles to complex verb phrases. Lexically or morphosyntactically marked forms constitute 63% of all nonclausal questions. Marking occurs within the constituent structure in 71% of all nonclausal questions. Particles and *wh*-words constitute 52% of all instances of within-the-constituent marking.

Of the remaining 37% of nonclausal questions with no associated marker, 23% are interpretable as next-turn repair initiators (NTRI's), while requests for confirmation constitute an additional 5%. This leaves 15 cases — or 10% — of nonclausal questions whose interpretation must be explained on other grounds. These forms function as offers which occur at dinner involving food, try questions, candidate understandings, requests for action and evaluation, topic/sequence solicitations and a repeat of a prior form which was misheard. Note: it some cases, the percentages don't add up to 100% because of rounding.

# Chapter 7

# Nonclausal Questions: Function

## 7.1. Multiple Functions of Nonclausal Questions

In this chapter, I will examine some functions of nonclausal questions in conversation. All the nonclausal questions in the data are functioning to do questioning; however, as we have seen in the case of declarative questions (Chapter 5), nonclausal questions in their social context also exhibit functions which can be given more detailed descriptions than doing questioning.

## 7.2. Functional Distribution of Nonclausal Questions

The nonclausal questions in the data have been categorized functionally as:

- Forms implicated in repair
  next-turn repair initiators (NTRI's)
  candidate solutions
- Forms not implicated in repair
  topic/sequence solicitations
  preferred responses
  candidate understandings
  backdowns from a prior assertion
  try questions
  offers
  requests for evaluations
  object locators
- Instances of *really* which receipt news or interesting information

The 153 nonclausal questions in the data distribute functionally as follows:

| | | |
|---|---|---|
| Forms Implicated in Repair | 92 | 60% |
| Forms Not Implicated in Repair | 49 | 32% |
| *Really* | 12 | 8% |
| **Total** | **153** | **100%** |

**Table 7.1.**
**Functional Distribution of Nonclausal Questions by Function**

This table shows that over half of all nonclausal questions in the data are implicated in repair. In fact, all but one of the nonclausal forms implicated in repair are NTRI's. The single exception is a candidate solution to a word search. Forms not implicated in repair constitute 32% of nonclausal forms, while instances of *really* constitute the remaining 8% of nonclausal forms. Repair work in conversation is a unified function described by Schegloff Jefferson, and Sacks (1977); Jefferson (1974) and by Schegloff (1987, 1989, 1990, 1992).

Following Schegloff *et. al.* (1977), I will present the types of other-initiated nonclausal repairs found in the data. Next, I will examine those nonclausal questions which function as topic solicitations, preferred responses, candidate understandings, backdowns, etc. and their interpretation. Then I will discuss the instances of the news receipt *really* in the data. This form has some characteristics of an NTRI in addition to characteristics of a receipt marker. The receipt markers will be only briefly discussed because a full description would require a much larger collection of data. Finally, I will also consider when questions can be done with particles, words and phrases instead of full syntactic clauses. The discussion will show why nonclausal forms are eminently suited to initiate repair work in conversation as NTRI's.

## 7.3. Next-Turn Repair Initiators (NTRI's)

An NTRI indicates the understanding the speaker has of the trouble source utterance, how much is comprehended and how much needs to be repeated or dealt with in some other way. NTRI's only pinpoint the trouble source (the repairable element) in the prior utterance (Chapter 2). Three relevant factors involved in the interpretation of basic NTRI's are:

(1) Next-turn position,
(2) The form of the NTRI and
(3) Rising terminal intonation.

While other-initiated repairs most often occur in next-turn position, they may interrupt the utterance with the trouble source or occur subsequent to the next turn. Similarly, while rising terminal intonation is associated with other-initiated repairs which appear in next turn (Cruttenden 1986:92), other intonation contours are possible. The following NTRI types follow Schegloff, Jefferson and Sacks (1977) and are presented in the order of their capacity specifically locate a trouble source. They appear in order from least specific locator to most specific locator:

*Type 1 (Huh, What)*

The most *basic* kind of NTRI is *huh* or *what*. The speaker needs to hear virtually nothing to produce this type of NTRI. These forms are quite minimal in lexical and phonological content. With rising terminal intonation, they target the entire prior utterance as the source of the trouble and are interpretable as requests for repetition of the entire trouble-source turn. This is an instance in which intonation *does* crucially determine function.

With basic NTRI's, falling intonation would not target the entire utterance (Type 2 below). In the following example, H is telling how she had called a former date and had hung up without saying hello. H produces an NTRI after a period of overlap:

```
(108)  N    You called Richard,=
       ( )  =hh-hh=
       H    = y(h)Yea(h)h
            and I h(h)ung up
            wh(h)en he ans[wer
       N                   [Oh: Hyla why::::[::,
       H                                    [*hhh
            well first of all
            I wasn't about to spend seventy five cents
            for three mi[nutes *uh] *eh=
       N               [Yea:h,   ]
            =That's true,=
       H    =*hihhhh that's a lot of money
            plus (.) uh then it's twenty five cents for extra minute a
            [fter that.]=
       N    [Yeah,     ]=
       H    =* hh y[ou know,    ]
       N          [How do you] know
            he [answered could you tell his voi:ce?]
       H      [so for four minutes its a bu:ck.    ]
            (0.2)
            "Hu:h?                                        ←
            (.)
       N    Could you tell his vo[i:ce,]
       H                         [Yea ]h I knew his voice,=
       N    =Oha:::[w,                             HGII 23:21
```

When produced with rising terminal intonation, a basic NTRI form is interpretable as a request for the repetition of the prior utterance.

In the following example, R is talking about his workplace:

```
(109)   A    A:nd um: it's not a bad place to be
             (0.4)
             because it's re:al (.)
             you know I got hummingbirds no:w?
             (0.2)
        R    "what?                                              ←
        A    I (h) *hh I have hu:mmingbirds.
        R    O:::h gre:at, [You should get a fee:der.
        A                  [yeah,                    Mannon 4: 67
```

R produces an NTRI *what* with rising intonation demonstrating some trouble with hearing (see also Selting 1992).

*Type 2 (Wh-word)*

*Wh*-words (*who, what, where, when, why, how*) may be used as NTRI's to query some element of the trouble source turn. They locate the source of the trouble as a referent, an event, a place, a time, a reason or an adverbial modifier. Using these words indicates some hearing of the prior utterance because their form varies depending upon whether the trouble involves the identification of a human or nonhuman referent (*who, what*), a location (*where*), an event (*what*), a time (*when*), a reason (*why*) or an adverbial modifier (*how*). When used in this way to target some element in the trouble source turn, these *wh*-words generally have level or falling intonation (see also Selting 1992). In the following example, V is relating what she wants to tell her mother regarding her father's recent elective knee surgery:

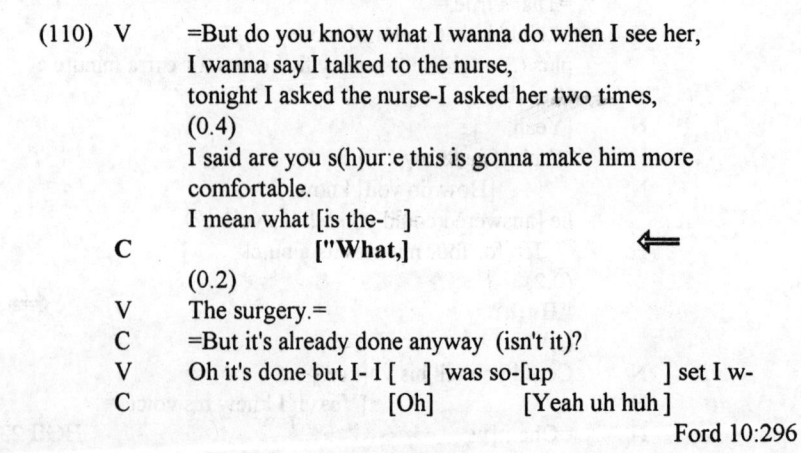

```
(110)   V    =But do you know what I wanna do when I see her,
             I wanna say I talked to the nurse,
             tonight I asked the nurse-I asked her two times,
             (0.4)
             I said are you s(h)ur:e this is gonna make him more
             comfortable.
             I mean what [is the-   ]
        C                ["What,]                                ←
             (0.2)
        V    The surgery.=
        C    =But it's already done anyway  (isn't it)?
        V    Oh it's done but I- I [    ] was so-[up       ] set I w-
        C                          [Oh]          [Yeah uh huh]
                                                         Ford 10:296
```

In this example, C produces an NTRI *what* with level intonation, demonstrating some trouble with identifying of the referent of *this*.

*Type 3a (Partial or Full Repeat + Wh-word)*
*3b (Partial or Full Repeat + Candidate Referent)*

A partial or full repeat plus a *wh*-word is another type of NTRI. This requires some hearing of the utterance. Below, L produces an NTRI which is a partial repeat plus a *wh*-word. This NTRI locates the trouble source in the prior turn as the identity of the referent of A:

```
(111)   E     Did I tell y-
              oh, yo:u heard it.
        L     Yeh, [ a ]bout K___?
        E          [[( )]
              No: about (1.2) A___.
        L     A___ "who,                                    ⇐
        E     is coming home,
        B     Oh [the one who left to go to ] Italy?
        N        [Oh yeah, I remember her ]
        L        [(                       ) ]
        E     She called and wants to come [home, ]=
        L                                  [Same  ]=Same terms as J.
                                                         Weber 3:8
```

E begins the sequence with a pre-announcement which she aborts and reconstructs as *Oh you heard it*. L offers a candidate referent which is then corrected by E. L then produces an NTRI by repeating the name of the referent she cannot identify and adding *who*. This NTRI is not given a second-pair part. Instead E continues her announcement. This clarifies the reference for the participants, as demonstrated in their subsequent responses. Although L's first response after the clause *is coming home* is unintelligible, her next turn shows that she has identified the referent of A because she knows the terms A's parents have set for letting her come home.

Following, N begins a story about a situation involving a friend whose daughter was giving her trouble. L, who is N's daughter, produces an NTRI which locates the trouble source in the prior turn as the referent of *my friend*:

```
(112)   N     I don't know,
              I'm dy::ing to know what happened up the street.
              We had the who:le thing going on with my friend
              (0.2)
              [who's up the  ] stree:t.=
        L     [with "J___? ]                                ⇐
        N     =Yeah.                                    Weber 8:116
```

L produces an NTRI by giving a partial repeat plus a candidate referent which N confirms. In fact, the candidate referent J is the daughter of N's friend, not N's friend. The NTRI, then, is actually clarifying the situation rather than the referent of *my friend*. (This example will be considered in greater detail later in this chapter).

*Type 4 (Partial Repeat Alone)*

A partial repeat alone, requiring some hearing of the utterance, may serve as an NTRI. Below, H and N had been talking about a play. H mentions that there was a review of it in the paper:

```
(113)   H      *hh Toda:y there was a who::le (.) review on it in
               [the paper.]
        N      [u-Whe:re.]
               (.)
               Oh real[ly I'm gonna loo:k, ]
        H             [In the View section.]
               (0.2)
        N      In the ["Vie:w?                              ⇐
        H              [*p*hh
               (.)
               Yeah
               but I don't want you to read it.
               (.)
        N      Okay,                                    HGII 9:1
```

N produces a partial repetition of H's prior turn which was overlapped. This repeat has terminally rising intonation. H responds to the NTRI with an affirmative token. This confirms that N correctly heard the utterance.

*Type 5 (You Mean + Candidate Understanding)*

*You mean* plus a possible understanding is also a type of NTRI. This not only requires some hearing, but also a sufficient understanding of the utterance to formulate a clarification or restatement. This possible understanding is produced to be confirmed or disproven by the speaker of the trouble-source turn.

Below, the participants had been discussing C's college-age daughter with respect to the college courses she had taken and her future goals:

```
(114)   D      [(           ) ]
        K      [No but no but= ]
        D      [(                     ) ]
        K      [=Wait a minute Wait a minute, ]
               She's she's interested  [in delivering   ] health,
```

NONCLAUSAL QUESTIONS: FUNCTION 157

```
L                    [(         ) ]
         not in health delivery systems.
C        Yeah,
         she's not interested in systems,
         she's interested in the delivery.
K        Ah it  [may be that the ah=
L               [( )
         =[system    system           ]
          [well [(then) [it'll be obsolete. ]
C                       [I made it    ] sound=
         =more intellectual [th [an it is.]
( )                     [( )  ]
K                       [Systems   ] can be delivered by
         computers, but uh the [actual delivery] can't be.
( )                     [(        )]
L        Oh no,
         There's all these diagnostic things,
         and all these uh    [           ]you know,
C                            [oh yeah but ]
         but she's interested in,
L        the doctor isn't there but he's into some terminal somewhere.
C        yeah well she's interested in (.) not [in th]at,
L                                              [( )]
C        She's interested in public health.
         and  and uh
         (0.1)
L        you mean   [sani      ]tation "type?       ⟵
C                   [°you know.]
         Yeah,
         that's right.
         (.)
         all those things.                       Shapley/Nel 6:11
```

L produces an NTRI which is realized by the discourse particle *you mean* plus a candidate understanding of public health. C responds with an affirmative token.

*Type 6 (Wh-word Used to Request More Information)*

There is a type of NTRI in which a *wh*-word occurs which does not refer to something mentioned in the prior utterance. This NTRI type demonstrates the need for more information in order to achieve a complete understanding of the utterance. *This type of question is an NTRI because it stops the projected course of the talk to locate the source of some trouble with understanding.* In the following example, N produces an NTRI with the *wh*-word *where*:

(115) H    *hh Toda:y there was a who::le (.) review on it in
           [the paper.      ]
      N    [u-"Whe:re.   ]                                    ⇐
           (.)
           Oh real[ly I'm gonna loo:k, ]
      H           [In the View section.]
           (0.2)
      N    In the [Vie:w?
      H           [*p*hh
           (.)
           Yeah
           but I don't want you to read it.
           (.)
      N    Okay,                                       HGII 9:3

This NTRI requests more information about the location of the review which H just mentioned. The NTRI is done in overlap with H's phrase *the paper* where she found the review.

Following, V has been describing her father's knee surgery. C produces an NTRI which requests more information about the conditions under which knee surgery patients get better:

(116) V    *hh but it is healing
           and she said
           we've seen it over and over
           an- and they get better.
      C    mm hm
      V    [No  ]
      C    [How] "fast?                                        ⇐
           (0.2)
      V    Three months.
           (0.3)
      C    M[m hm]
      V    [Thr  ]ee months of- of crutches.
      C    Mm hm.                                     Ford 11:322

C requests more information with the *wh*-word plus adverb *how fast*, which asks how fast the knee will heal. V responds in the next turn with *three months* and then produces more turn *three months of crutches*.

Because the trouble source is not explicitly located in the prior turn, this type of repair initiator is different from those previously mentioned. The trouble source is information *not* included in the utterance (at least up to that moment in which the NTRI is produced). The *wh*-word of this NTRI type, however, must be interpretable as relevant to the trouble-source utterance. In other words, not any *wh*-word can serve as an NTRI. The choice of *wh*-word and how it is interpreted, depends on the construction of the prior utterance. Schegloff, Jefferson and Sacks (1977) mention this type of NTRI in a footnote.

It could be argued that this type of question is simply a next turn requesting more information (*i.e.*, the question has nothing to do with trouble in understanding the prior utterance); however, NTRI's disrupt the projected course of the talk in order to deal with the trouble source. To decide whether *wh*-word utterances of this type are NTRI's, the crucial factor must be whether or not the projected course of the talk is stopped. The more projectable the course of the talk, the more obviously a *wh*-word disrupts the projection. Another crucial factor in deciding whether or not a *wh*-word question is an NTRI is whether the information requested *could* be relevant in clarifying the identity of some referent in the utterance.

### Type 7 *(Appender Question with Candidate Referent)*

There are other types of NTRI's to which Schegloff, Jefferson, and Sacks (1977) allude but do not discuss. One type not exemplified in their paper is an appender question. These NTRI's are syntactically integrated with the prior utterance, and they usually can be interpreted as forming the terminal constituent of the prior utterance (Shapley 1983). In the following example, L is explaining to his guests why he had to hurry to get home from work before they arrived for dinner. He was delayed because he had an unexpected visitor C who would not take the hint that L had plans and did not have time to sit and talk. Below, L is reporting the conversation in which C was discussing his children:

```
(117)  L      And then he started asking me about my kids,
              and (.) *hh   [telling me about his kids,] you know,
       ( )                  [ °ha ha °ha ha °ha ha    ]
              cause his (.) son J___, has just been (.)
              he's in Carnegie Hall now or something
              and made a big success.
              [(he he)]
       M      [with  ]his rock "group?                    ⇐
       L      He writes minimal-
              No he's a (now) a modern composer
              he's gotten out of all that crap now,
              he writes minimal music.           Shapley/Nel 14:16
```

M produces an NTRI in the form of an appender question which is unmarked in any syntactic or lexical way. The question is interpretable as forming the terminal constituent of the prior utterance *and made a big success.* In other words, this NTRI is integrated with the syntactic structure of the prior clause.

M's NTRI indicates that she knew J was a rock musician. J's success at Carnegie Hall, therefore, runs counter to M's expectation that Carnegie Hall is not associated with rock and roll. The kind of music that J played at Carnegie Hall is, therefore, in question. After M's NTRI, L produces a clause which he interrupts to answer M. The second-pair part answer begins with the negative token *no*. This is expanded with the clause *he's a (now) a modern composer*. The *now* confirms that what he is now, a modern composer, differs from what he was previously. This answer is further expanded with the clause *He's gotten out of all that crap now*. The phrase *that crap* apparently refers to what is involved in being a rock musician. This answer demonstrates that M's question was based on the accurate belief that J had been a rock musician. L continues *he writes minimal music*. This utterance redoes the clause which was produced and then interrupted by L immediately following M's NTRI. This repetition suggests that this is what L had meant to say before.

M's NTRI occurs during the course of an extended turn and is syntactically based on the prior turn. Its relevance is based on the shared knowledge that (1) J is a rock musician and (2) Carnegie Hall is not known for rock performances. M's expectations about J and the world (=Carnegie Hall) are called into question by L's prior utterance. It is not that M has had trouble understanding the talk, rather she has had trouble integrating her knowledge about J, the world and L's prior utterance.

Following, the NTRI appender questions are marked by a word tag. V is explaining why her father needed to have knee surgery:

(118)  V   Okay this is what t-the problem is,
           my dad's knee- leg was very bow-legged.
           It was like thirt[een degrees ]
       C                  [all his "life.] (.) "right?         ⇐
       V   Well: more in old age (h).=
       C   =Uh huh.                                        Ford 2:37

C produces the NTRI *all his life. right?* This is a prepositional phrase marked by a word tag and is interpretable as forming a final constituent of the prior clause *my dad's knee- leg was very bow-legged*. It is relevant because it offers a candidate specification of the temporal period during which V's father had been bow-legged. *Right?* with rising intonation unambiguously marks the turn as doing questioning. This candidate, built with a word tag, expects confirmation, which V rejects in a way which suggests she is disconfirming the candidate NTRI.

Below, D is describing a drink which is found in Nepal:

(119)  D   When a pe(r)-
           when a ol:d man reaches seventy seven
           they have this big ceremony
           (i wa)s like his re:bir:th or something

| | |
|---|---|
| D | and they do wha' |
| | they (.) carry him on his ba:ck |
| | and put him in a chariot |
| | and (.) carry him around |
| | all the (.) ki:ds drag him around through the village an' stuff |
| | (they do all this) |
| | The(n they have a) big fea:st |
| | and they drink |
| | they have these bi:g (.) jars full of this (.) mm- |
| | (0.1) |
| | It's like fermen:ted wi(n) er- fermented ri:ce. |
| | It's like (.) |
| | they (.) |
| | y'know ri- |
| W | rice wine? |
| | (0.3) |
| D | It's not like wi- |
| | I mean it's it's not like wi:ne. |
| | It doesn't taste like wine |
| | but it's |
| W | fermented.= |
| D | =white and milky |
| | but it's [fermented |
| **H** | **["oh yeah,** ← |
| | (0.3) |
| | **in "bo:wls?** |
| W | oh that [sounds disgusting |
| D | [y- yeah well it's in these big |
| | (0.1) |
| | [va:ses, [you know. |
| W | [vats. |
| H | [Yeah. |
| D | [huge. |
| H | [Yeah. |
| D | But what I didn't realize at the time was |
| | I had always been thinking |
| | well a:ll anything alcoholic has been (.) distilled |
| | and is oka:y. |
| | (0.2) |
| | but this isn't. |
| | (0.3) |
| | it's just made from (.) |
| | I [meant they jus- |
| J | [oh yea:h, |

D     It's just ferme:nted. It's not disti:lled.

*Riggenbach 6: 141*

H produces the utterance *oh yeah*. Schiffrin (1987:91) states that *oh* can serve as "a marker of recognition of familiar information — more specifically, old information which has become newly relevant" (see also Heritage 1984). The *oh yeah* suggests that H recognizes the referent D is describing. This is followed by a (0.3) delay and then the appender question *in bowls?* which can be interpreted as forming the final constituent of the prior clause *but it's fermented*. The NTRI offers a candidate prepositional phrase which specifies the kind of containers in which the drink is fermented. H's utterance expects to be confirmed. It is requesting more information which can be used to identify the referent D is in the process of describing. D's answer is constructed to show orientation to the fact that it disconfirms the candidate NTRI.

*Type 8 (Appender Question with Wh-word)*

Appender type NTRI's differ from other NTRI's because the repairable is not within the trouble-source utterance. Rather, the trouble located by the NTRI is information *not* included in the trouble-source utterance. The relevant factor involved in the *interpretation* of appender questions is the compatibility of the syntactic structure of the trouble-source turn and the appender question.

Appender questions may include a *wh*-word which demonstrates some trouble with identifying a referent, an event, a place or a time.[1] Following, the speaker N is relating what the dermatologist told her:

```
(120)   N       But he goes,
                (.)
                he:-he goes
                you have a really mild case
                he goes,
                (.)
        H       of "wha[:t.  ]                              ⇐
        N              [You] sh-
                (.)
                A:cne-e,=
        H       =Oh:  , hhh (hhh)                    HG II 4:4
```

H produces an NTRI with the prepositional phrase *of what*. This NTRI is locating a problem with the referent of *case* (the particular disorder). This NTRI is interpretable as locating a post-modifying phrase of *case* as the trouble source. Because such a post-modifier does not appear in the trouble-source turn, the NTRI is an appender question of sorts. Instead of offering a candidate disorder (*of acne*), a *wh*-word *what* is produced in the place of the element whose identity is being queried *(of what)*. N produces the answer *acne* which is receipted with the particle *oh*. This NTRI involves referent identification but does not include a partial repeat as in example 111; rather, it utilizes an appender form plus a *wh*-word.

In these NTRI's, the speaker is requesting more information — sometimes with a candidate referent and sometimes with a *wh*-word. NTRI's which consist of *wh*-words which question elements not referred to in the trouble source utterance also request more information (example 115 above). The difference between these two types is that a *wh*-word requesting more information is an open-class question; its speaker does not have to offer any candidate for confirmation or disconfirmation. In appender questions with candidate referents, the NTRI speaker demonstrates more of a grasp of the situation encoded by the utterance, although comprehending the trouble-source utterance is required in both types of appender NTRI's.

As is the case of *wh*-words which request more information (Type 6), appender-question NTRI's do not locate a trouble source in the prior utterance — rather, the trouble source is information which has *not* been included in the prior turn. Appender questions stop the course of the projected talk and initiate repair by offering a candidate guess at the "missing" information which the recipient judges necessary for understanding. Appender NTRI's are a kind of understanding check which clarifies what has been said.

*Type 9 (Candidate Substitution)*

This is a type of repair initiator in which a candidate referent is offered to identify a referent previously mentioned in the trouble-source utterance. In this example, L produces an NTRI which is a candidate referent substitution:

```
(121)  E    Did I tell y-
            oh, yo:u heard it.
       L    "Yeh, [ a   ]bout "K__?                    ⇐
       E         [[( )  ]
            No: about (1.2) A__.
       L    A__ who?
       E    is coming home,
       B    Oh [the one who left to go to ] Italy?
       N       [Oh yeah I remember her   ]
       L       [(                     ) ]
       E    She called and wants to come [home, ]=
       L                                 [Same  ]=Same terms
            as J__                                Weber 3:8
```

L produces a candidate substitution for the referent *it* in the pre-announcement *oh you heard it* in the prior turn. This NTRI is realized as a prepositional phrase *about K___*. Although not a partial repeat, the NTRI evokes the projected but aborted interrogative, *Did I tell you about —*, which was realizing the pre-announcement.

The NTRI is requesting clarification of the referent who was to be the subject of the announcement.

In summary, these types of NTRI's are arranged in a hierarchical order, increasing in the amount of specificity with which they target the trouble source. Specificity indicates how much of a grasp the speaker has on the utterance and/or the situation. Multiple NTRI's normally increase in strength or specificity, *e.g.*, a speaker generally would produce *huh* then *who,* rather than *who* and then *huh*.

### 7.4. NTRI's and Preference Structure

In addition to locating a repairable, NTRI's may project disagreement in conversation (Chapter 2). In the following example, J previously had described what he had done to his roommate. The roommate had invited a young woman over for dinner. J and the girl began picking on the roommate; and at one point, both of them disappeared outside when he left the room:

```
(122)  P    John, now you know that's not nice.
       J    I know it wasn't nice=
       P    =y- you apologize to that boy.=
       J    =Oh:. I will
            (0.2)
            but (0.4) Donna was having a good time, hha too.
            *hh
       P    (Oh, my [God)
       J           [Yeah=he should understand the humor of it all.
       P    THAT'S NOT FUNNY=
       J    It's fu::ny ha ha [haha
       P                      [That is not funny Jo::hn=
       J    =*hhhh= it's very funny.
       P    Is it like the first time they dated?
       J    "Huh?"                                              ←
       P    It's like the first time that (.)
            it was like a date?
       J    Oh, they weren't really on a date.
            They were more on like (0.5) just having uhm:::=
       P    =JO::HN, now you know that was a DATE=
       J    Now, Pa:t[ri:ck
       P             [(ish-) is he a freshman?
       J    Yes
       P    Jo::hn=that was a date.=
       J    It was a date to him
            but to her-she: was told that they were gonna study
            philosophy.
```

| | | |
|---|---|---|
| J | *hh an she already been there an hour an they hadn't studied anything. | |
| P | No::w, Jo::hn, no::[w comon, John. | |
| J | [hahaa | Kinjo 6:10 |

J responds to P's question *is it the first time they dated* with a basic NTRI *huh*. When P redoes the utterance as a declarative clause question, P denies they were on a date. He begins to offer an alternative description of the occasion and cannot come up with a plausible category. P then insists that J knew that it was a date, but J still resists that categorization. P asks if the young man was a freshman. Upon hearing that he was, indeed, a freshman, P reasserts that the evening constituted a date. J then backs down from his original claim that *they weren't really on a date* by stating that, although it was a date to his roommate, it was not a date to the young woman.

J's NTRI (in response to P's question about the appropriate categorization of the evening) projects disagreement with any suggestion that the evening was "really" a date. J at first denies the evening was a date, but eventually backs down from that claim as a result of P's further questioning. Apparently, picking on your roommate while he is having a date, especially a first date, leaves J vulnerable to more severe criticism than if the roommate and his guest were not really on a date.

NTRI's can project disagreement even when they are not a response to a question. In the following example, M is reporting his events of the previous weekend. K interrupts with an NTRI. Two stretches of talk, connected by brackets and ascribed to the same speaker, indicate two possible hearings:

| | | |
|---|---|---|
| (123) | M | But - the bad thing was that um:, |
| | | (0.4) |
| | | I had to move my Dad's furniture |
| | | (0.6) |
| | | from his place in Santa Monica= |
| | | I had- to- have let the movers in (-) |
| | | so. |
| | | (0.6) |
| | | Being totally drunk from that orgy on Saturday night |
| | | I had to get up |
| | | (0.2) |
| | | and go down (0.1) to Santa Monica with Hillary, |
| | | (0.3) |
| | | and let these damn movers in. |
| | | (0.2) |
| | | ten o'clock in the morning (-) |
| | | it was raining: |
| | | it was mess [y 'knhh* |
| | K | ["Huh* *hh    ← |

166   VARIETIES OF QUESTIONS IN ENGLISH CONVERSATION

    K    (0.4)
          On "Sunday?                  ⇐
          (0.2)
    M    mm hm
          (0.2)
    R    That's strange             ⇐
    M    S::o
          (0.4)
    K    sh (-) y[ou're sure it      ⇐
          y' [sure it was Sunday Mark.  ⇐
    M        [End-
          (0.1)
          Yeah it was [Sunday*
    R              [uh huh huh* hih h[ih*
    M                              [After S*aturday night usually
          its Sunday
          (en)
          (tha-)
          (0.1)
          hih hih
    S    Mm
          (0.1)
    K    Yeah
          but in y[ou're condition you never know
    M           [' was stumbling around
          (0.1)
          Well no I kno:w.
          (0.6)
          Whole weekends are shot to hell ["wha-(-)wha-" ]
                                            [why oh why   ]
                                                          SN4 11:26;12:1

M is describing how he had to get up early the morning after his Saturday night orgy. He states that it was raining and messy. This comment results in a basic NTRI from K. There is no response from M and after a (0.4) silence, K produces another NTRI. She produces the question *On Sunday?* This is a prepositional phrase which is interpretable as an appender question; however, it is not asking for clarification of the date/time or for more information. It is clear that M was referring to Sunday morning. It, by implication, is suggesting that K had some reason to disagree with Mark's statement that it was raining on Sunday morning. K responds to this with an affirmative token.

    R produces the utterance *that's strange,* aligning herself with K's pre-disagreements. K produces another utterance questioning M's description of Sunday morning as rainy and messy. She questions M's memory with regard to what the day was, not whether or not it was really raining. The assumption is you can get confused about the day of any particular weather event but not the experience of the weather. M does not back down from his assertion that it was Sunday morning which was rainy and messy. Neither K nor R actually go on and disagree explicitly with M.

This example demonstrates a speaker's use of a series of forms beginning with a basic NTRI with which she deals with a questionable fact asserted by M. The forms show increasing specificity in locating the trouble source. The speaker initiating repair first produces a basic NTRI — *huh*. This type of NTRI can be produced by a speaker who has no comprehension of the trouble-source turn. This form has minimal lexical and phonological content.

The speaker initiating repair next produces an NTRI appender question — *On Sunday?* In contrast to the *huh*, this form has more lexical and phonological content and has syntactic structure. The speaker initiating repair then produces an NTRI which is realized as a syntactic clause interpretable as an interrogative clause — *y' sure it was Sunday Mark*. This series of NTRI forms exhibits increasing specificity in locating the trouble source. The NTRI forms become increasingly longer and exhibit increasingly more complex syntactic structure.

Because NTRI's can be used to mark dispreferred responses, NTRI's may not seem to be a preferred second-pair part response; however, we could ask if an utterance's construction can have the effect of stimulating an NTRI from a recipient. In the following example, D is answering a question concerning what made him the sickest during his recent stay in Nepal. Previously, he related how he had drunk fermented rice at a celebration and had become sick several weeks later. D's wife, C, becomes a co-teller of the story about how ill D eventually became. W produces a nonclausal appender question in response to C's use of the passive form of the verb *escort*:

(124) C   I knew
　　　　　he was gonna go on this thing
　　　　　and and I (.)
　　　　　and he was rea:lly sick
　　　　　but I didn't want to be like (.) the momma
　　　　　and say don't go.
　　　　　Go ahead.
　　　　　You'll have a good time.
　　　　　It's all right.
　　　　　Next da:y, he was escorted home by (hh)
　　　　　[(he was)
　　　W  [on a "stretcher?　　　　　　　　　　⇐
　　　C   Just abou:t.
　　　　　(1.2)
　　　W  How awful. [Oh: Go:d
　　　H         [Uhh.　　　　　　　　　Riggenbach 7:180

W's question is a request for more information with respect to the prior clause which was aborted. C produces a passive clause which she aborts before completing the *by* phrase in which the semantic agent of the clause is identified. After the passive is aborted, C begins a new clause with *he was*. Passive clauses in which the *by* phrase makes explicit the agent are rare in English ( Quirk *et al* 1985; Thompson 1987; Fox 1987). W's question which goes to completion overlaps C's clause (which begins *he was* and is subsequently aborted). This question is a request for the circumstances in which he *was escorted home*.

The passive form of this verb puts the patient *he* in subject position and suppresses the agent (the person who escorted D home). *He* refers to D. The story is about D's illness. The use of this structure suggests that someone else was the agent. The fact that the *by* was produced but the agent was not produced draws attention to the missing agent or agents. The subsequent talk reveals the speaker knew the name of the agent. The NTRI (*on a stretcher*) by offering a candidate understanding is asking for more information. It is occasioned by the use of the verb *escorted* in the passive form in conjunction with the fact that the utterance was aborted after the *by* of the *by* phrase. This example suggests that an NTRI may be stimulated by certain types of self-repaired utterances.

This section demonstrates that nonclausal NTRI's can function to project disagreement and to mark dispreferred second-pair parts. When an NTRI follows a first-pair part question, it breaks continuity between the first-pair part and the second-pair part answer (Sacks 1987[1973]). The NTRI is itself a first-pair part question which makes a second-pair part relevant. The NTRI and its second-pair part constitute an insert sequence between the original first-pair part and its second-pair part.

NTRI's can project disagreement in response to statements as well. The possibility was raised that NTRI's may be stimulated by self-repairs of certain syntactic constructions. Responses to appender questions can reflect preference structure in the same way that responses to other types of questions can reflect preference structure, (examples 125 and 126).

In the following example, V is telling why her father needed to have knee surgery:

```
(125)  V    Okay this is what t-the problem is,
            my dad's knee- leg was very bow-legged.
            It was like thirt[een degrees ]
       C                    [all his "life.] (.) "right?        ⇐
       V    Well: more in old age (h).=
       C    =Uh huh.                                    Ford 2:37
```

In this example, V produces *well*, a marker of a dispreferred response. The rest of V's answer *more in old age* implies that he was very bowlegged only in old age. In other words, V's answer implies that her father was not, in fact, very bow-legged all his life. This second-pair part is constructed in such a way that it is not a preferred response.

In the following example, D is describing a drink which made him sick:

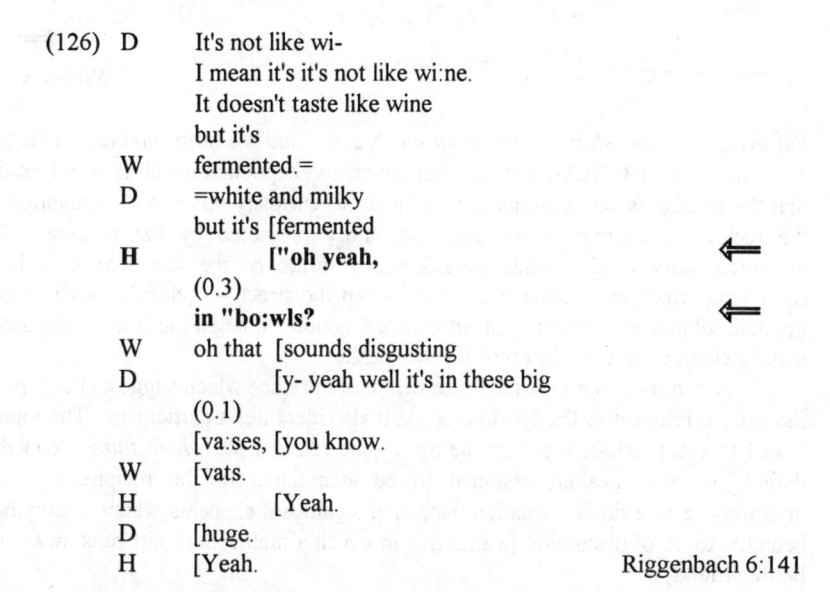

(126)  D    It's not like wi-
             I mean it's it's not like wi:ne.
             It doesn't taste like wine
             but it's
        W    fermented.=
        D    =white and milky
             but it's [fermented
        H           ["oh yeah,                    ⇐
             (0.3)
             **in "bo:wls?**                      ⇐
        W    oh that [sounds disgusting
        D            [y- yeah well it's in these big
             (0.1)
             [va:ses, [you know.
        W    [vats.
        H             [Yeah.
        D    [huge.
        H    [Yeah.                         Riggenbach 6:141

D gives an affirmative token followed by a marker of a dispreferred response — *well*. He answers that it is *in these big vases* and then states the qualification *huge*. In other words, it is not fermented in bowls. This response is initially shaped as a preferred response and then constructed to show orientation to the fact that it is a dispreferred answer.

### 7.5. Other Functions of NTRI's

Questions can function simultaneously in several ways. A nonclausal question can function to initiate repair as an NTRI and, thereby, project disagreement and act as a marker of a dispreferred response. A close examination of NTRI's reveals that this type of question can function in other very subtle ways to achieve the participants' interactional goals. The following section presents a detailed analysis of an NTRI which serves to make a claim on the part of the speaker for co-telling rights to a story-in-progress. This exchange takes place between a mother and daughter. The mother begins a story about a family who lives on their block. Throughout, the mother and daughter compete over the perspective from which the story will be told — that of the parent vs. the child/young adult:

(127)  N    I don't know,

```
N    I'm dy::ing to know what happened up the street.
     We had the who:le thing going on with my friend
     (0.2)
     [who's up the ] stree:t.=
L    [with "J__? ]                              ⇐
N    =Yeah.                              Weber 8:116
```

*I'm dying to know what happened up the street.* This is a story preface. This turn constructional unit (TCU) displays that something happened which is so interesting that the speaker is very curious about it, and this curiosity serves as a motivation for the recipient's interest in the upcoming story projected by the preface. The projected story is also made interesting by virtue of the fact that it is local, something which has occurred close by — up the street — (close enough to be a possible subject of interest). This utterance functions to begin the storytelling and to make a claim of an extended turn for the speaker.

N continues her extended turn with more preface which suggests the topic of the story is relevant to the previous story; it also identifies a participant. The topic is linked to the previous topic by the use of the referent *the whole thing*, coded as definite by the speaker, assumed to be identifiable to the recipients. It is interpretable as a similar situation, including significant elements which already have been the topic of discussion (a situation in which a high school girl runs away with her boyfriend).

The speaker is telling the story in reference to the previous story. At the same time, the new story will provide additional information in such terms that the previous story can be interpreted further. This *whole thing going on*, the situation about to be the subject of the story, is kept relevant, and therefore, tellable, by the use of the pronoun *we*. The projected situation (what happened up the street) is tied to the speaker and her daughter by *we had* and continues to be relevant and interesting by this personal connection. The projected story is made relevant not only because it is about a similar situation, but also because there is a personal connection between the speaker, her daughter and this similar situation.

This personal connection introduced by *we had* is further clarified by the prepositional phrase *with my friend*. The projected situation, which has so far received its meaning by being another case of the situation in the previous story, is connected to the speaker through the relationship the speaker has with a participant. The speaker refers to the participant as *my friend*. The referent is identifiable to the recipients because it is given in a semantic frame.

The following pause may have been the result of eating or serving, and I will not examine it because there is no videotape of the conversation. Whatever its motivation, there is an interval of time after which the speaker and her daughter both begin speaking. The speaker continues by adding a relative clause. Because the speaker is taking an extended turn, the silence is a pause, not a gap. A pause is a period of silence within a speaker's turn, while a gap is a period of silence between two speakers' turns. A speaker may turn a period of silence which would be interpretable as a gap into a pause by taking more turn, *i.e.*, by adding on to what has already been produced.

The relative clause locates the friend — up the street. This is the same phrase used to locate the interesting happening. By repeating the phrase, the speaker relates two incidents (*what happened* and *we had the whole thing going on with my friend*) by (1) their syntagmatic relation to the phrase and (2) their both being located *up the street*. This all gets interpreted as follows: there is an interesting thing which happened, which is similar to what we were just talking about and which has to do with my friend who lives up the street.

L, N's daughter, takes a turn in overlap with N's relative clause. Neither speaker stops talking. L does a next-turn repair initiator (NTRI), asking for clarification. The NTRI begins with *with* plus a candidate referent, *J*. She is asking for clarification of the situation, however, not the referent of J. This becomes clear to the analyst by the end of the story. The referent of *my friend* is a woman called A, while the referent of J is A's daughter, a high school girl who has run away from home to be with her boyfriend. How can we demonstrate that the NTRI is seeking a clarification of the situation and not a referent without referring to ethnographic data?

For the moment, let us assume the guest recipients in the interaction did not know the referent of the story participant introduced as *my friend*. There are reasons to think that the speaker has made this assumption. The noun phrase (NP) which introduces the participant is not a name, *i.e.*, a recognitional NP. By using the form *my friend*, the speaker has not provided grounds for identifying the referent, rather the relationship of the referent to herself. The repair initiator *with J* is constructed with typical form for clarification repairs (a partial repeat plus a candidate understanding). Given our assumption, the repair initiator would be interpreted as asking for clarification of the referent of *my friend*. The recognitional form used by L is addressed to N, not to the other recipients of the story-in-progress.

In fact, J is L's friend, the daughter of N's friend. L's NTRI indicates she has interpreted *the whole thing* as a situation and is asking for clarification. She is offering a candidate understanding of another participant in the situation, not for the referent of *my friend*.

N responds to the NTRI with an answer, *Yeah*. Note: she did not interrupt her own turn constructional unit (TCU) which was in overlap with the NTRI, nor did she pause after the relative clause or before the answer to the NTRI. This answer implies that she heard the turn which overlapped her talk and answered it without hesitation when she completed her own turn. It further displays that the NTRI was understood as a request for clarification of another participant in the situation, not for clarification of the referent.

This use of the NTRI is the first of several moves on behalf of the daughter to become a co-teller of the story from the perspective of the daughter in the story, not the mother. N is telling the story from the mother's perspective as something which happened to her — her kid ran away. L will see it from the daughter's perspective.

This detailed analysis has revealed that speakers not only make multiple uses of questions, but also achieve very subtle interactional effects with the simplest of syntactic forms. Such functions cannot be intuited; they must be discovered by a close examination of the data. Unless the full range of communicative functions realized in conversation is explored, researchers interested in language use will never be able to adequately describe how people manage to do things with words.

## 7.6. Candidate Solutions to Same-Turn Repairs

Nonclausal questions can be used as a candidate solution to a word search initiated by another speaker. A word search is a type of self-initiated repair. Example 128 exhibits a word search and candidate solution done with a nonclausal question. D is trying to describe a drink which is found in Nepal:

```
(128)   D      When a pe(r)-
               when a ol:d man reaches seventy seven
               they have this big ceremony
               (i wa)s like his re:bir:th or something
               and they do wha'
               they (.) carry him on his ba:ck
               and put him in a chariot
               and (.) carry him around
               all the (.) ki:ds drag him around through the village an'
               stuff
               (they do all this)
               The(n they have a) big fea:st
               and they drink
               they have these bi:g (.) jars full of this (.) mm-
               (0.1)
               It's like fermen:ted wi(n) er- fermented ri:ce.
               It's like (.)
               they (.)
               y'know ri-
        W      rice "wine?                                          ⬅
               (0.3)
        D      It's not like wi-
               I mean it's it's not like wi:ne.
               It doesn't taste like wine
               but it's
        W      fermented.=                              Riggenbach 5:133
```

After the speaker makes three aborted tries to describe this drink, W supplies a candidate solution to this problem with the utterance *rice wine*. This candidate is rejected, and D continues with his attempt to describe the drink.

Nonclausal forms implicated in repair constitute 60% of all instances of nonclausal questions. With the exception of the single instance of a candidate solution to a word search, all the nonclausal questions implicated in repair are NTRI's. Although the previous literature has not recognized a typical function for nonclausal questions, these data exhibit a strong association between nonclausal questions and repair-initiating function.

**7.7. Functions of Nonclausal Questions *not* Implicated in Repair**

An examination of the data reveals several functional types of questions: topic/sequence solicitations or introductions, responses to pre-announcements, candidate understandings, backdowns, try questions, offers, requests for evaluations, etc.

*7.7.1. Topic/Sequence Solicitations*

Some nonclausal questions prefer a response which presents or develops news. Following, a nonclausal first-pair part is built to display a preference for a second which presents more news:

```
(129)  N     Anything else to "report,          ⇐
             (0.3)
       H     Uh::::::m::::,
             (0.4)
             Getting my hair cut tomorrow,=
       N     Oh really?
             (.)
       H     Yea:   [:::h,
       N            [Oh ( so soo:[d]?)
                       (for foo:d?)
             (0.4)
       H     Wha:t?
             (0.2)
       N     Cause member
             you said
```

```
N         you w [ere gonna   m]ake an appo[intment n, ]
H               [owhhhhhhhoo]             [Oh:    y  ]eah.*=
                                                         HG II 15:24
```

This example is interpretable as "do you have anything else to report."

In the next example, M begins a new sequence with the question: *So you dating Keith?* K answers this but does not expand her answer. M then produces another question which K does expand upon. M constructs this question with the *wh*-word plus particle *what about* (Keenan and Schieffelin 1976). This question solicits information about a former friend of Keith's:

```
(130)  M    So you dating Keith?
            (0.1)
       K    He's a friend.
            (0.6)
       M    What about that girl he used to "go with for so  long  ⇐
            (0.1)
       K    Alice? (-) I d [on't* think (ing about)
       M                   [myeh*
            (0.5)
            Wha-/
            (0.2)
       K    I dunno where she is
            but I-
            (0.9)
            Talks about her every so often
            but I dunno where she is
            (0.6)
       M    hm                                          SN4 27:7
```

This example is constructed as follows: *wh*-word particle + determiner + noun + relative clause in which the relativized NP (*that girl*) plays the semantic role of patient in the relative clause. *That girl* is referred to in terms of Keith, who was mentioned in M's previous turn. When Keith, as a topic, is not taken up by K, M tries again to initiate another topic by mentioning Keith's former steady girlfriend. Fox (1987) observes that patient-relative clauses serve "to anchor or show the contextual relevance of what is mentioned in the head NP" (see also Prince 1981). By using the *what about* plus a patient-relative clause, M is able to initiate a new topic (Keith's girlfriend), while at the same time treating this topic as contextually relevant. The use of the referent's name instead of the relative clause would not display the contextual relevance explicitly; rather the relevance would be implicit.

Example 131 is another nonclausal question constructed as follows: noun plus relative clause in which the relativized NP (*nice Jewish boy*) plays the semantic role of experiencer in the relative clause. This clause forms a bridge between (1) a prior candidate characterization and subsequent acceptance of that characterization and (2) an expansion of a prior topic:

(131)    N    How did you get his number,
                     (.)
         H    I(h) (.) c(h)alled information in San Francisco(h) [uh!
         N                                                     [Oh:::::.
                     (.)
                     very cleve:r, hh=
         H    =Thank you    [: I- *hh-*hhhhhhhh    ]hh=
         N                     [What's his last name, ]
         H    Uh:: Freedla:nd. *hh    [hh
         N                            [Oh [:,
         H                                  [('r) Freedlind
         N    =Nice Jewish bo:y?
                     (.)
         H    O:f cou:rse,=
         N    ='v    [cou:rse, ]
         H            [hh-hh-hh] hnh *hhhhh=
         N    **=Nice Jewish' boy who doesn't like to write letters?** ⬅
                     (.)
         H    eYe::h, *hhh And he ma:de such a big dea::l about it
                     he, s    [:    ] pent- ] *hh
         N                    [I    ]kno:: ] ::::w.=
         H    =He    [said that he would write ]
         N               [That's what I don't un      ]der=
         H    =fir::s:::t an ::,
                     (.)
         N    I know
                     see that's what I don't understand
                     that's why I still think he might write you,
                     (0.3)
                     It just takes him awhi:le,
                     (.)
         H    khh-hh-hhe writes one word a day, hhih [hn
         N                                               [Yeahhh
                     (.)
                     Dea:r? hh next day. Hyla,=
         H    =*u *u *hhh
                     (.)
         N    Ho:w?
                     (.)
         H    *hhhi:    [ nh] heh-heh,
         N                [A: ]re?

```
N        (.)
H        _you:.=
         =*eh-*u[h,
N              [*hhh
         (0.2)
H        *hhihhh I think I'll get the le(h)tter next
         yea(hhh[h)r
N               [Yea(h)h,=
         =hhhhh *hh You'll get a ten page lett(hh)er [hh
H                                                      [eh-eh-uh
         *hhhihhh=
         =(w(h)en th(h)ey [make it)  ]
N                         [will it be ]=
         wo:[rth waiting [fo(h)r?  ]
H        [*hhhh          [hhhhhhh] *hh=
N        =hnh=
H        =*ahhh *uh,=
N        =hh-kh
         (.)
( )      (ᵒhh)
         (.)
H        [*hh   [ mean [time he's  ]=
N        [By    [then  [you could ]
H        =married with s[ix k(h)i(h)ds,       ]
N                       [By then you could ]=
         be marri(h)ed (h)w(h)ith six k(h)i[(h)ds ]
H                                          [hhhh ]          HG II 25:26
```

N repeats her previous candidate characterization *nice Jewish boy* and adds a relative clause whose verbal complement, the infinitive phrase *to write letters*, evokes the beginning of this sequence. The sequence begins with N asking *Did you get the mail today*. This question is prompted by N's knowledge that H still hopes to receive a letter from Richard (=the nice Jewish boy). This nonclausal question, then, returns the talk to the topic (the expected but not-yet-received letter) which had been deflected by H's confession that she had called Richard.

The relative clause is a transitive clause whose subject is the relativized NP. Fox (1987) identifies transitive relative clauses as agent relatives (Dixon 1979) "linking the current utterance to the preceding discourse, using the object of the relative as a bridge" (pp. 858-9). In order to serve as the anchor or bridge between two referents, an NP must be mentioned or evoked in the preceding talk. In the instances of agent relatives (A-relatives) described by Fox, the head NP is anchored to the preceding discourse by the object of the relative clause. Fox notes these agent relatives are rare in her data. Because objects of transitive verbs tend not to be good anchors, agent relatives are less frequent than patient relatives (example

130). Objects tend not to be good anchors because they generally code new rather than given information in the discourse (Du Bois 1981a, b, 1985, 1987).

In this example, the A-relative functions differently from those agent relatives described by Fox (1987). The subject of the relative is *nice Jewish boy*. This subject NP does not need to be anchored to the preceding discourse because it repeats an utterance N produced just two turns previously. The object of the transitive verb is the infinitive phrase *to write letters*. *Letters* is a nonreferential NP (Du Bois 1980). Unlike the objects of agent-relatives described by Fox, *letters* does not code referents already given in the discourse. The phrase *to write letters*, however, evokes the beginning of this sequence when N asks H if she has already gotten the mail that day. The repetition of *nice Jewish boy* as the head NP provides an anchor for the relative clause which *reintroduces* the topic of the letter which has not yet arrived.

### 7.7.2. *Preferred Responses to Pre-Announcements*

A number of nonclausal questions in the data are responses to pre-announcements which are also first-pair parts in their own right. Following, the speaker H returns to a previous topic — the subject of a Dear Abby column. She had been unable to recall the subject of the column. She produces a pre-announcement which is followed by a preferred response *what*. Note: the pre-announcement is marked by *oh* signaling that the speaker has retrieved some information (Schiffrin 1987:91, Heritage 1984).

```
(132)   H    =O::h no I remember what yesterday was,=
        N    ="Wha [t.                                    ⇐
        H         [Forget it
             I made that up.
             hh- [hh
        N         [What was [it.
        H                    [Yes [th(hh)e other [day, ]
        N                         [Sh(hh)e       [make]s it up,=
             =*hhhh Hey that's a pretty good one,=
        H    =eh-eh *he:::hhh Yesterday, (.) wa:s, *hhh this girl,
             *hh °e- fifteen year old girl her mother didn't let her wear
             sho:rt skirts
             or midriff to [:ps or h ]alter to:::ps or a::n:ything,=
                           [Uh hu:h ]                      HGII 36:1
```

H's utterance that she has recalled the Dear Abby column functions to solicit a request from N that she tell what she remembers.

Below, the speaker H produces a question which functions as a pre-announcement:

(133)  H    A:::nd what e:lse.
            *hhh Do you know what I did today
            I was so proud of my [ sel    ]f,=
       N                        ["What.]              ←
       H    =*hhh I we:nt- (0.2)
            Alright like I get off at work at one,=
       N    Uh hu:h,=
       H    And I hav- (.) my class starts at two:.
            *hh so within that one hou:r,
            I got to school
            ((etc. on this topic))                HGII 18:5

N's *what* is the preferred response to H's question *Do you know what I did today I was so proud of myself;* it functions to solicit more about what happened. The response is done in overlap with H's pre-announcement. *What* is produced very quickly, the vowel is reduced and the terminal intonation is falling. As a lexical element constituting a turn, it is minimally produced as a word, signaling nothing more than "continue."

Following, a nonclausal question *like what* is the preferred response to a pre-announcement of a discovery stated in general terms.[2] The preferred response solicits a request for a specific example of the general announcement. The response is also not in next-turn position. There is a lot of laughter in this conversation which has not been included in the transcription because it would make the text very difficult to read:

(134)  C    There's no way to terminate an evening with A___ X___,
            I've noticed.
            I love, A, uh
            I'm very appreciative of his coming to see me,
       L    oh yeah
            but it's (.)
       C    he doesn't (.) have any concept of time, you know
            [you can say things like=
       D    you [ can't say something like
       C    =well, I guess
            now (that) the paper's being tossed on your front lawn
            (.)
            I guess
            it's about time to go to work, you say,
            ((laughter))
            The next morning.
       D    (night A___?)
       C    and he's still noodling (.) at the piano.

| | |
|---|---|
| C | (.) |
| | playing with the dog. |
| | (0.1) |
| L | yes. |
| M | Oh, I guess I |
| | (.) |
| | he's usually sleeping here, |
| | so I just (.) go to bed. |
| | ((laughter)) |
| | Everybody else goes to bed, |
| | and he finally gets |
| | (.) |
| L | Yeah, |
| | and he finally starts crashing at about four a.m. or something. |
| M | Yeah |
| | (3.0) |
| C | Well, I find he's very good company, |
| | and [I always like to see him,= |
| M | [Well he's charming, and interesting= |
| C | =just delightful, and interesting] and |
| M | to talk to. yeah. ] |
| | I think, though it |
| | I've discovered |
| | that he throws out these (.) rather (.) unusual statements, you see. |
| ( ) | ( ) |
| K | (Oh, I see) ( ) |
| M | And then everybody keeps feeding him, |
| | and then he throws [out another] one, |
| ( ) | (yeah) |
| D | [like "what.] ⬅ |
| M | well, (.) like he started |
| | (.) |
| | my conversation |
| | I just transcribed |
| | started out with |
| | actually (.) spinach takes iron from the body. |
| | ((laughter)) |
| C | okay (that's ) |
| L | and you know how it is. |
| | (.) |
| | (I mean) he's perfectly capable of inventing the whole thing, |
| | although it may also be true. |
| C | yeah, |

```
          L    (and then) cause cause he went through a good deal of
               the so-called chemistry of of the reaction=
          M    well, he used chelate a lot,
               [which     ] sounded very impressive.ha ha
          L    [(the word)]
               the word  chelate came in qui- quite frequently,
               it's chelated or not chelated or rechelated
          M    [But it seems to me ]
          L    [(             )]
          M    you're getting into something like rhetoric,
                 or public speaking (.) [at th-this (.) stage,
          ( )                           [ha ha
          M    I mean, it isn't really conversation,
               it's techniques of (.) something else.
```
                                              Shapley/Nel 17:22

M responds with a verbatim quotation to D's request for specific cases of unusual statements produced by A. This turn is expanded upon by L, M's husband. L and M continue to expand on the answer as a party.

Nonclausal questions which elicit further talk are not similar to NTRI's in function even though they may use the same form, *e.g., what*. This demonstrates that the sequential slot in which the form occurs is critical in its interpretation. When *what* follows a pre-announcement, it is interpretable as a preferred second if the terminal intonation falls and as a basic NTRI requesting repetition, if the terminal intonation rises.

### 7.7.3. Backdowns

Nonclausal questions can be used by speakers to modify *their own prior utterance*. In the following example, H has been summarizing the plot of a play they are going to see that evening. N then produces an uptake:

```
(135)     N    =But, so basically it's kind o[f a love story in a [wa:y,=
          (H)                                 [*hhhhh              [*hh
          H    We:ll no:t=
          N    ="Pa:rt of  [i:t.  ]                                    ⟵
          H                [really] s  [o mu:ch. ] Y]ah there's-    ]=
          N                            [Pa:rt of i ]t. ] Right?     ]=
          H    =there's one part be[twee:n,  ]
          N                        [But it's m]ost[ly about the au:nt?  ]
          H                                       [between this Jewish ] gu:y
               and the:*hh and the (w)  gi:rl.
```

```
H    *hh tha[:t,    ]
N           [That]'s the conflict, =
H    =Tha [t's ] i- yeah=
N         [Ri ]ght?                                    HG II 13:2
```

N produces an uptake of the plot summary and receives a dispreferred answer marked by *well* followed by the negative form *not*. N modifies her original uptake at this time with the nonclausal *Part of it*— interpretable as modifying her own prior statement to change her characterization of the play as *basically* a love story to *in part* a love story. N repeats this form plus the word tag *right*. H responds to the backdown with an affirmative token and then mentions one part of the play which could be considered a love story (between *this Jewish guy and the girl*). N's backdown from her original characterization and its repetition exhibit preference structure in conversation. It is the responsibility of both participants to achieve preferred responses. In this case, N changes her uptake to get an agreeing response.

### 7.7.4. Candidate Understandings

Several examples in the data have nonclausal questions which offer candidate understandings of a prior utterance. In producing a candidate understanding, a speaker presents a recipient with an empathetic characterization of some aspect of the recipient's experience. Below, the participants had been discussing the fact that C changed her name back to her maiden name after she was divorced. C comments on her daughter's feelings about this fact:

```
(136)  C    Yes I think
            M___ thought of it as a (.) stand for women.
            (So ) she (was) (.) she [(thought it ) was=
       ( )                           [( )
       C    =the only thing to do.
       K    Yeah
            I never really (.) talked to uh

            I guess
            I did talk to M___ a little about uh her women's studies
            course.
            which I gave a lecture to.
            Did [she ever tell you about that?
       C       [Oh did you?
            No:, she never really told me about (much) much about the
            course.
       M    What did you lecture about women's studies?
       K    Well, they put together this women's studies course.
```

```
        A:h
C       Yeah she was in some subset.
        What was tha[t.
K                  [Let's see (.)
        I'm try [ing to think
C               [third world [women? or something],
L                            [(       )           ]
        Oh that's like black studies, you mean?
C       Yeah righ[t.
K                [I'm trying to think how they (.)
        characterized it. Um
( )     he he
D       It (.) It hasn't gone that far ( )
K       Um, I guess
        it was just called women's studies.
        but uh I was trying to, (.)
        I was talking on sex differences
        and trying to put together a very sophisticated
        developmental argument,
C       ((laughing))
        ( you know ) so that  they could use on the barricades,
K       Right, exactly, you know I had I (.)
        [I you know
C       [a slogan or tw[o
K                     [actually it was one of my most uh animated
        lectures.
        I mean I was really all=
C       =scholarly, though huh?
K       It wa:s: (.) a bit (.)
        you know
        it wasn't exactly schol[arly.
L                              ["sparkling with footnotes,   ⇐
        "[j]uh?                                              ⇐
D       ( )
        [((laughter))                              ]
K       [No, no. but it was, it was, you know it ]
        there was there was a certain coherence to it,
        I     mean [you [know
( )              [((laughter))
L                       [Oh
K       [ha ha ha there was a ha ha ha = ]
( )     [((laughter))                   ]
K       [a theoretical idea behind it. ]
( )     [((laughter))                 ]
```

K       And uh I saw these glazed faces ((laughs))
        and uh as soon as I got through,
        uh, you know I didn't get through
        I you know (just) came to the end
        and said
        how about some questions,
        and the first question I got was (0.2)
        why do you keep talking about mothers.
        (0.8)
                [laughs)) in- in- instead of parents.   ]
( )             [((laughter))                           ]
L       parent persons?
( )     ((laughter))
D       [( )person ((laughs))
( )     [((laughter))
K       well uh you know sorry about that.
        But uh=
L       (P) P (person ) parents.
K       =um mothers are [(.)              ]generally the people
L                       [that's a question.]
K       we generally see in the laboratory with the (.) babies.
        and and uh *hh in the in in the    [ ( ) (pres-)  ] present
        day society=
C                                          [sexist        ]
K       =they (. ) are the most likely people to be taking care of
        (.) babies.
        It went on from there.
        D [own hil  [l.=
( )       [((laughter))
C                   [down.
( )                 [((laughter))         ]
        [They didn't like it, huh?]

K       I'm afraid this elegant ha ha theoretical exposition just
        [went ha ha (.) ]
( )     [((laughter))   ]
        went uh (.) ( [t$^s$])by them apparently.
C       ( )
K       [It turned out to be entirely a class of ( ).
( )     [((laughter))
        I mean it was a (.)
        It's orientation was: sli:ghtly to the radical side of where
        I was,

```
            ( )      where (.) I had always found myself rather comfortable.
                                                              Shapley/Nel 3:4
```

K describes her lecture as *one of my most animated*. She then begins a repair which she does not complete. K's repair is overlapped by C's characterization of K's lecture as *scholarly, though*. *Scholarly*, then, is added to *animated* in effect. This is accepted (*It was a bit*) and then rejected (*It wasn't exactly scholarly*), demonstrating preference structure in conversation for agreeing answers. At this time, L produces a candidate characterization of the lecture with the nonclausal question *sparkling with footnotes, huh*. This too gets rejected. K then goes on to characterize the lecture as coherent and based on a theoretical idea.

The candidate characterization of the lecture as *sparkling with footnotes* is done as a joke. It is offering a description of a certain type of lecture with which the participants would all be familiar as academicians, regardless of their respective fields. K's rejection of the characterization without hesitation confirms her understanding of this type of lecture. The characterization suggests a type of lecture in which footnotes are generously distributed. The use of the adjective *sparkling* likens them to gems. When lecturing to undergraduates, a professor who treats footnotes as valuable diamonds winds up with a talk which is too precious and overdone.

The example following demonstrates another instance of a candidate understanding. The participants are discussing a former date of H's who lives in another city and has not written to her since they last saw each other. H had called him the previous night and had hung up without saying anything:

```
(137)   N    How did you get his number,
             (.)
        H    I(h) (.) c(h)alled information in San Francisco(h)    [uh!
        N                                                          [Oh::::.
             (.)
             very cleve:r, hh=
        H    =Thank you [: I- *hh-*hhhhhhhh        ]hh=
        N               [What's his last name,     ]
        H    Uh:: Freedla:nd. *hh[hh
        N                        Oh [:,
        H                           [('r) Freedlind
        N    =Nice Jewish "bo:y?                                   ⟵
             (.)
        H    O:f cou:rse,=
        N    ='v   [cou:rse, ]
        H          [hh-hh-hh] hnh *hhhhh=                    HG II 25: 21
```

N offers the candidate characterization *nice Jewish boy*. This is not merely offering a candidate characterization of the referent's religious/ethnic background; it is checking, in fact, if he is an acceptable marriage prospect. H's response *of course* and N's receipt of that response with the same phrase, demonstrate the "of courseness" of his eligibility for marriage. H would not be calling him long distance and suffering so much, if he were not eligible.

*7.7.5. Try Questions*

In the data, there are several instances of try questions (informed guesses which are themselves questions requesting confirmation). Below, the participants at a dinner-table conversation are discussing Colonel Sanders' problems with the corporation that bought his company:

(138)  L    He sold the company.
             and [( subsequently)
         M    [Then he tried to get them to remove his name
             because he said they were awful and greasy.
             ((laughter))
         ( )   (       )
         L    The first thing he tried to do though,
             was
             (3.0)
             (( intervening talk from other conversation about the
             food; serving of food))
             He formed another company in his wife's name.
             and they opened a restaurant called the Colonel's lady.
             and the (.) people who owned Colonel Sander's
             incorporated (.) successfully
         T    successfully sued the[m
         L                     [successfully sued them.
             and got them to change the name.
             ( ) as being too close.
             Apparently in selling the company
             he somehow gave away his name.
         T    I see.
         M    What's the next rank above Colonel.
             ((laughter))
             Could he get promoted.
         ( )   ((laughter))
         T    °I don't know.
         L    **°Lieutenant "Colonel?**                      ←
             (1.0)
         M    What comes after Colonel,
             Major?

```
              T       I think that's befo [re.
              M                     [or general.         Shapley/Fer 11:275
```

M asks what the next rank above Colonel is. T answers *I don't know*, and L produces a try question *Lieutenant Colonel*. This is not confirmed by any of the participants. M's next utterance redoes his question as to what rank comes after Colonel. He offers an alternative between Major or General as candidate ranks above Colonel. In producing these candidates, he is implicitly rejecting the try question *Lieutenant Colonel*.

### 7.7.6. Other Functions

Some questions in the data are not NTRI's and do not fit into any of the other categories described above. One nonclausal question in the data marks the speaker's surprise. In this example, the speaker N solicits a new topic from H. H answers she is getting her hair cut. N responds to this with the particle *oh* and *really*. When H does not expand her affirmative response to this, N produces a question done with the particle *oh* and an adverbial phrase *so soon:*

```
     (139)  N    Anything else to report,
                 (0.3)
           H     Uh::::::m::::,
                 (0.4)
                 Getting my hair cut tomorrow,=
           N     Oh really?
                 (.)
           H     Yea:   [:::h,
           N            [Oh  ( so "soo:[d]?)           ←
                              (for foo:d?)
                 (0.4)
           H     Wha:t?
                 (0.2)
           N     Cause member
                 you said
                 you w [ere gonna m ]ake an appo [intment n, ]
           H         [owhhhhhhhoo]              [Oh:    y ]eah.*=
                                                       HG II 16:7
```

The question utterance *so soon* is interpretable as demonstrating surprise over the fact that H was getting a hair cut the next day. Although the transcription indicates two possible hearings for this turn, later talk clarifies that N produced the utterance *so soon*; H interpreted the utterance, however, as *for food*. (On the basis of the subsequent clarification, I am taking N's utterance to be *so soon* pronounced *so soo[d].*) Preceding N's response to the prior answer, the particle *oh* codes the receipt of unanticipated information (Schiffrin 1987:89). This further demonstrates that N's expectation was that H was not going to get her hair cut within the next 24 hours.

H produces an NTRI in response to N's *so soon*. N interprets this not as a request for repetition, rather as expressing some problem with the prior utterance, *i.e.*, as expressing some problem with N's surprise. This analysis is supported by the fact that N gives evidence to support why she found H's announcement surprising or at least unanticipated. H responds with an elongated *oh* and then *oh* plus an affirmative token in overlap with N's explanation. The elongated *oh* codes H's processing of N's answer with respect to the NTRI *what*. Given N's response to the NTRI (a reason for surprise), H is able to reinterpret the trouble source utterance as *so soon*. H then produces *oh yeh*. *Oh* plus an affirmative token codes the recognition of familiar information which is newly relevant. The question *so soon*, then, is not a request for confirmation.; it only gets produced because the prior talk was unanticipated given the speaker's expectation.

The utterance *so soon* is not an appender question which is syntactically integrated with the prior utterance. This form is doing a temporal evaluation of the event which H reports will happen the next day. It takes the entire prior turn as relevant and evaluates it with respect to its temporal dimension.

There are a number of other instances in the data which do not fall into any of the previous functional categories, discussed in Chapter 6 in relation to unmarked nonclausal questions. These utterances function to make offers, to request evaluations and to point out an object. Undoubtedly, an examination of more data would reveal other functions which speakers accomplish with nonclausal questions.

## 7.8. News Receipts

There are five instances of *really* in the data which are similar to NTRI's because they have a wide functional distribution. They can appear after statements and are used to receipt information which is new and interesting, or in some respect, unanticipated. Below, D had been describing how he had had a traditional Nepalese drink which eventually made him sick:

```
(140)   D    Oh maybe two or three weeks later it was the triple
             wha:mmy.
             Y' know
             (1.0)
             wor:ms an:
        W    "REA:lly?                                          ⇐
        D    Yeh, [amoe:bas y- (hh-hh) the whole thing.=
        W         [Oh
        C    (hm-mm)
```

W    =Oh: G(h):od.Oh:. Da:vid.                    Riggenbach 7:165

W produces an emphatic *really* after worms are mentioned. This is confirmed and then receipted by *oh*. In this sequential position, *really* is displaying appropriate interest in such a startling unusual statement.

W produces *Oh God* and *Oh David* after *amoebas* and *the whole thing*. These latter forms suggest W is coding a shift in the intensity of her orientation to the information. She is registering an increasing intensity of empathy for the speaker's condition (Schiffrin 1987:95).

In the following example, K is discussing turn-taking behavior:

(141) K      But, u:h but the question of how long a turn is, is interesting.
             I mean when you (.) i-
             its (.)
             well th-these notions about turn taking are (.) are really quite simple.
             You know, when when a turn is over, somebody else takes a turn.
             (That ), even kids know that.
             They're very good at turn taking.((laughs))
      C      How do you know when its your [turn.
      K                                    [but (.)when
             when you know [that a turn is finished.       ]
      La                   [( well alot of times kids=   )]
                =push the other kids out before their turn is
                [finished. ha ha
      K         [I mean actually,
             THIS is what's not supposed to happen.
             is this kind of overlap.
             and other people who have done conversational analysis CLAIM
      La     ha ha
             that adults don't have overlaps,
             and (.) [children do.  ] ((laughs))
      ( )            [(children do)]
             ((laughter))
      M      "rea::lly?                                          ⬅
      K      yes
      L      try transcribing a ta [pe ( )
      D                            [( )
      K                                 [so so if you tr- exactly,
             you'll find just
             see L___ and I just overlapped.

```
D      (    [              )]
M           [That's not true. ]
            ALL of our books are full of overlaps.
D      (alright )
K      Ah hah.
L      No no one believes that.                        Shapley/Nel 11:10
```

M produces *really* after a statement by K concerning what people claim about overlaps in conversations among children and adults. This could be interpretable as displaying receipt of an interesting bit of new information. Several turns later, however, it becomes apparent that M disagrees with the claim that adults do not have overlaps. She mentions that *our books are full of overlaps*. This suggests that she is also disagreeing with the K's statement that there are people who make the claim that there is no overlap in adult conversation. Evidence to the contrary is both accessible and plentiful — in *all our books*, so she wonders who would make such a claim.

### 7.9.   Conclusion

In these data, NTRI's are realized overwhelmingly by nonclausal forms vs. declarative clauses. Nonclausal forms are eminently suited to initiating the work of repair, *i.e.*, locating a trouble source in a prior turn. An explanation for their suitability is found in the relation of nonclausal forms to the structure of the prior turn. Shapley (1983) examined nonclausal forms of all functional types in conversation (statements, exclamations, questions). She has shown that most nonclausal forms are sufficiently constrained by the preceding linguistic context in form and semantic content to be defined in terms of that context. She states:

> ...they occur in the form of phrasal constituents or combinations of constituents, semantically related to that context. That is, the fragments were interpretable as a part of a source sentence, with the surface syntax carried over by the fragment speaker (p. 1).

Shapley classifies nonclausal forms into two types: completive and noncompletive. Completive nonclausal forms (classified as additions or substitutions) are semantically and/or syntactically related to the prior utterance, while noncompletive nonclausal forms have an evaluative meaning only.

As we have seen, some NTRI's use *wh*-words which locate problematic elements — referents, events, places, times. Others utilize partial repeats to further locate problematic elements by virtue of the repetition itself. Partial repeats also serve to further specify *wh*-words or candidate referents. In all these instances, there is a direct relationship interpretable between the NTRI and an *explicit* element of the prior utterance.

*Wh*-words also request more information rather than locate an explicit element of the prior turn. The information requested is semantically related to the prior turn (it could have been part of the prior turn but was not included by the speaker).

Appender question NTRI's are interpretable by virtue of the syntactic structure of the prior utterance; they can be understood as an *addition,* or an added constituent. This constituent, added across speaker turns, specifies the problematic element which was "missing" from the prior turn from the point of view of the speaker of the NTRI. In Shapley's terms, appender questions are classified as completive forms.

In summary, NTRI's are interpretable by direct reference to the syntactic structure of the prior turn with the exception of a *wh*-word which requests more information. This NTRI type is related semantically to the prior utterance. Although all utterances are interpretable in terms of their sequential position in the talk (in terms of the utterance/s they succeed), this does not mean that every utterance is interpretable in terms of the *syntax* of the prior utterance.

With regard to linguistic (vs. extralinguistic) elements, utterances are interpretable in terms of their own morphosyntax in conjunction with intonation as well as the functional interpretation of the prior utterance. In order to interpret an NTRI (identify the trouble source it is locating), a recipient must make crucial reference to the morphosyntax of the prior utterance as well as the NTRI itself. When the role of morphosyntax is considered with respect to the interpretation of NTRI's, NTRI's are interpretable in terms of their own morphosyntactic form and the *morphosyntactic structure* of the prior turn. As with any other utterance in the real world, other factors (in addition to morphosyntax), are relevant to interpretive procedures, *e.g.*, sequential position in the talk and intonation.

We have seen that questioning not implicated in repair is also done with nonclausal forms. These nonclausal questions exhibit a broad range of functions; many of them refer to some entity in the physical environment, *e.g.*, food items (Chapter 6). Those nonclausal questions interpretable in terms of the prior discourse differ from nonclausal NTRI's insofar as they are not so much constrained by the syntax of the prior turn as by the meaning of the prior turn.

# Chapter 8

# The Many-to-Many Relations of Lexical and Morphosyntactic Markers of Question Function

## 8.1. Introduction

The linguistic problem addressed in this study is the form/function problem. This problem is expressed as an absence of a one-to-one correlation between syntactic form and communicative function. Specifically, questioning can be done by any syntactic-clause type as well as by forms which do not constitute a syntactic clause.

In this text, I have examined both declarative clauses and nonclausal forms which do questioning. Declarative clauses and nonclausal forms are used by speakers to accomplish many other communicative functions in addition to realizing questions. How, then, do recipients interpret such forms as questions? Although morphosyntax plays a role in realizing question function in conversation, it must be evaluated in conjunction with intonation, sequential position in the discourse and the accessibility of the information questioned.

The many-to-many relation between form and function has been discussed with regard to the role of intonation associated with utterances which realize question function. In Chapters 1 and 4, we have seen that there is no such thing as unambiguous question intonation. Any contour which can appear on a clause which asks a question can also appear on one which makes a statement. Nevertheless, there are typical correlations between intonation contours and communicative functions and, in *some* cases, intonation is the crucial factor in determining question function (Couper-Kuhlen 1986).

Lexical and morphosyntactic markers associated with question function exhibit the same many-to-many relationship to communicative functions which have been discussed with regard to intonation. In other words, these markers appear with utterances which realize functions other than questioning, as well as with utterances which do questioning.

In this chapter, I will present some examples to show that lexical and morphosyntactic markers associated with question function may also be associated with an utterance which does *not* do questioning. Intonation, sequential position and information accessibility are relevant to the interpretation of these utterances as statements rather than questions.

## 8.2. Lexical and Morphosyntactic Markers

The markers identified as suggestive of question function appear in the data with a variety of utterances which do not do questioning. The following discussion, however, is restricted to the occurrence of these lexical and morphosyntactic markers with *declarative clauses* and *nonclausal forms* which function, not as questions, but as statements.

*Lexical Elements*

In the example below, the subject plus verb phrase *I don't know* is not associated with question function. H produces an extended turn during which she explains why she did not meet a friend:

```
(142)   N     What's doing,
              (.)
        H     Ah:, noth[i: n:,     ]
        N              [Y' didn't g]o meet Grahame?=
        H     =*pt *hhhhhahh Well, I got ho::me,
        N     =u-hu:h?
              (.)
              a::::n he hadn't called yet
              an there weren't any messages or anythi[n:g    ]e-]
                                                    [Uh  h]u ]:h
        H     a:n hh then I kind of got on the pho:ne
              an I heard a couple of clicks
              an hhhhhhh *hh I don't know if he was trying to  ⇐
              call =                                            ⇐
              =but "I'm too tired=                              ⇐
              =to go all the way back to Westwood anyw[ay, ]   ⇐
        N                                             [Ye : ]:ah,
                                                     HGII 1: 25
```

H expresses a gap in knowledge with the phrase *I don't know*. Although an expression of a gap in the speaker's knowledge may be a marker of question function, this example shows that it need not always be interpreted as such. Thus, the interpretation of *I don't know* in this example contrasts with the same phrase in the following example.

Below, N produces a declarative clause in which she expresses a gap in her knowledge relating to a play the participants are going to see that evening. This clause was classified as a marker of question function associated with the following declarative question:

```
(143)  H    Yeh but I don't want you to read it.
            (.)
       N    [O  ]kay,      ]
       H    [Plea]se don't.]
            *hh
            b[ecause-  ]
       N     [See "I do]n't know what its a           ⇐
             [bout yer n ]ot gonna                    ⇐
       H    [Yeah,     ]
       N    "tell [me?]                               ⇐
       H          [*p*]
            becau:se there's one point in there
            where it gives away s:something th[at- ]
       N                                      [Oh:]
            rea [lly:?    ]
       H        [i-is a sho]:cker =
            =and I don't want y[ou to kno:w, ]
       N                       [Okay I wo  ]:n ['t,
       H                                       [Cause it'll
            affect you more=
            =[when you see it.]
       N     [I'll read it a: f  ]ter,
```
                                                          HGII 9:15

Although H acknowledges that N is not familiar with the play, she does not respond with an answer. As we have seen in Chapter 4, however, N subsequently redoes the question and receives a response (example 23). The prior example demonstrates that *I don't know* plus a complement clause is not always interpretable as asking a question relevant to the information in the complement clause; therefore, it is not simply the expression of a speaker's lack of knowledge which is a marker of question function.

The expression of a speaker's lack of knowledge in a matrix clause is a marker of question function *when* the complement clause encodes a state of affairs about which the recipient is believed to have some knowledge (Labov and Fanshel 1977:101). In example 142, H produces the utterance *I don't know if he was trying to call but I'm too tired to go all the way back to Westwood anyway*. This is interpretable as expressing a gap in knowledge (whether or not Grahame was trying to call H). N has no particular access to whether or not Grahame was trying to call H. Marked by the conjunction *if*, the complement is a hypothetical clause. H produces more turn after the complement of the *I don't know* clause without any pause; and N does not respond at the end of the *I don't know* clause, which would indicate she interpreted it as doing questioning.

When the matrix clause expresses a gap in the speaker's knowledge and *neither* participant has any special access to knowledge about the state of affairs encoded in the complement clause, the utterance *may* function as a question. According to Labov and Fanshel's rule of confirmation: "if there is any doubt about the status of a particular event, it automatically falls into the class of D(isputable)-events" (Labov and Fanshel 1977:100). They state:

> If A makes an assertion about a D-event, it is heard as a request for B to give an evaluation of the assertion.

By evaluation, they mean agreement, disagreement and "more extended types of evaluation" (p. 101). In the following example, the complement clause is interpretable as a D-event (disputable). H expresses a gap in her knowledge regarding the procedures of the telephone company. This is not information which N has any special access to — it is not a B-event for N; rather, it is a D-event (one about which there is some doubt). Note: the utterance appears with the associated discourse marker *so* and the tag *or not*. Both *so* and *or not* are themselves markers associated with question function. It is not clear, therefore, to what extent *I don't know* is contributing to the functional interpretation of the utterance as a question.

```
(144)   N      You called Richard,=
        ( )    =hh-hh=
        H      = y(h)Yea(h)h
               and I h(h)ung up
               wh(h)en he ans[wer
        N                    [Oh: Hyla why::::[::,
        H                                     [*hhh
               well first of all
               I wasn't about to spend seventy five cents
               for three mi[nutes *uh] *eh=
        N                  [Yea:h,   ]
               =That's true,=
        H      =*hihhhh that's a lot of money
               plus (.) uh then it's twenty five cents for extra minute a
               [fter that.]=
        N      [Yeah,    ]=
        H      =* hh y[ou know,   ]
        N             [How do you] know
               he [answered could you tell his voi:ce?]
        H         [so for four minutes its a bu:ck.  ]
               (0.2)
               Hu:h?
```

H   (.)
N   Could you tell his vo[i:ce,]
H            [Yea ]h I knew his voice,=
N   =Oha:::[w,
H          [hhhih*hh=
N   =Ho:w was it to hear his    [voice,  ]
H                               [ah:    ]::,
    *u-*ehhh I wanted to tape [record ihhhhh
N                             [Did you wanna=
H   heh [heh]
N   [say [hi ]:, so ba:d?=
H   =Wha:t?=
N   =Didn't you wanna  really say hi:,=
H   =Ye:s, but as soon as he said hello I hung up.=
N   [ºOh ::::::,                    ]
H   [So 'I don't know if I'll get char ]ged the seventy- ⇐
    five "c(hh)ents(h ) or not,= ⇐
N   =No I don't think you will but- (.) (you ) might get charged
    something,
    (0.3)
H   ↓Oh:.                                          HG II 24:9

This example demonstrates that the phrase *I don't know* which expresses a gap in the speaker's knowledge may function as a marker associated with question function when the information in the complement clause is a D-event. In this case, however, there are other markers associated with the utterance which may play a crucial role in determining the question function of the utterance.

The same lexical element may appear in utterances which do questioning as well as in utterances which do not. The information status of the complement clause is relevant, as is the co-occurrence of other markers.

*Word Tag*

Below, C produces two utterances followed by the word *right*. In these cases, however, *right* is *not* functioning as a word tag associated with question function:

(145) D    We use to do some really a:wful things though
           some of the girls uh- in the hotel
           (I mean) we use to call it Menopause Manor.
           (y' know)
           khm khmm because of all the old ladies.
           (0.8)
           ((swallow)) t!a:nd, we'd get on the elevator

D	and we'd be smoking awa:y y'know,
	(0.4)
	°They g- ekhhuh! ekhuuh! ekh!
	*hh S'we use to take smoke and blow it in front of their fa:ces
	and, *hhhh m(h)y (h)one roommate she was really embarrassing
	she really was.
	She use to knock on doors
	and y' know these little old ladies would open
	and sh::sh::sh:::!
	and she'd s:qui(h)rt th(h)m (h)a(h)a(h)ll=
C	=[Oh Go::d, ]
D	=[ih ih ih! uh] *hhh!=
	=We use to do te::rrible thin[gs.
C	                              [Oh the:y use to have a really (good) ti[me (there)]
D	        [Oh::    ]:=
	Go:[d I know.    ]
C	   [(in the hotel.) ]
	(0.7)
D	It was (just) incredible,
	    (really)
C	But the- the year after we left they.
	(0.3)
	u-they: uhm,
	I think,
	you must not'v been that far behind me
	cause pretty soon there [after they-
D	                        [I was sixty si:x.=
	=so I think we just mis[sed each other,]=
C	                       [Yeah you were]
	[tw   ]o years behind me=
D	[=Yeah,]
C	= (at any rate )
	(           )
	cause I graduated in sixty four but-
	(0.5)
	uh:m, they closed down the hotel (uh-) right there- after.
	                                              (what-)
	(0.3)
D	Well in my year [actually, in sixty six ] they uh (m),
C	                [Built the new do:rm.]
	(0.5)
D	We were there I guess (for the:-) until Ja:nuary

D	or something like tha::t
	and the:n, y' know.=
C	=(Th') had the new "do:rms. "Right.   ⇐
	I did see the new do:rm.
	(That's the only)
	(Last year on a house tour.)
D	It wasn't ba::d.
	We lived in it en:d uh,
	(0.5)
	It was pretty ni:ce.
	It really wa:  [s.
C	               [°(Yeah it [ wa:s. Yeh).           ]
D	                          [It was nice and it was] clean:,=
C	=[Right.]
D	=[It was] new:
	and they [have  ]y'know like made the be:ds and,
C	         [°Right]
	(0.5)
D	° fu  [rniture (and s]tuff.)
C	      [(Y') had (choice) "furniture. "Right.=   ⇐
	(trellised)
	=W 'we had that over in our p- uh,
	(0.8)
	u-They had bought that for our house.
	°When they furnished the house.            Clacia 7:11
	                                           Clacia 7:24

C produces the utterance *(Th') had the new do:rms. Right.* Both intonation and sequential position are relevant factors in the interpretation of the utterance as a statement rather than as a question requesting confirmation. This utterance redoes the last clause of C's prior turn which is overlapped. C, therefore, is repeating information she had just stated. Both *(Th') had the new do:rms* and *right* have terminally falling intonation. With the word tag *right*, this contour differs from other utterances in the data which are doing questioning (in those cases, the declarative clause had terminally level or falling intonation, and the tag had terminally rising intonation) (see also Quirk 1985).

C subsequently produces the utterance *(Y') had (choice) furniture. Right.* Sequential position does not appear to be a crucial factor determining statement function for this utterance — intonation, however, is crucial. C is not requesting confirmation about the furniture in the new dorms; she is confirming that she *knows* about the furniture.

These examples contrast with the example below in which *right* functions as a word tag associated with question function:

(146) B    What's thi:s. ((signs)) *hhh ha ha
     L    That's She knows what that [is.
     M                              [That?
          they taught me the other night.
          It's, it's (.) you know,
          this is (.) your mother, ((signs))
          and this is (.) your grandmother, ((signs))
          and this is(.) mother-in-law ((signs)) ((laughter))
     B    Must be Italian.
          ((laughter))
     M    That's a joke. Actually it's not.
     L    **The mother and grandmother are "right, "right?** ⇐
     M    Yeah.                              Shapley/Boys 16:550

*Particles*

In the following example, C produces the particle *hm* which displays C's attention and interest in V's story. This particle is functioning as a continuer:

(147) V    and he said
          we'll probably have to put an artificial knee in in five years:.
          (0.2)
          for my Dad.
     C    "°hm,=                                              ⇐
     V    =because his knee is is deteriorating and weak.
                                                    Ford 5:141

This example may be contrasted with the following one in which the same particle is functioning as a question (specifically, an NTRI):

(148) C    Well it was a funny feeling to make him leave.
          What did I have to do,
          Oh, I know what it was.
          I was having fifty people to lunch the next day.
          ((laughter))
          It was just a couple of months ago he was here.
          It was in January.
          I was having luncheon for fifty the next day.
          An[d he called.
     K       [Why were you having luncheon for fi- for fifty.
     C    "Hm?                                                ⇐
     K    Why were you having luncheon for fifty.=
          =It seems a biza[rre thing to do.              ]

L  [(cause) it's one way to get] rid of A___.
                                    Shapley/Nel 18:27

What specifics in these two cases account for the difference in function? Both occur during the course of narrative; both are produced by recipients of the narrative. The only difference is intonation. When it functions as an NTRI, *hm* takes rising intonation. When it functions as a continuer, *hm* takes level or falling intonation.

*Second-Person Subjects*

In the next example, the second-person subject *you* is not serving as a marker of question function although the speaker's utterance is interpretable as relating to a B-event (Chapter 4). This conversation takes place during a dinner: N is the hostess/cook; L is her daughter; B and E are guests:

(149) L    What's the da:rk green thing.
           (0.4)
      N    Pardón?= ((French))
      E    =he=
      L    =What's this?
      N    That's Japanese eggplant.
           (0.1)
           **"You like it.**                                    ⇐
      B    Oh it's Japa[nese eggplant.]
      E             [It's goo:d.     ]
      B    °It's delicious.                          Weber 5: 51

L asks her mother, N, about the identity of a vegetable on her plate. N answers by identifying the vegetable as Japanese eggplant and then takes more turn in which she tells her daughter that she (the daughter) *likes it*. Guest B then takes a turn in which she responds to the identification of the vegetable as news. E and B both then give a positive assessment of the food.

Why is the utterance *You like it* not interpretable as a request for confirmation? An individual certainly has access to knowledge relating to what s/he likes in terms of foods. An utterance by speaker A about a food preference of B's, on the face of it, should be interpretable as a request for confirmation. In this case, however, it is not.

Although the sequential position and the information status of the utterance might suggest it is doing questioning, the intonation in this example explicitly determines its function as a statement rather than as a question. The *you* has pitch prominence and is spoken with falling terminal intonation. In order to be interpretable as a request for confirmation, this utterance (in this sequential position) would have to have the pitch prominence on the verb with rising terminal intonation.

Utterances like example 149 which are interpretable *as statements* are not unusual among individuals who are in an intimate relationship, *e.g.*, parents and children, husbands and wives.

Contrast this example with the next, which exhibits the same stress on the second-person subject in conjunction with falling terminal intonation:

```
(150)   E      Did I tell y- Oh, "yo:u heard it.           ⇐
        L      Yeh, [a ]bout K__?
        E           [( )]
               No:, about (1.2) A__.                    Weber 2:4
```

The utterance is interpretable as a request for confirmation in terms of A- and B-events. As previously, the second-person subject has pitch prominence, and there is falling terminal intonation. The prior-aborted interrogative clause appears to be a factor, however, in the interpretation of this utterance as a request for confirmation rather than as a statement.

Examples 149 and 150 may be contrasted with the next example, interpretable as a question:

```
(151)   M      I came to talk to Ruthie about borrowing her (0.1) notes
               (-) from (0.1) econ.
        R      O[h ( ).
        S      [You didn't come to talk to "Karen?          ⇐
               (0.5)
        M      No
               (0.2)
               Karen: (0.3) Karen and I are having a fight.    SN 4 4:2
```

The speaker's utterance is a statement about a B-event and is interpretable as a request for confirmation. Note: the second-person subject is unstressed (unlike the preceding two examples), and the verb receives pitch prominence.

### *Repetitions Which Are Not NTRI's*

Below, N repeats H's prior utterance. This repetition is not functioning as an NTRI, rather as third-position receipt (Chapter 2):

```
(152)   N      What's his last name,
        H      Uh:: Freedla:nd. *hh[hh
        N                          [Oh[:,
        H                             [('r) Freedlind.=
        N      =Nice Jewish bo:y?
               (.)
        H      O:f "cou:rse,=                              ⇐
```

N      ='v["cou:rse,]
H      [hh-hh-hh ] hnh *hhhhh=                    HG II 25: 22

N produces the question *Nice Jewish bo:y?* H then produces the second-pair part answer *O:f cou:rse* with terminally level intonation. N receipts this answer by repeating it. Although N's *'v cou:rse* repeats the entire prior utterance, it is not displaying any trouble with understanding. In order to be interpreted as an NTRI, this repetition (in the sequential slot for a third-position receipt) would have to be produced with rising terminal intonation.

Below, R produces an answer by repeating the question:

(153)  A    *hhh (Well) w [hen do you find out,
       R                  [ye:ah,
            *hhh ey- I don't kno:w,
            (0.4)
            I don't kno:w,
            (0.4)
            *hh Chances are it's no::
            and I gotta start thinking that way (.) so
       A    (Yuh) just in "case?                              ⇐
       R    Just in "case,=                                   ⇐
            =[Yeah  ]                                         ⇐
       A    =[(*Yeah)]
            (B-)                                              Kinjo 6: 141

A's question is realized by an affirmative token plus *Just in case?* R's answer reverses the order of A's question — *Just in case, yeah.* This utterance is not displaying any trouble in understanding the prior question. In order to be interpreted as an NTRI, this repetition (in the sequential slot for a third-position receipt) would have to be produced with rising terminal intonation.

Contrast these examples with the example below. N repeats the prior utterance with rising terminal intonation in order to signal some trouble with hearing:

(154)  H    *hh Toda:y there was a who::le (.) review on it in
            [the paper. ]
       N    [u-Whe:re.]
            (.)
            Oh real[ly I'm gonna loo:k, ]
       H          [In the View section.]
            (0.2)
       N    In the ["Vie:w?                                   ⇐
       H           [*p*hh

H    (.)
     Yeah
     but I don't want you to read it.
     (.)
N    Okay,                                                HGII 9:1

Note: the utterance which is the source of the trouble is overlapped. The overlap, itself, supports the interpretation that N's repetition is produced as a result of some trouble with hearing the prior utterance.

This section has presented a number of examples of utterances which, while not functioning as questions, are realized by lexical and morphosyntactic elements associated with question function (Chapters 4 and 6). I have considered how intonation, sequential position and the accessibility of information interact to occasion statement vs. question function. I have also examined two cases in which repetitions of the immediately prior utterance are not functioning as NTRI's. Intonation appears to be the crucial determinant of statement vs. NTRI function in these cases.

## 8.3.   Misinterpretations

Utterances can be misinterpreted as doing questioning. We may ask what accounts for the possible interpretation of the utterance as a question. In the following example, V is taking an extended turn describing her father's knee surgery, her mother's reaction to the surgery and her own reaction to both her father's surgery and her mother's behavior:

(155)  V    and she's saying
            his leg's gonna be an inch sho:rter?
       K    °teh oh shit   [( )  ]
                           [This] is what my Mom's saying.
            (0.4)
       V    Because they took it out-
            this is her
            the doctor didn't say  his leg's gonna be an inch shorter
            she's saying it,
            *hh and that it's unnecessary:,
            and that there's no re:ason fo:r it
            and on and on and on and on.
       K    (Well if) your Mom's so wrong about so much stuff
            why would she b-all of a sudden be an expert on   [that.]
       V                                                      [an  ]
            it was like

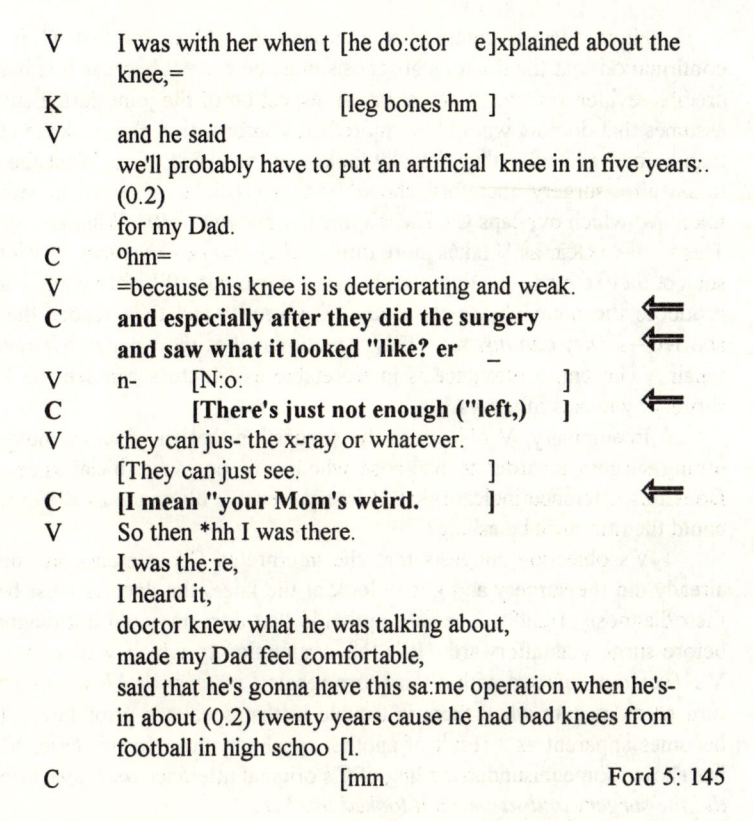

| | |
|---|---|
| V | I was with her when t [he do:ctor e]xplained about the knee,= |
| K | [leg bones hm ] |
| V | and he said |
| | we'll probably have to put an artificial knee in in five years:. |
| | (0.2) |
| | for my Dad. |
| C | ᵒhm= |
| V | =because his knee is is deteriorating and weak. |
| C | and especially after they did the surgery ⇐ |
| | and saw what it looked "like? er ⇐ |
| V | n-   [N:o:                                      ] |
| C | [**There's just not enough ("left,)**    ] ⇐ |
| V | they can jus- the x-ray or whatever. |
| | [They can just see.                            ] |
| C | [**I mean "your Mom's weird.**            ] ⇐ |
| V | So then *hh I was there. |
| | I was the:re, |
| | I heard it, |
| | doctor knew what he was talking about, |
| | made my Dad feel comfortable, |
| | said that he's gonna have this sa:me operation when he's- |
| | in about (0.2) twenty years cause he had bad knees from |
| | football in high schoo [l. |
| C | [mm                    Ford 5: 145 |

C and K are recipients of V's story. C produces the utterance *and especially after they did the surgery and saw what it looked like? er.* V responds as if the utterance is a request for confirmation; she produces a negative token and an account.

First, consider in detail C's utterance and V's response to see if doing questioning is a possible interpretation of C's utterance. C produces the utterance after a multiclausal turn of V's in which she is describing her mother's version of her father's condition. In contrast to this version, she then states what the doctor actually said. Introduced by *he said*, this takes the complement clause *we'll probably have to put an artificial knee in in five years*. After a pause, V produces the transition repair *for my Dad.*

The repair, however, does not report "what the doctor said." C responds with ᵒ*hm* which signals her interest in the continuation of the story. V takes more turn — *because his knee is is deteriorating and weak.* At this point, it is ambiguous whether V is resuming her report of the doctor's words or whether she is giving a reason why the doctor thought an artificial knee would be necessary in the future. C then produces the utterance *and especially after they did the surgery and saw what it looked like? er.*

How does V interpret C's utterance? V infers that C is requesting confirmation that the doctor's prognosis must be correct because it is based on very credible evidence from an actual visual inspection of the joint during surgery. This assumes that doctors would have more/better information about a knee after surgery than before, *i.e.*, after they actually looked at the inside of it. What the doctor had to say after surgery, therefore, should be very credible. V responds with a negative token *No* which overlaps C's *There's just not enough (left)*. What is V objecting to? This is made clear as V takes more turn — *they can jus- the x-ray or whatever*. The subject *they* refers to the doctors; the word *just* is cut off before completion. V then produces the noun phrase *the x-ray or whatever* and then redoes the clause she aborted — *They can just see*. This repetition makes *the x-ray or whatever* an insert repair. The entire utterance is interpretable as "doctors can see the knee before surgery by means of x-rays."

In summary, V objects to the suggestion that the doctors must see a knee during surgery in order to diagnose whether or not an artificial knee is required. Does this utterance indicate that V interpreted C's utterance as a question? What could the utterance be asking?

V's objection suggests that she interpreted C's utterance as "because they already did the surgery and got to look at the knee, the doctors must be correct in their diagnosis, right?" The assumption is that doctors could not diagnose as well before surgery as afterward. It is this assumption to which V objects. C overlaps V's *They can just see* with a third-turn repair *I mean your Mom's weird*. A third-turn repair occurs when there is trouble in that speaker's prior turn. The trouble becomes apparent as a result of another speaker's turn. In this case, V's utterance has shown some misunderstanding of C's original utterance *and especially after they did the surgery and saw what it looked like? er*.

We may ask in what way *I mean your Mom's weird* clarifies the meaning of *and especially after they did the surgery and saw what it looked like? er*. V's "answer" deals with doctors and medical technology. C's clarification repair makes no mention of anything medical, rather it refers to V's mother. In order to understand, we must consider how C may have intended *and especially after they did the surgery and saw what it looked like? er* to be interpreted.

V is talking about her mother's reactions and reporting what her mother had to say about the surgery. She then makes it clear that *what her mother is saying* is not *what the doctor actually said*. K takes a turn to question V's mother's authority to speak on the issue — *(Well if) your Mom's so wrong about so much stuff why would she b-all of a sudden be an expert on that*. He is implicitly claiming the mother is not an expert on knee problems.

V continues her story by relating what the doctor said. C's utterance *and especially after they did the surgery and saw what it looked like? er* is interpretable as contrasting V's mother's opinion with what the doctors had said. This utterance supports K's claim that V's mother is not an expert. V's mother's statement conflicts with the doctors'; and the fact that the doctors had actually seen the knee supports his/her judgment.

Note: C begins her turn with *and*, a connective. To which prior utterance is C providing a connection? The utterance is connected in terms of argumentation to K's prior utterance. It is interpretable as "why should she be an expert on that (leg bones) *especially after they (the doctors) did the surgery and saw what it ( the knee) looked like*? C then takes more turn *There's just not enough (left)*, interpretable as stating that the doctor saw there was not enough existing knee remaining. C's clarification *I mean your Mom's weird* supports the above interpretation of *and especially after they did the surgery and saw what it looked like? er*. Only a "weird" person would disagree with the experts, especially after the experts have visually examined the knee during surgery.

The factors involved in V's interpretation of *and especially after they did the surgery and saw what it looked like? er* as a question are sequential position and intonation. C produces the utterance during the course of a narrative. V, as the teller, has access to relevant medical information. C's utterance appears to be interpreted by V as a request for confirmation, and the utterance has rising terminal intonation. C's third-turn repair, however, indicates that she did not intend the utterance to be a question requesting confirmation.

## 8.4. Distribution of Markers in Declarative Statements

The lexical and morphosyntactic markers associated with declarative questions also appear in declarative statements. Are these markers associated with declarative statements with the same frequency as with declarative questions? When the first 10 declarative statements occurring in each conversation in the data are examined, the 140 declarative statements exhibit the following distribution of markers:

| | | |
|---|---|---|
| Associated Marker | 48 | 34% |
| No Associated Marker | 92 | 66% |
| Total | 140 | 100% |

Table 8.1.
Declarative Statements with an Associated Marker
vs.
Declarative Statements with No Associated Marker

Declarative statements *without* associated lexical and morphosyntactic markers appear more frequently (66% of all instances) than declarative statements *with* associated markers (34% of all cases). Contrast this distribution with the marking associated with declarative questions in Table 4.9 — declarative questions have an associated marker in 85% of all cases.

Declarative statements and questions also differ with respect to markers per form. Ninety-nine percent of declarative statements with an associated marker contain only one marker, with only two exceptions (1%). One case has two discourse markers (*well, then*), and the other, has a clause introduced by *if* with a second-person subject (*if you ever cook corn again*).

Contrast this distribution with the marking associated with declarative questions in Table 4.10 in which declarative questions have one marker in 54% of all cases. For slightly less than half of all cases, declarative questions have more than one marker.

The following table exhibits the temporal distribution of markers per form for declarative statements:

| | | |
|---|---|---|
| Within marking | 9 | 18% |
| Prior marking | 41 | 82% |
| Subsequent marking | 0 | 0 |
| **Total** | **50** | **100%** |

Table 8.2.
**Temporal Distribution of Markers per Form for Declarative Statements**

Markers appearing *within* the clause constitute 18% of all markers. This percentage includes seven *you* subjects. Of the remaining two cases, one is the subject plus verb phrase *I don't know* and the other is the particle *oh* which marks the object of the clause rather than the clause itself. The remaining 82% appear prior to the declarative clause, and there are no subsequent markers.

The temporal distribution of markers per form for declarative statements is different from that of declarative questions. The following table exhibits the temporal distribution of markers per form for declarative questions when the second-person subject *you* is considered a marker associated with question function. Note: *you* as a marker was not included in Table 4.5.:

| | | |
|---|---|---|
| Within marking | 52 | 34% |
| Prior marking | 49 | 32% |
| Subsequent marking | 51 | 34% |
| **Total** | **152** | **100%** |

Table 8.3.
**Temporal Distribution of Markers per Form for Declarative Questions**

When *you* is included as a lexical marker, the temporal distribution of markers associated with declarative questions is approximately equal in all temporal domains. Compare this table to Table 8.2. — declarative statements have fewer instances of markers appearing within the clause than declarative questions. Declarative statements have no subsequent marking; whereas, declarative questions have subsequent marking in 34% of all instances of marking.

The types of markers which appear with declarative statements are mainly conjunctions, adverbs, particles and second-person subjects. The following defines the markers which appear with declarative statements:

| Conjunctions | but | 2 | | | |
| | so | 11 | | | |
| | if | 1 | } | 14 | 28% |
| Adverbs | now | 2 | | | |
| | then | 6 | } | 8 | 16% |
| Particles | well | 10 | | | |
| | oh | 5 | | | |
| | oh + yes | 1 | | | |
| | oh + yeah | 1 | | | |
| | you know | 1 | | | |
| | okay | 2 | } | 20 | 40% |
| Verb | I don't know | 1 | } | 1 | 2% |
| 2P Subject | you | 7 | } | 7 | 14% |
| Total | | 50 | | | 100% |

Table 8.4.
Types of Markers Associated with Declarative Statements

A variety of markers are associated with declarative statements, although declarative statements have a smaller variety of associated markers than declarative questions. There are no *wh*-words associated with declarative statements in these data. When conjunctions (*but, so*) and adverbs (*now, then*) appear with declarative statements, the utterance is usually an element in a narrative sequence in which the speaker of the declarative statement is also the speaker of the prior utterance. When these same conjunctions and adverbs appear with declarative questions, however, the speaker of the question is usually *not* the speaker of the prior utterance.

Eight of the ten instances of *well* which appear with declarative statements appear in utterances which are answers to questions. The function of *well* as a response marker has been described by Wootten (1981), Owen (1983), Pomerantz (1984) and Schiffrin (1987). No declarative question, however, functions as a second-pair part answer. Labov and Fanshel (1977:156) note that *well* can shift talk toward shared topics. This function of *well* appears to be relevant to its function in declarative questions.

In summary, only a subset of markers associated with declarative questions are also associated with declarative statements. An examination of these markers suggests that the discourse environment of declarative statements differs from that of declarative questions. Because this work is not a full statistical study of the distribution of morphosyntactic and functional types, these results are meant only to be suggestive of the different discourse environments in which declarative questions and statements are realized. This is an interesting area for further research.

## 8.5. Conclusion

This study has discussed several aspects of the fact that there is not a one-to-one relationship between form and function. We have seen that syntactic clause type and intonational contour both stand in a many-to-many relation with communicative function. With regard to question function, any clause type may function as a question; in addition, these same clause types may also realize non-question functions. As Pike notes (1945, cited in Bolinger 1972:9), any intonational contour which can appear on a question can also appear on a statement (see also Bolinger 1989). These same many-to-many relations also apply to lexical and morphosyntactic markers associated with question function. While these markers are associated with declarative and nonclausal questions, they also function in declarative and nonclausal statements.

In presenting the results of this study to various audiences, I have been presented with the argument that it is the rising terminal intonation of the utterance which signals question function for declarative clauses and nonclausal forms. There are, I think, three relevant responses to this.

First, the role lexical and morphosyntactic elements play in the interpretation of declarative and nonclausal questions in no way detracts from the role intonation plays in their interpretation. Secondly, rising terminal intonation on declarative clauses and nonclausal utterances (particles, words, phrases), *in and of itself* does not exclusively determine question function. Moreover, Stenström (1984) and Geluykens (1988) have shown that declarative questions show variation with regard to rising vs. falling terminal pitch movement. My data confirm these findings. Furthermore, Couper-Kuhlen (1986:156) presents instances of declarative clauses, words and phrases which have rising terminal intonation but are not functioning as questions. In other words, there is no such thing as unambiguous question intonation (Bolinger 1989). Thirdly, there is no doubt that rising terminal intonation does crucially determine question function in *some* cases, *e.g.*, in the case of particles which are functioning as NTRI's.

A few people make the point that because the lexical and morphosyntactic markers associated with declarative and nonclausal questions also appear with non-questions, these markers do not determine question function. There are several relevant responses to this.

First, these markers, in and of themselves, are not determining question function. They are *associated* with question function. These morphosyntactic elements play a role in the functional interpretation of an utterance as a question. Independently, these elements do not necessarily determine the interpretation of an utterance as a question.

Secondly, the same arguments against the claim that intonation determines question function can also be made with regard to these lexical and morphosyntactic markers. Some of the same markers which appear in declarative or nonclausal questions can be found in declarative or nonclausal statements. These markers do not, therefore, unambiguously signal question function. Even such elements as particles (*huh*) and single *wh*-words (*what*) can realize nonquestion functions, *e.g.*, an exclamatory function.

The interpretation of question function involves *several* factors and their interaction. Morphosyntactic elements are relevant and have been exemplified with instances found in the data. I have also described other factors in the interpretation of question function, *viz.*, intonation, sequential position and accessibility of information. By presenting examples of statements realized by lexical and morphosyntactic elements which are also associated with question function, I have attempted to provide instances which are the discourse equivalents of "minimal pairs." A change in one or more factors precipitates a change in functional interpretation.

Language makes multiple uses of its resources — word order, morphology, lexical elements and intonation. These resources combine with the sequence of utterances and the flow of information to establish many-to-many relations between forms and functions. Although linguists and philosophers who study language may consider this to be a problem, it may be more appropriate to consider these relations to be a solution. As a result of many-to-many relations of form and function, language users manage to create worlds of meaning and achieve an astounding variety of communicative accomplishments.

# Chapter 9

# Conclusions

## 9.1. Introduction

In Chapter 1, I set two goals for this work:

(1) My first goal was to show that morphosyntactic form correlates with doing questioning when questioning is identified functionally.

(2) My second goal was to consider how the structure of the morphosyntactic forms which do questioning are motivated by their function in the talk.

In this chapter, I will discuss:

(1) How these goals have been met.

(2) The speakers' typology which I have constructed for questions in English conversation and its relationship to the various syntactic strategies which other languages use to indicate questioning (interrogativity).

(3) Finally, I will also consider the relevance of this study for the notion of typical question forms in English.

## 9.2. Goal 1

When question function is broadly defined, morphosyntactic form correlates with this function. In other words, noninterrogative forms which do questioning tend to be marked lexically or morphosyntactically, as in the following table:

Table 9.1.

|  | Marked Forms | Forms with No Associated Marker |
|---|---|---|
| Declarative | 85% | 15% |
| Nonclausal | 63% | 37% |
| **Total** | **100%** | **100%** |

Declarative Questions vs. Nonclausal Questions
Marked Forms vs. Forms with No Associated Marker

Eighty-five percent of all declarative questions in the data have a marker associated with question function, while only 15% have no associated marker. Sixty-three percent of all nonclausal questions, on the other hand, have a marker associated with question function, and 37% have no associated marker. In Chapter 1, the question of the interface between form and function was posed. Coulthard (1977) describes this problem in terms of how a relatively small number of grammatical options can realize a relatively large number of communicative functions.

The first goal was to explore how morphosyntactic options interact with intonation and sequential position to realize question function. An examination of declarative and nonclausal questions has shown that the role of morphosyntax in the interpretation of these questions is far greater than realized. Morphosyntax interacts significantly with intonation, sequential position and information accessibility to signal question function for noninterrogative questions.

In Chapter 8, I presented utterances with the same form which differed in their communicative function (including the markers identified in Chapters 4 and 6). In these instances, utterances with the same form may function as statements or questions. These examples indicate that variation in intonation, sequential position and information accessibility can crucially affect the function of an utterance. It is not a single factor, in itself, which determines question function; rather, the interpretation of question function is sensitive to the interaction of morphosyntactic form, intonation, sequential position and information accessibility (Chisholm 1984, Bolinger 1989, Tsui 1991).

## 9.3. Goal 2

My second goal was to demonstrate that morphosyntactic form emerges from the discourse uses of the form. In other words, the form/function correlations exhibited in the data are not arbitrary; they are functionally motivated (García 1975, 1979, Thompson 1983, 1987a, 1987b, Du Bois 1985, 1987a, 1987b, 1988, Hopper

1987, 1988, Hopper and Thompson 1980, 1984, Bentivoglio and Weber 1986, Weber and Bentivoglio 1991, Geluykens 1992, Hopper and Traugott forthcoming).

Declarative and nonclausal questions exhibit specific patterns of morphosyntactic marking. The relevant aspects of morphosyntactic marking to be explained in terms of specific discourse functions of declarative and nonclausal questions are:

- The percentage of marked forms vs. forms with no associated marker
- The number of markers per form; and
- The temporal distribution of markers per form.

The difference between the marking patterns of declarative and nonclausal questions can be explained in terms of function when the function is described more specifically than doing questioning.

With respect to the percentage of marked forms vs. forms with no associated marker, Table 9.1. indicates that more declarative questions exhibit marking than nonclausal questions (85% vs. 63%). This difference also can be related to differences in the functions of declarative vs. nonclausal questions.

With respect to the number of markers per form and their temporal distribution, we may ask why declarative and nonclausal questions also show different patterns of marking. The following table presents the distribution of markers per form (see also, Table 4.10. and Table 6.4.):

|  | 1 Marker per form | $1^+$ Marker per form | Total |
|---|---|---|---|
| Declarative | 54% | 46% | 100% |
| Nonclausal | 90% | 10% | 100% |

Table 9.2.
Declarative Questions vs. Nonclausal Questions
Number of Markers per Form

Different syntactic forms correlate with differences in the number of markers per form. If a declarative clause has any markers, more than half the time it will have one marker; and slightly less than half of the time, it will have more than one marker. At this level of functional analysis, then, the number of markers per form cannot be strongly predicted. In contrast, we can predict that if a nonclausal question has any markers, it will have one marker fully nine times out of 10. Following, (Section 9.4.) this skewed distribution is related to differences in function between declarative and nonclausal questions.

The next table presents the temporal distribution of markers when the second-person subject *you* is included as a marker (see Table 4.3. for a comparison of declarative clause markers which exclude *you*):

|  | Within | Before | Subsequent | Total |
|---|---|---|---|---|
| Declarative | 34% | 32% | 34% | 100% |
| Nonclausal | 71% | 16% | 13% | 100% |

Table 9.3.
Declarative Questions vs. Nonclausal Questions
Temporal Distribution of Markers
(includes *you*)

Different morphosyntactic forms correlate with differences in the distribution of temporal marking. When *you* subjects are included, declarative questions have marking within the structure of the clause 34% of the time, while nonclausal questions exhibit marking 71% of the time.

In contrast, declarative questions have an associated marker in 66% of all instances either before or after the clause (32% + 34%), nonclausal questions have an associated marker in 29% of all instances either before or after the form (16% + 13%). In summary, declarative questions have nearly equal instances of marking in all three temporal domains, while for nonclausal questions, more than two out of three instances of marking appears within the structure of the form. This difference in distribution relates to the difference in function between declarative and nonclausal questions.

## 9.4. Functional Explanations of Morphosyntactic Patterns

The relevant aspects of morphosyntactic form associated with question function are:

(1) The percentage of forms which appear with associated markers;
(2) The number of markers per form; and
(3) The temporal distribution of markers per form.

The differences in percentages for declarative and nonclausal questions for these factors are interesting because they reflect morphosyntactic patterns which are functionally motivated. These form/function patterns of noninterrogative questions result from the choices speakers make in conversation to accomplish interactional and informational goals. Questions are realized in different ways — by different morphosyntactic forms and with different associated patterns of marking — depending on what the question is doing in the talk. Declarative and nonclausal forms in conjunction with their associated patterns of marking are well suited to their respective functions.

## 9.4.1. Declarative Questions

How does the percentage of marked declarative questions (vs. those with no associated marker) as well as the number of markers per form and their temporal distribution relate to the typical function of declarative questions? Typically, declarative questions request confirmation in terms of A- and B-events; they are rarely next-turn repair initiators (NTRI's). Unlike many nonclausal NTRI's, repetitive elements as well as *wh*-marking within the clause in general do not play a significant role in the interpretation of declarative questions (although they do play a role in the interpretation of nonclausal NTRI's). Other types of associated markers, however, do play a significant role in the interpretation of declarative questions; speakers use them to mark declarative questions 85% of the time. We may infer that speakers employ this marking to facilitate the interpretation of declarative questions *as questions* rather than as statements (Table 8.1.).

Declarative questions not implicated in repair are well suited to confirm information related to some prior utterance. In these data, the prior utterance to be confirmed is most often immediately prior and is produced by another speaker, *i.e.*, not the speaker of the declarative question. In terms of speaker turns, then, the declarative question often has a different speaker from the utterance which precedes it. *The declarative question relates to the prior utterance through its subject.*

Fully 94% of all subjects of declarative questions in the data not implicated in repair are personal pronouns (*you*), demonstrative pronouns (*that, these*) or noun phrases with demonstrative adjectives (*these beans*). The subjects most often refer to the recipient of the utterance (*you*) or to a referent explicitly mentioned in the prior utterance. The information for which the speaker requests confirmation is realized in the verb phrase of the declarative question. This part of the utterance is not a repetition or restatement of previously mentioned information, rather it elaborates or it draws an inference from the prior utterance. Because the information for which confirmation is requested was not mentioned previously, syntactic clause structure is required to encode it. This functional need to use clause structure may be contrasted with repair function; it is not the case that speakers *need* to use a complete syntactic clause to locate a source of trouble in a prior turn. As we have seen in Chapter 6, nonclausal forms are frequently employed to do repair.

When the number of markers per form in declarative questions are considered, slightly more than half of all forms have one marker, while slightly less than half have more than one. If declarative questions are generally marked to facilitate their interpretation as questions, why do some of these questions receive more than one marker? Although beyond the scope of this study, the discourse environments and interactional motivations which condition the appearance of multiple markers are areas for further research.

Consider the temporal distribution of markers associated with declarative questions. We have seen that 32% of markers associated with declarative questions appear before the clause. We might say that these questions resemble *yes/no* requests for confirmation in that the marking occurs early, if not immediately, in the utterance. It is also true that *wh*-questions are marked early, if not immediately, in the turn by both a *wh*-word and subject/verb inversion (except in those instances in which the subject is itself a *wh*-word). For the 34% of markers which appear within the clause, most of that marking consists of verbs and second-person *you* subjects which occur early in the turn.

There are, in fact, only three cases of within-the-clause marking which do not exhibit this early-in-the-turn marking. The exceptions are: two cases of NTRI's with *wh*-words within the clause and one case of the use of a gap strategy. When these three cases are excluded, the instances of prior marking and marking early in the turn within the clause constitute 64% of all instances of marking. This pattern resembles the *temporal* dimension of the marking which characterizes interrogative questions.

Some declarative questions are marked only by tags. In conjunction with intonation, tags unambiguously signal question function. Although how the discourse environment conditions the use of declarative questions marked only by tags is beyond the scope of this study, a more detailed analysis of requesting confirmation might reveal significant differences in function for declarative questions marked only by tags vs. those with prior and within-the-clause marking, both of which occur early in the turn (see also Brown 1981).

This section has discussed the functional motivation of the morphosyntactic patterns of declarative questions. The relevant patterns are whether or not the clause has morphosyntactic marking, the number of markers per form and the temporal distribution of the markers.

### 9.4.2. Nonclausal Questions

What does the percentage of marked nonclausal questions (vs. those with no associated marker), the number of markers per form and their temporal distribution signify for the function of nonclausal questions? In other words, why are fewer nonclausal questions marked than declarative questions, and why do marked nonclausal questions typically have a single marker within the structure of the nonclausal form?

Table 9.1. illustrates that 63% of all nonclausal questions are marked, while 37% have no associated marker. Table 7.1. indicates that over half of nonclausal questions are NTRI's. When these nonclausal NTRI's are considered, we see why not all nonclausal NTRI's need to be marked to accomplish their repair function. Marked nonclausal NTRI's use a particle or a *wh*-word to target the trouble source in the prior turn (example 108 and 109) or in conjunction with a repetition of *part* of the prior turn (example 111). Because it is usually *not* necessary to repeat the entire prior clause to target the source of the trouble, most NTRI's in the data which work by repetition are not realized by a complete syntactic clause but by a repeated word or phrase.

Nonclausal NTRI's do not need to be marked, however, in order to locate the source of trouble in the prior turn. One type of unmarked nonclausal NTRI uses *only* a partial repetition of the prior turn (example 113) — another is an appender question (example 117). These NTRI's utilize the constituent structure of the trouble source utterance by adding an additional "final" constituent (L: *he's made a big success.* M: *with his rock group?*) Appender questions solicit more information by adding a constituent which can be integrated into the syntactic structure of the prior utterance. Nonclausal questions use a greater percentage of forms with no associated marker than do declarative questions, in part, because nonclausal questions which are NTRI's can be unambiguously interpreted *as questions* without any associated markers in any sequential position.

NTRI's are sequentially relevant after any utterance. Information accessibility in terms of A- and B-events is irrelevant to the interpretation of NTRI's. As mentioned in Chapters 2 and 6, the next-turn position and the repetitive elements themselves constitute a kind of marking for NTRI's. For appender questions, interpretation is made on the basis of the syntactic structure of the prior utterance and that of the appended nonclausal form. Rising terminal intonation also appears to be crucial for the interpretation of nonclausal forms as NTRI's (Cruttenden 1986:108). Nonclausal questions with no associated marker are, therefore, as well suited to doing repair as marked nonclausal NTRI's.

Those nonclausal questions in the data which are not NTRI's serve a broad variety of functions. The interpretation of many of these utterances depends upon the recipient's visual access to an entity in the physical environment. Many other of these utterances make reference to a story. They are semantically and/or syntactically related to the prior utterance.

Nonclausal questions which exhibit marking associated with question function have just one marker 90% of the time. Many of these nonclausal questions are NTRI's, and the morphosyntactic markers are particles or *wh*-words which appear either alone or in conjunction with repeated elements of the prior turn. This pattern of marking is, of course, well suited to locate a source of trouble in the prior turn. Some nonclausal questions which are not NTRI's are also marked, *e.g.*, responses to pre-announcements (*what*).

The fact that nonclausal markers appear within the constituent form 71% of the time is also related to the repair function of 60% of these forms. The single repair function of NTRI's is to *locate* the source of the trouble. We have seen that 52% of within-the-constituent-form marking for nonclausal questions is constituted by *wh*-words and particles (Table 6.3.). In most instances, these markers constitute the entire form.

## 9.5. Universals of Question Function

Moravcsik (1991) notes the universality of structures which do questioning and states that languages show "considerable resemblance" in the way they utilize morphology, word order and intonation to determine question function vs. statement function. Note: the types of morphosyntactic question marking which have been presented in Chapters 4 and 6 can be found in other languages of the world.

### 9.5.1 Question Marking Strategies

The major types of marking associated with question function which have been discussed in this work are the following:

*Lexical Elements*

Some verbs which take a complement clause can be markers of question function (*know, wonder, hear*). In some (*know, wonder*), the complement of the matrix clause constitutes an embedded question. Embedded questions appear commonly in the languages of the world and are often introduced by markers which signal question function. In English, *wh*-words and the conjunctions *whether* and *if* mark embedded questions (example 22 and 144). There are many other languages which employ such markers in embedded clauses, *e.g.*, Georgian (Harris 1984); however, embedded questions may appear without such markers, as in Mandarin (Li and Thompson 1984).

*Question Pronouns*

Question pronouns (*wh*-words in English) in languages are often related to indefinite pronouns. In interrogative clauses in English, *wh*-words appear at the beginning of the clause, and there is subject/verb inversion (with the exception of those cases in which the *wh*-word is itself the subject). As we have seen, *wh*-words may appear in declarative clauses in non-initial positions; these questions are usually NTRI's. In other languages, non-NTRI questions may have question pronouns in clause initial position without any subject/verb inversion, *e.g.*, Russian (Comrie 1984); but, the conjunction of initial question pronouns and subject/verb inversion is rare (Chisholm 1984:5). In some languages, question pronouns exhibit a great deal of freedom as to where they can appear in a clause, *e.g.*, Bengali (Saha 1984) and Mandarin (Li and Thompson 1984).

*Prior Question Marker/Pronoun*

In English, question function may be projected over a clause, phrase or word by a prior marker (*what, how about*). This strategy also is found in other languages. In Bengali, a question marker may appear before a clause to project question function (*ki* 'what' (Saha 1984)). As in English, two intonation contours distinguish this syntactic type from question pronouns appearing within a clause. In Russian, the conjunction *a* is used to ask a question of a topic in the same way *how about* is used in English.

### Particle, Word and Clause Tags

Particles are commonly used to signal questions in languages of the world. In my data, the particle *huh* or *uh* comes at end of the utterance and affects the entire utterance. (Other particles in English are *eh* and *hah*.) In other languages, question particles are often related to disjunctive conjunctions and may appear in positions other than clause final — before the clause (Polish), after the first constituent (Ute) or after the focused constituent (Russian) (Moravcsik, 1991). Like English, Mandarin uses a particle tag only at the end of the utterance (Li and Thompson 1984). Word tags are also used in other languages, *e.g.* Mandarin.

### Alternative Questions

Noninterrogative forms in English may pose alternative questions. There are two types of alternative declarative questions in the data: clause plus *or not* and clause plus *or what*. *Or not* constitutes the negative alternative to the affirmative clause preceding it. Li and Thompson (1984) report that Mandarin has grammaticized the disjunction of the affirmative and its negative counterpart. The disjunctive particle and the repeated material is generally omitted in the negative clause. In the second type of alternative question in the data, *or what* presents an open-ended alternative to the affirmative clause which precedes it.

### 9.5.2. Implication for Typological Studies

Typological studies contrast similarities and differences in the languages of the world. The discovery of language universals has obvious implications for cognitive science; universal structures and functions of language may reveal significant aspects of cognition. Given this relationship between typological studies and cognitive science, typological investigations need to focus on the structures speakers actually use (Chisholm 1984). This study is relevant to typological studies because it presents the actual structures English speakers use to do questioning when that action is functionally defined. From the perspective of the study of language universals, infrequent syntactic structures are as important as those more frequently used.

## 9.6. Typical Questions

Chapter 1 discussed clause structures which typically realize question function. Why talk about typical questions in English? We all believe that typical questions are realized by interrogative clauses (*wh-* and *yes/no* questions which exhibit subject-verb inversion). When data are considered from the point of view of frequency of clause types, however, we see that interrogative questions comprise 59% of all questions, while the remaining 41% are declarative clauses or nonclausal forms (Table 6.1.). In some sense, then, 41% of all the questions in these data are not typical, *i.e.*, not interrogative. Because this work is not a large distributional study of syntactic clause types which accomplish questions in English conversation, these percentages are only suggestive. Nevertheless, they do raise some interesting issues about ways of asking specific functional types of questions.

Any discussion of *typical question forms* must include additional specification of communicative function to accurately reflect the way speakers ask questions in conversation. When function is considered in this more specified way, we may ask, for example, what is the typical syntactic form speakers use to do other-initiated repair in conversation? We know from this study that when only noninterrogative forms are considered, we can confidently say that NTRI's are typically realized by nonclausal forms rather than by declarative clauses.

Of the 101 NTRI's in the data, 90% are nonclausal forms and 10% are declarative forms. Similarly, when only noninterrogative forms are considered, a request for confirmation in terms of A- and B-events not implicated in repair is typically done by a declarative clause. Of the 87 requests for confirmation in the data which also are not implicated in repair, 78% are declaratives and 22% are nonclausal forms. Of course, *yes/no* questions (not analyzed in this study) also function to request confirmation. In summary, declarative questions and nonclausal questions are typically used by speakers to accomplish certain specific functions — to request confirmation and to effect repair.

This section has considered the notion of a typical question in English. Given the frequency with which speakers in conversation use noninterrogative questions and the correlation of these questions to specific question functions, it is appropriate to expand the notion of the typical question to include some additional specification of function.

## 9.7. Implications for Other Areas of Language Study

### 9.7.1. Descriptive Linguistics

From the perspective of description alone, speakers have a number of morphosyntactic options available when they do questioning with declarative clauses or nonclausal forms. These options include the use of lexical elements, discourse markers and *wh*-words. Both intonation and the accessibility of information are relevant to the interpretation of noninterrogative questions. Descriptive linguistic studies which do not include data from naturally occurring conversations may omit functionally important constructions.

### 9.7.2. Speech Act Theory

This study is relevant for linguists and speech-act theorists who are interested in the form/function problem. Further discussion of this issue should involve the many options available to speakers in conversation which have not been specifically noticed or related to form/function correlations. In other words, options for syntactic marking are available to speakers who do questioning with declarative clauses and nonclausal forms. This study shows the importance of looking at conversational data in any attempt to explain *how* people manage to use language to do things.

The fact that language in use contrasts so strikingly with the language imagined by those working on the theory of speech acts is, I suggest, an issue for speech-act theory. The data demonstrate that the morphosyntactic options available to speakers to mark noninterrogative questions are used frequently. These options interact with other factors (intonation, sequential position and information accessibility) and require complex interpretive procedures. In contrast, speech-act studies present "recreated" examples of utterances which lack this complexity.

### 9.7.3. Formal Linguistics

Although the assumptions are different, functional linguists' descriptions of language use in naturally occurring conversations are of real value to formal linguists. Such descriptions can reveal dynamic aspects of the grammar of a language not accessible to intuition. The use of prior markers to project question function to declarative clauses, for example, is something speakers know and use in a variety of ways to accomplish their goals in interaction. Although the distribution of morphosyntactic structures may not be relevant within formal linguistics, the frequency of the types of questions described in this study suggests that they are part of the grammar which speakers must learn — somehow. As such, these forms are just like other parts of the grammar and should, therefore, be explained by formal linguists on their own terms.

### 9.7.4. Cognitive Science

This study also highlights that when conversational data are examined, and the temporal dimension of language seriously considered, morphosyntactic patterns associated with communicative functions are revealed. Because they are associated with communicative functions in a motivated way, these patterns are learnable. This study, then, has implications for cognitive science in terms of both interpretation and language acquisition. To the extent that cognitive science is interested in language processing (interpretation) and language acquisition (learnability), the correlations between morphosyntactic patterns and communicative functions have implications in both these areas of research.

# Notes

## Chapter 1. The Problem: The Relation between Discourse and Grammar

1. I am indebted to Manny Schegloff for teaching me what I know about the analysis of conversation in terms of the sequential structure of the talk. Although this work is not conversation analysis itself, it has come about, in large part, as a result of my studying how conversation is organized functionally by participants.

2. It is possible to say something with a full mouth, so that no articulation occurs; only the intonation contour is produced. It is often possible to guess the unarticulated meaning in these situations.

3. The term 'marker' has been used in the literature to refer to morphosyntactic elements associated with utterances which function as questions. In the following statement from Bolinger (1957), Q-marker refers to question marker, and NQ refers to a nonquestion, *i.e.*, an utterance which does not function as a question. He mentions "both outright Q-markers and other expressions which, while often used in NQs, suggest questionness by their frequency in Qs — example I suppose..."(p. 9). Stenström (1984) also uses the term 'marker' in relation to functional questions.

## Chapter 2. Analytical Procedures and Principles

1. There is one case of an imperative clause which, though not constructed by its speaker as a question, appears to be misinterpreted as a question by its recipient.

2. Cruttenden (1986:48) notes that terminals, *i.e.*, the last pitch direction on the last syllable of an intonation-group, "are only significant when they reverse the preceding pitch direction" (p. 45). He points out that "the last pitch movement is certainly important but need not be terminal, *i.e.*, it need not occur actually on the last syllable of the intonation-group" (p. 58). This point is exemplified in the following two patterns. The dots represent syllables, with the larger dots representing stressed and/or accented syllables. The lines represent the limits of a speaker's pitch range. A line attached to a dot represents pitch movement.

                Unfortunately                    John didn't do it

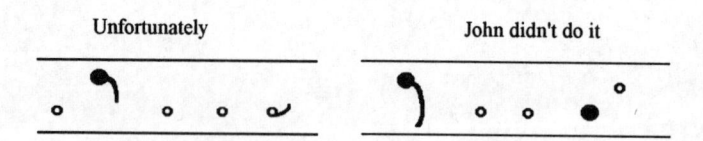

In the first case, there is a rise on the unstressed *-ly* and in the other case, there is a rise between *do* and *it*. Thus, for *John didn't do it*, the last pitch movement does not actually occur on the last syllable.

## Chapter 3. Methodology

1. Heidegger's admonition.

## Chapter 4. Questions in Declarative Form: Morphosyntactic Patterns

1. It has been noted that negative statements imply some expectation with respect to the affirmative situation (Sacks 1972a, Schegloff 1972, Labov and Fanshel 1977). Labov and Fanshel state: "An assertion that x has not occurred presupposes that someone expects (for some reason) that x would occur (p. 104)." In this study, negative declarative questions with no associated marker are interpretable as requests for confirmation in terms of A- and B-events. Although it would have been possible to make a case for considering negation a marker associated with question function, I did not treat it as such. I excluded negation as a marker in an attempt to take the most conservative possible approach to morphosyntactic marking. If, in fact, negation were counted as a marker associated with question function, the correlation between morphosyntactic marking and declarative questions would be even stronger.

## Chapter 5. Declarative Questions: Function

1. Requests for confirmation in terms of A- and B-events exclude NTRI's which are interpretable on other grounds.
2. This excludes NTRI's.

## Chapter 7. Nonclausal Questions: Function

1. Schegloff refers to this type of NTRI as a post-positioned interrogative (personal communication).
2. Utterances which are similar to this are often NTRI's. This utterance may even be considered a borderline case. The crucial issue in this instance is whether it is functioning to

clarify the speaker's understanding of the category "unusual statements" or to solicit an amusing story.

## Appendix

(1)  N    This is so (good.)
          I never u- drink during the week.=
     ( )  =[ heh]
          =[ ha ]
     B    =[mmh ] We'll be so (ho)rry, (.) [tomorrow.
     L                                     [toMOrrow ha ha ha
     E                                     [(toMOrrow
     L    hehehehehehe
          (.8)
     N    I fall asleep too fast,                        ←
     L    hehehehe                              Weber 4:34

(2)  B    Can you imagine ( .) letting somebody ( 0.2) do that?
          O:h                                             ←
     N    At that age.
          Well that's what goes on with Ann's daughter
          (etc. on this topic)                  Weber 12:194

(3)  C    He:y. Where c'n I get a::, uh, 'member the old twenny
          three Model T spring,
          (0.5)
          Backspring 't came up like that,
     Kid  Come on let's go get it! Come on Mi:chael,=
          =[ c'mon
     (1.0)
     C    [Dju know what I'm [talk ] what I'm talkin a[bout, ]
     M                       [Ye:h,]                  [ I thi]=
          =nk - I know whatchu mean,
     C    Wh'r c'n I get o:ne.
          (0.8)
     Kid  Mi:ke!

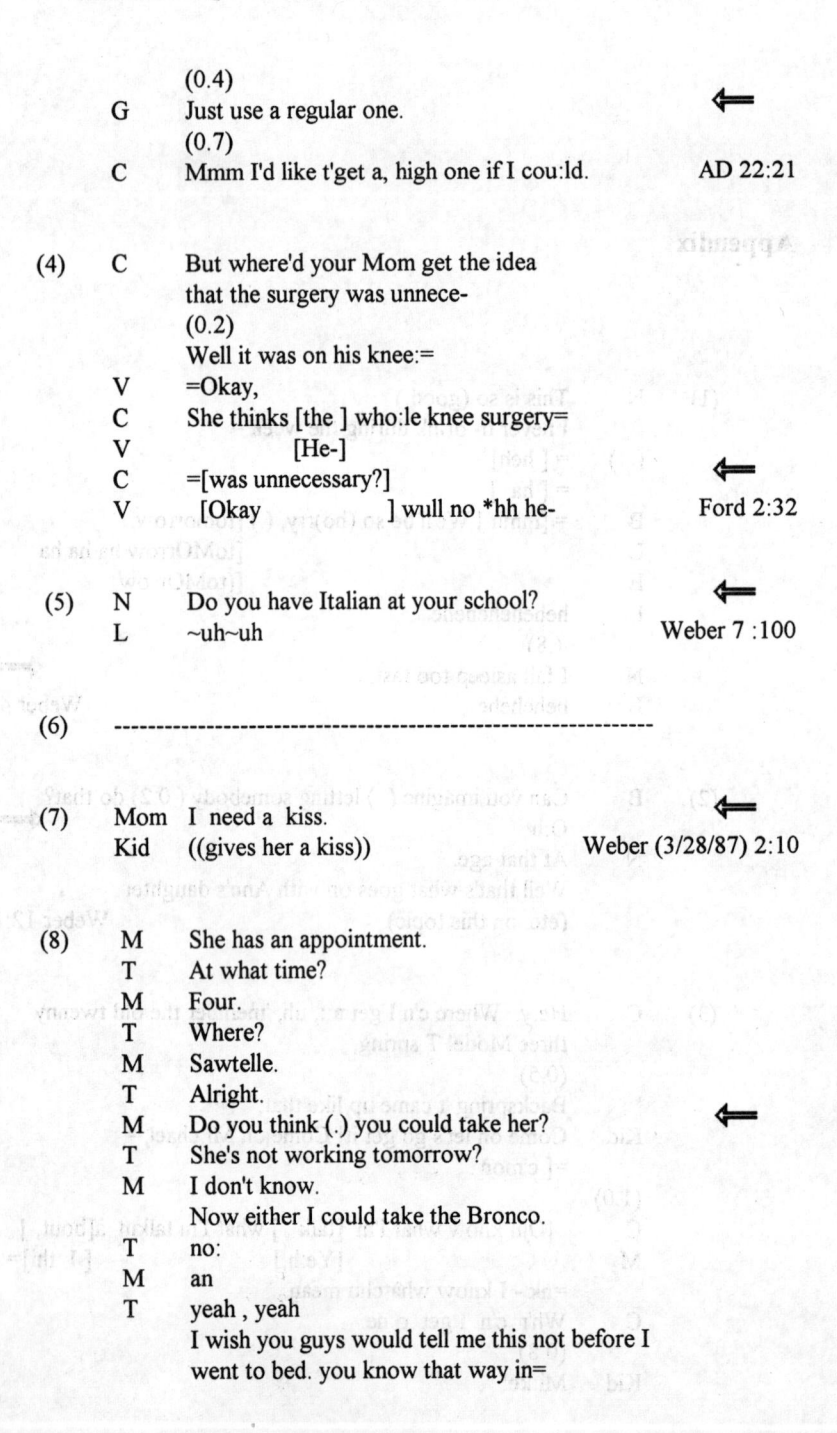

```
         (0.4)
    G    Just use a regular one.                    ←
         (0.7)
    C    Mmm I'd like t'get a, high one if I cou:ld.    AD 22:21


(4) C    But where'd your Mom get the idea
         that the surgery was unnece-
         (0.2)
         Well it was on his knee:=
    V    =Okay,
    C    She thinks [the ] who:le knee surgery=
    V               [He-]
    C    =[was unnecessary?]
    V     [Okay         ] wull no *hh he-           Ford 2:32


(5) N    Do you have Italian at your school?        ←
    L    ~uh~uh                                     Weber 7:100


(6) ---------------------------------------------------------------


(7) Mom  I need a kiss.                             ←
    Kid  ((gives her a kiss))                       Weber (3/28/87) 2:10


(8) M    She has an appointment.
    T    At what time?
    M    Four.
    T    Where?
    M    Sawtelle.
    T    Alright.
    M    Do you think (.) you could take her?      ←
    T    She's not working tomorrow?
    M    I don't know.
         Now either I could take the Bronco.
    T    no:
    M    an
    T    yeah, yeah
         I wish you guys would tell me this not before I
         went to bed. you know that way in=
```

=case I do have plans I don't make the plans.
Weber (7/16/86) 4:1

(9)　　N　　ºPass the salad,

⬅

Weber 9:132

# References

Ashby, William J. 1988. "The Syntax, Pragmatics, and Sociolinguistics of Left and Right Dislocations in French". *Lingua* 75:203-29.
Atkinson, Martin. 1979. "Prerequisites for Reference". *Developmental Pragmatics* ed. by E. Ochs & B. Schieffelin, 229-49. New York: Academic Press.
Atkinson, J. Maxwell & Paul Drew. 1979. *Order in Court: The Organization of Verbal Interaction in Judicial Settings*. London: Macmillan.
Atkinson, J. Maxwell & John Heritage, eds. 1984. *Structures of Social Action*. Cambridge: Cambridge University Press.
Austin, John L. 1962. *How to Do Things with Words*. Oxford: Clarendon Press.
Ayer, A. J. 1936. *Language, Truth and Logic*. London: Gollancz.
Bentivoglio, Paola & Elizabeth G. Weber. 1986. "A Functional Approach to Subject Word Order in Spoken Spanish". *Studies in Romance Linguistics* ed. by O. Jaeggli & C. Silva-Corvalán, 23-40. Dordrect, Holland/Riverton, USA: Foris.
Benveniste, Emile. 1966. *Problèmes de Linguistique Générale 1*. Paris: Gallimard.
—————. 1971 [1966]. *Problems in General Linguistics* trans. by M. E. Meek. Coral Gables, Florida: University of Miami Press.
Bilmes, Jack. 1985. "'Why That Now?' Two Kinds of Conversational Meaning". *Discourse Processes* 8:19-56.
Bloom, Lois. 1970. *Language Development: Form and Function in Emerging Grammars*. Cambridge: MIT Press.
—————. 1976 [1973] "One Word at a Time". *Janua Linguarum* Series Minor, 154. The Hague: Mouton de Gruyter.
Bolinger, Dwight. 1952. "Linear Modification". *Publications of the Modern Language Association of America* 67:1117-14.
—————. 1954. "Meaningful Word Order in Spanish". *Boletín do Filología* 7:45-56. Santiago: Universidad de Chile.
—————. 1957. "Interrogative Structures of American English". *Publication of the American Dialect Society*, no. 28. University, Alabama: University of Alabama.
—————. 1972. *Intonation: Selected Readings*. Harmondsworth, England: Penguin.
—————. 1977. *Meaning and Form*. New York: Longman.

───────. 1978. "Intonation Across Languages". *Universals of Human Language* (= Phonology, II ed. by J. Greenberg, C. Ferguson & E. Moravcsik, 471-524). Stanford: Stanford University Press.

───────. 1982. "Nondeclaratives from an Intonational Standpoint". *Papers from the Parasession on Nondeclaratives Chicago Linguistic Society* ed. by R. Schneider, *et al.*, 1-22. Chicago: Chicago Linguistic Society.

───────. 1986. *Intonation and Its Parts*. Stanford: Stanford University Press.

───────. 1989. *Intonation and Its Uses*. Stanford: Stanford University Press.

Brazil, David. 1985. *The Communicative Value of Intonation in English*. Birmingham: English Language Research & Bleak House Books.

Brown, Gillian, Karen Currie & John Kenworthy. 1980. *Questions of Intonation*. London: Croom Helm.

Button, Graham & Neil Casey. 1984. "Generating Topic: The Use of Topic Initial Elicitors". *Structures of Social Action, Studies in Conversational Analysis* ed. by J. M. Atkinson & J. Heritage. (= Studies in Emotion and Social Interaction, 3:167-90). Cambridge: Cambridge University Press.

Chafe, Wallace. 1970. *Meaning and the Structure of Language*. Chicago: University of Chicago Press.

───────. 1976. "Givenness, Contrastiveness, Definiteness, Subjects, Topics, and Point of View". *Subject and Topic* ed. by C. Li & S. Thompson, 25-56. New York: Academic Press.

───────. 1979. "The Flow of Thought and the Flow of Language". *Discourse and Syntax* (= Syntax and Semantics, 12th ed. by T. Givón, 159-81). New York: Academic Press.

───────. 1980. "The Deployment of Consciousness in the Production of a Narrative". *The Pear Stories: Cognitive, Cultural, and Linguistic Aspects of Narrative Production* ed. by W. Chafe, 9-50. Norwood, N.J.: Ablex.

───────. 1982. "Integration and Involvement in Speaking, Writing, and Oral Literature". *Spoken and Written Language: Exploring Orality and Literacy* ed. by D. Tannen, 35-53. Norwood, N.J.: Ablex.

───────. 1984. "Cognitive Constraints on Information Flow". *Berkeley Cognitive Science Report No. 26*. Berkeley: University of California.

Chisholm, Jr., William, ed. 1984. *Interrogativity*. Amsterdam & Philadelphia: John Benjamins.

Comrie, Bernard. 1984. "Interrogativity in Russian". *Interrogativity* ed. by W. Chisholm, Jr., 7-46. Amsterdam & Philadelphia: John Benjamins.

Coulthard, Malcolm. 1977. *An Introduction to Discourse Analysis*. London: Longman.

───────. 1985. *An Introduction to Discourse Analysis*. London: Longman.

Coulthard, Malcolm & Martin Montgomery, eds. 1981. *Studies in Discourse Analysis*. London: Routledge & Kegan Paul.

Coulthard, Malcolm & David Brazil. 1979. "Exchange Structure". *Studies in Discourse Analysis* ed. by M. Coulthard & D. Brazil, 82-106. London: Routledge & Kegan Paul.

————. 1981. "The Place of Intonation in the Description of Interaction". *Georgetown University Roundtable on Languages and Linguistics 1981* ed. by D. Tannen, 94-112. Washington, D.C.: Georgetown University Press.
Couper-Kuhlen, Elizabeth. 1986. *An Introduction to English Prosody*. Baltimore: Edward Arnold.
Cruttenden, Alan. 1986. *Intonation*. Cambridge: Cambridge University Press.
Crystal, David. 1969. *Prosodic Systems and Intonation in English*. (= Cambridge Studies in Linguistics, 1.) London: Cambridge University Press.
————. 1975. *The English Tone of Voice*. London: Edward Arnold.
Dale, Philip, Elizabeth Loftus & Linda Rathbun. 1978. "The Influence of the Form of the Question on the Eyewitness Testimony of Preschool Children". *Journal of Psycholinguistic Research* 4:269-77.
Dixon, Robert M. W. 1979. "Ergativity". *Language* 55:59-138.
Diver, William. 1969. "The System of Relevance of the Homeric Verb". *Acta Linguistica Hafniensia*. 12:45-68.
————. 1980 [1975]. "Introduction". *Columbia Working Papers in Linguistics*, 2:1-20. New York: Columbia University, Dept. of Linguistics. corrected reprint, Fall 1980.
Drew, Paul. 1985. "Analyzing the Use of Language in Courtroom Interaction". *Discourse and Dialogue* (= Handbook of Discourse Analysis, 3rd ed. by T. Van Dijk 133-48). New York: Academic Press.
Du Bois, John W. 1980. "Beyond Definiteness: The Trace of Identity in Discourse". *The Pear Stories: Cognitive, Cultural, and Linguistic Aspects of Narrative Production* ed. by W. Chafe, 203-74. Norwood, N.J.: Ablex.
————. "The Sacapultec Language". Ph.D. dissertation, Berkeley: University of California, 1981.
————. 1985. "Competing Motivations". *Iconicity* ed. by J. Haiman, 343-65. Amsterdam & Philadelphia: John Benjamins.
————. 1987a. "The Discourse Basis of Ergativity". *Language* 63:805-55.
————. 1987b. "Absolutive Zero: Paradigm Adaptivity in Sacapultec Maya". *Lingua* 71 (special issue on Ergativity ed. by R. M. W. Dixon.), 203-22.
————. "Discourse as Pattern Model For Grammar". Paper presented at Coherence and Grounding in Discourse Conference, June, 1984.
Du Bois, John, Stephan Schuetze-Coburn, Danae Paolino & Susanna Cumming. 1992. *Outline of Discourse Transcription*. In Sandra A. Thompson, ed., *Discourse and Grammar* (Santa Barbara Papers in Linguistics, vol. 2). Santa Barbara, California: University of California, Department of Linguistics, 1988; and in Jane A. Edwards and Martin D. Lampert, eds., *Talking Data: Transcription and Coding Methods for Language Research*. Hillsdale, N.J: Lawrence Erlbaum.
Duranti, Alessandro & Elinor Ochs. 1979. "Left-Dislocation in Italian Conversation". *Discourse and Syntax* (= Syntax and Semantics, 12th ed. by T. Givón, 377-416). New York: Academic Press.

Esau, Helmut. 1982. "The 'Smoking Gun' Tape: Analysis of the Information Structure in the Nixon Tapes". *Text* 2:293-322.

Firth, J.R. 1957 [1935]. "The Techniques of Semantics". *Papers in Linguistics 1934-1951* 7-33. London: Oxford University Press, 1957.

Fónagy, Ivan. 1978. "A New Method of Investigating the Perception of Prosodic Features". *Language and Speech* 21:34-49.

Ford, Cecilia E. "Grammar in Interaction: Adverbial Clauses in American English Conversations". To be published by Cambridge: Cambridge University Press.

Ford, Cecilia E. & Sandra A. Thompson. "Interactional Units in Conversation: Syntactic, Intonational, and Pragmatic Resources for the Projection of Turn Completion". To appear in *Grammar in Interaction*, ed. by E. Ochs, E. Schegloff & S. Thompson.

Fox, Anthony. 1973. "Tone Sequences in English". *Archivium Linguisticum* 1:17-26.

Fox, Barbara. 1987. "The Noun Phrase Hierarchy Revisited". *Language* 63:856-70.

Friedrich, Paul. 1979 [1966]. "Structural Implications of Russian Pronominal Usage". *Language, Context, and the Imagination*, 63-125. Stanford: Stanford University Press.

Friedrich, Paul. 1979. *Language, Context, and the Imagination*. Stanford: Stanford University Press.

García, Erica. 1975. *The Role of Theory in Linguistic Analysis: The Spanish Pronoun System*. New York: American Elsevier.

——————. 1979. "Discourse without Syntax". *Discourse and Syntax* (= Syntax and Semantics, 12th ed. by T. Givón, 23-49). New York: Academic Press.

Garfinkel, Harold. 1984 [1967]. *Studies in Ethnomethodology*. Cambridge: Polity Press.

Garvey, Catherine. 1979. "Contingent Queries and Their Relations in Discourse". *Developmental Pragmatics* ed. by E. Ochs & B. Schieffelin, 363-72. New York: Academic Press.

Geluykens, Ronald. 1987. "Intonation and Speech Act Type: An Experimental Approach to Rising Intonation in Queclaratives". *Journal of Pragmatics* 2:483-94.

——————. 1988. "On the Myth of Rising Intonation in Polar Questions". *Journal of Pragmatics* 12:467-85.

——————. 1989a. "The Syntacticization of Interactional Processes". *Belgian Journal of Linguistics* 4:91-103.

——————. 1989b. "R(A)ISING Questions: Question Intonation Revisited". *Journal of Pragmatics* 13:567-75.

——————. 1992. *From Discourse Process to Grammatical Construction: On Left Dislocation in English*. Amsterdam: John Benjamins.

Gibbon, Daffyd. 1984. "Intonation as an Adaptive Process". *Intonation, Accent and Rhythm: Studies in Discourse Phonology* ed. by D. Gibbon & H. Richter. Berlin: Mouton de Gruyter.

Givón, Talmy. 1979. *Understanding Grammar*. New York: Academic Press.
—————. 1984. *Syntax: A Functional-Type-Logical Introduction*, vol. 1. Amsterdam & Philadelphia: John Benjamins.
Goffman, Erving. 1967. *Interaction Ritual*. New York: Doubleday.
—————. 1974. *Frame Analysis*. Cambridge: Harvard University Press.
—————. 1976. "Replies and Responses". *Language in Society*. 5:257-313.
—————. 1981. *Forms of Talk*. Philadelphia: University of Pennsylvania Press.
Goldberg, Julia. 1983. "A Move toward Describing Conversational Coherence". *Conversational Coherence* ed. by R. Craig & K. Tracy, 25-46. Beverly Hills: Sage.
Goodwin, Charles. 1979. "The Interactive Construction of a Sentence in Natural Conversation". *Everyday Language: Studies in Ethnomethodology* ed. by G. Psathas, 97-121.
—————. 1981. *Conversational Organization*. New York: Academic Press.
Goodwin, Charles & Marjorie Goodwin. 1986. "Gesture and Coparticipation in the Activity of Searching for a Word". *Semiotica* 62. 1/2:51-75.
—————. 1987. "Concurrent Operations on Talk: Notes on the Interactive Organization of Assessments". *International Pragmatic Association Papers in Pragmatics*, 1:1-54.
—————. 1992. "Context, Activity and Participation". *The Contexturalization of Language* ed. by Peter Auer & Aldo di Luzo, 77-9. Amsterdam: John Benjamins.
Goody, Esther G. 1978. *Questions and Politeness*. Cambridge: Cambridge University Press.
Grimes, Joseph. 1968. *The Thread of Discourse*. (ERIC Microfiche ED. 019669).
—————. 1971. "Kinds of Information in Discourse". *Kivung* 4:64-74.
—————. 1975. *The Thread of Discourse*. The Hague: Mouton de Gruyter.
Grimes, Joseph & Naomi Glock. 1970. "A Saramaccan Narrative Pattern". *Language*. 46:408-25.
Halliday, M.A.K. 1967. *Intonation and Grammar in British English*. The Hague: Mouton de Gruyter.
—————. 1970. "Language Structure and Language Function". *New Horizons in Linguistics* ed. by J. Lyons, 140-65. Baltimore: Penguin.
—————. 1977 [1975]. *Learning How to Mean*. New York: Elsevier North-Holland.
—————. 1985. *An Introduction to Functional Grammar*. London: Edward Arnold.
Harris, Alice. 1984. "Interrogativity in Georgian". *Interrogativity* ed. by W. Chisholm, Jr., 63-112. Amsterdam & Philadelphia: John Benjamins.
Heritage, John. 1984. *Garfinkel and Ethnomethodology*. Cambridge: Polity Press.
Holmes, Janet. 1985. "Functions of *You Know* in Women's and Men's Speech". *Language in Society* 15:1-22.
Hopper, Paul. 1987. "Emergent Grammar". *Berkeley Linguistic Society* 13:139-55.

———. 1988. "Emergent Grammar and the *a Priori* Grammar Postulate". *Linguistics in Context* ed. by D. Tannen, 103-20. Norwood, N. J.: Ablex.
Hopper, Paul J. & Sandra A. Thompson. 1980. "Transitivity in Grammar and Discourse". *Language* 56:251-99.
———. 1984. "The Discourse Basis for Lexical Categories in Universal Grammar". *Language*. 60:703-52.
Hopper, Paul J. & Elizabeth C. Traugott. *Grammaticalization*. To be published by Cambridge: Cambridge University.
Jefferson, Gail. 1972. "Side Sequences". *Studies in Social Interaction* ed. by D. Sudnow, 294-338. New York: Free Press.
———. 1975. "Error Correction as an Interactional Resource". *Language in Society* 3:181-99.
———. 1978. "Transcript Notation". *Studies in the Organization of Conversational Interaction* ed. by J. Schenkein, xi-xvi. New York: Academic Press.
———. 1984. "On the Organization of Laughter in Talk about Troubles". *Structures of Social Action* ed. by J.M. Atkinson & J. Heritage, 346-69. Cambridge: Cambridge University Press.
Keenan, Elinor Ochs & Bambi Schieffelin. 1976. "Foregrounding Referents: A Reconsideration of Left-Dislocation in Discourse". *Berkeley Language Society* 2:240-57.
Kim, Kyu-hyun. "WH-Clefts and Left Dislocation in English Conversation with Reference to Topicality in Korean". Ph.D. dissertation, Los Angeles: University of California, 1992.
Kirsner, Robert. 1969. "The Role of *Zullen* in the Grammar of Modern Standard Dutch". *Lingua* 24:101-54.
———. "On Deixsis and Degree of Differentiation in Modern Standard Dutch". Ph.D. dissertation, New York: Columbia University, 1972.
Laberge, Suzanne & Gillian Sankoff. 1979. "Anything *You* Can Do". *Discourse and Syntax* (= Syntax and Semantics, 12th ed. by T. Givón, 419-40). New York: Academic Press.
Labov, William. 1964. "Phonological Correlates of Social Stratification". *American Anthropologist*. 66:164-76.
———. 1966. *The Social Stratification of English in New York City*. Washington: Center for Applied Linguistics.
———. 1972a. *Sociolinguistic Patterns*. Philadelphia: University of Pennsylvania Press.
———. 1972b. *Language in the Inner City*. Philadelphia: University of Pennsylvania Press.
Labov, William & David Fanshel. 1977. *Therapeutic Discourse*. New York: AcademicPress.
Lehiste, Ilse. 1970. *Suprasegmentals*. Cambridge: MIT Press.
Lerner, Gene H. 1987. "Collaborative Turn Sequences: Sentence Costruction and Social Action". Ph.D. dissertation, Irvine: University of California.

——————. 1989. "Notes on Overlap Management in Conversation: The Case of Delayed Completion". *Western Journal of Speech Communication* 53: 167-77.

——————. 1991. "On the Syntax of Sentences in Progress". *Language in Society* 20: 441-458.

Levelt, Willem J. & Stephanie Kelter. 1982. "Surface Form and Memory in Question Answering". *Cognitive Psychology* 14:78-106.

Levinson, Samuel. 1983. *Pragmatics*. Cambridge: Cambridge University Press.

Li, Charles & Sandra A. Thompson. 1984. "Interrogativity in Mandarin". *Interrogativity* ed. by W. Chisholm, Jr., 47-61. Amsterdam & Philadelphia: John Benjamins.

Longacre, Robert E. 1968. *Discourse, Paragraph, and Sentence Structure in Selected Philippine Languages*. Santa Ana: Summer Institute of Linguistics.

——————. 1972. *Hierarchy and Universality of Discourse Constituents in New Guinea Languages*. 2 vols. Washington, D. C.: Georgetown University Press.

——————. 1983. *The Grammar of Discourse*. New York: Plenum Press.

Los Angeles, University of California. "What Discourse Analysis Reveals about Tag Questions: Implications for TESL". [by Cheryl Brown], 1981.

——————. "Fragments" [by Marian Shapley] 1987.

Malinowski, Bronislaw. 1935. *Coral Gardens and Their Magic, a Study of the Methods of Tilling the Soil and Agricultural Rites in the Trobriand Islands*. (= The Language of Magic and Gardening, 2) London: Allen & Unwin.

——————.1946 [1923]. "The Problem of Meaning in Primitive Languages" *The Meaning of Meaning*, ed. by C. K. Ogden & I.A. Richards, 296-336. New York: Harcourt, Brace & World.

McLemore, Cynthia. "The Pragmatic Interpretation of English Intonation". Ph.D. dissertation, Austin: University of Texas, 1991.

Merritt, Marilyn. 1976. "On Questions Following Questions in Service Encounters". *Language in Society* 5:315-57.

Moravcsik, Edith. 1991. *Oxford International Encyclopedia of Linguistics*. Oxford: Oxford University Press.

Ochs, Elinor. 1988. *Culture and Language Development*. Cambridge: Cambridge University Press.

Ochs, Elinor & Bambi Schieffelin. 1983. *Acquiring Conversational Competence*. London: Routledge & Kegan Paul.

Ochs, Elinor, Bambi Schieffelin & Martha Platt. 1979. "Propositions Across Utterances and Speakers". *Developmental Pragmatics* ed. by E. Ochs & B. Schieffelin, 251-78. New York: Academic Press.

O'Connor, J.D. & G. F. Arnold. 1973. *Intonation of Colloquial English*. London: Longman.

Ogden, C.K. & I.A. Richards. 1946 [1923]. *The Meaning of Meaning*. New York: Harcourt, Brace & World.

Ong, Walter. 1967. *The Presence of the Word*. New Haven: Yale University Press.

—————. 1977. *Interfaces of the Word: Studies in the Evolution of Consciousness and Culture*. Ithaca: Cornell University Press.

Owen, Marion. 1981. "Conversational Units and The Use of 'Well...'". *Conversation and Discourse: Structure and Interpretation* ed. by P. Werth, 99-116. New York: St. Martin's Press.

—————. 1984 [1983]. *Apologies and Remedial Interchanges*. New York: Mouton de Gruyter.

Pierrehumbert, Janet. 1987. *The Phonology and Phonetics of English Intonation*. Bloomington: Indiana University Linguistics Club.

Pike, Kenneth. 1945. *The Intonation of American English*. Ann Arbor: University of Michigan.

—————. 1954. *Language in Relation to a Unified Theory of the Structure of Human Behavior*. The Hague: Mouton de Gruyter.

—————. 1975. "On Describing Languages". *The Scope of American Linguistics* ed. by Robert Austerlitz, 9-39. Lisse, Belgium: The Peter de Ridder Press.

Pomerantz, Anita. "Second Assessments: A Study of Some Features of Agreements/Disagreements". Ph.D. dissertation, Irvine: University of California, 1975.

—————. 1978. "Compliment Responses: Notes on the Cooperation of Multiple Constraints". *Studies in the Organization of Conversational Interaction* ed. by J. Scheinkein, 79-112. New York: Academic Press.

—————. 1984. "Agreeing and Disagreeing with Assessments: Some Features of Preferred/Dispreferred Turn Shapes". *Structures of Social Action* ed. by J. Maxwell Atkinson & J. Heritage, 57-101. Cambridge: Cambridge University Press.

Prince, Ellen. 1981. "Toward a Taxonomy of Given-New Information". *Radical Pragmatics* ed. by P. Cole, 223-55. New York: Academic Press.

—————. 1985. "Fancy Syntax and Shared Knowledge". *Journal of Pragmatics* 9:65-81.

Quirk, Randolph, Sidney Greenbaum, Geoffrey Leech & Jan Svartik. 1985. *A Comprehensive Grammar of the English Language*. New York: Longman.

Reid, W. H. 1974. "The Saussurian Sign as a Control in Linguistic Analysis". *Semiotexte*. 1:31-51.

Rommetveit, Ragmar. 1974. *On Message Structure*. London: John Wiley & Sons.

Sacks, Harvey. Lecture Notes, Irvine: University of California, School of Social Science, 1965.

—————. Lecture Notes, Irvine: University of California, School of Social Science, 1971.

—————. 1972a. "On the Analyzability of Stories by Children". *Directions in Sociolinguistics: The Ethnography of Communication* ed. by J.J. Gumperz & D. Hymes, 325-45. New York: Holt, Rinehart & Winston.

———————. 1972b. "An Initial Investigation of the Useability of Conversational Data for Doing Sociology". *Studies in Social Interaction* ed. by D. Sudnow, 31-74. New York: Free Press.

———————. 1984. "Notes on Methodology". *Structures of Social Action* ed. by J. M. Atkinson & J. Heritage, 21-27. Cambridge: Cambridge University Press.

———————. 1987 [1973]. "On the Preferences for Agreement and Contiguity in Sequences in Conversation". *Talk and Social Organization* ed. by G. Button & J. Lee, 54-69. Cleavedon, England: Cleavedon Press.

Sacks, Harvey, Emanuel Schegloff & Gail Jefferson. 1974. "A Simplest Systematics for the Organization of Turn-Taking in Conversation". *Language* 50:696-735.

Sadock, Jerrold. 1984. "Interrogativity in West Greenlandic". *Interrogativity* ed. by W. Chisholm, Jr., 189-214. Amsterdam & Philadelphia: John Benjamins.

Saha, P. K. 1984. "Interrogativity in Bengali". *Interrogativity* ed. by W. Chisholm, Jr., 113-43. Amsterdam & Philadelphia: John Benjamins.

Santa Barbara, University of California. "Ergativity and Preferred Argument Structure in Sacapultec Discourse". [by John W. Du Bois] 1981.

Schegloff, Emanuel. 1972. "Notes on Conversational Practice: Formulating Place". *Studies in Social Interaction* ed. by D. Sudnow, 75-119. New York: Free Press.

———————. 1979. "Relevance of Repair to Syntax-for-Conversation". *Discourse and Syntax* (= Syntax and Semantics, 12th ed. by T. Givón, 261-86). New York: Academic Press.

———————. 1981. "Discourse as an Interactional Achievement". *Georgetown University Roundtable on Languages and Linguistics 1981* ed. by D. Tannen, 71-93. Washington, D.C.: Georgetown University Press.

———————. 1984 [1976]. "On Some Questions and Ambiguities in Conversation". *Structures of Social Action* ed. by J. M. Atkinson & J. Heritage, 28-52. Cambridge: Cambridge University Press.

———————. 1987. "Some Sources of Misunderstanding in Talk-in-Interaction". *Linguistics* 25:201-18.

———————. 1989. "Reflections on Language, Development, and the Interactional Charcter of Talk-in-Interaction". *Interaction in Human Development* ed. by Marc H. Bornstein & Jerome S. Bruner, 139-53. Hillsdale, N.J: Lawrence Erlbaum.

———————. 1990. "On the Organization of Sequences as a Source of 'Coherence' in Talk-in-Interaction". *Conversational Organization and Its Development*, ed. by Bruce Dorval. Norwood, N.J.: Ablex.

———————. 1992. "Repair After Next Turn: The Last Structurally Provided Defense of Intersubjectivity in Conversation". *American Journal of Sociology*. 97:1295-1345.

Schegloff, Emanuel, Gail Jefferson & Harvey Sacks. 1977. "The Preference for Self-Correction in the Organization of Repair in Conversation". *Language* 53:61-82.

Schegloff, Emanuel & Harvey Sacks. 1973. "Opening up Closings". *Semiotica*. 8:289-327.
Schenkein, J. N. 1978. *Studies in the Organization of Conversational Interaction*. New York: Academic Press.
Scheutze-Coburn, Stephan, Marian Shapley & Elizabeth G. Weber. 1991. "Units of Intonation in Discourse: A Comparison of Acoustic and Auditory Analyses". *Language and Speech* 34:207-34.
Schiffrin, Deborah, ed. 1984. "Meaning, Form, and Use in Context: Linguistic Applications". *Georgetown University Roundtable on Languages and Linguistics 1984*. Washington, D.C.: Georgetown University Press.
——————. 1987. *Discourse Markers*. Cambridge: Cambridge University Press.
Searle, John R. 1969. *Speech Acts*. Cambridge: Cambridge University Press.
——————. 1975. "Indirect Speech Acts". *Speech Acts* (= Syntax and Semantics, 3rd ed. by P. Cole & J.L. Morgan, 59-82). New York: Academic Press.
——————. 1979. *Expression and Meaning*. Cambridge: Cambridge University Press.
Selting, Margret. 1992. "Prosody in Conversational Questions". *Journal of Pragmatics* 17:315-45.
Shapley, Marian. "Some Constraints on Fragments". Master's thesis, Los Angeles: University of California, 1983.
——————. "Fundamental Frequency Variation in Conversational Discourse". Ph.D. dissertation, Los Angeles: University of California, 1989.
Sinclair, John McH. "Indescribable English". unpublished inaugural lecture, University of Birmingham, 1966.
Sinclair, John McH. & R.M. Coulthard. 1975. *Towards an Analysis of Discourse*. London: Oxford University Press.
Stenström, Anita-Brita. 1984. *Questions and Responses in English Conversation*. (= Lund Studies in English, 68) Malmö, Sweden: CLK Gleerup.
Stevenson, C. L. 1944. *Ethics and Language*. New Haven: Yale University Press.
Stewart, Susan. 1978. [1979]. *Nonsense*. Baltimore: Johns Hopkins University Press.
Svartvik, Jan. 1980. "*Well* in Conversation". *Studies in English Linguistics for Randolph Quirk*, 167-77. London: Longman.
Swadesh, M. 1946. "Chitimacha". *Linguistic Structures of Native America* ed. by H. Hoijer. New York: Viking Fund Publications in Anthropology.
Tannen, Deborah. 1981a. "Analyzing Discourse: Talk and Text". *Georgetown University Roundtable on Languages and Linguistics 1981*. Washington, D.C.: Georgetown University Press.
——————. 1981b. "The Machine-Gun Question: An Example of Conversational Style". *Journal of Pragmatics* 5:383-97.
——————. 1984a. *Coherence in Spoken and Written Discourse*. Norwood, N.J., Ablex.

―――――. 1984b. *Conversational Style: Analyzing Talk Among Friends.* Norwood, N. J.: Ablex.
―――――. 1984c. "Spoken and Written Narrative in English and Greek". *Coherence in Spoken and Written Discourse* ed. by D. Tannen, 21-41. Norwood, N.J.: Ablex.
―――――. 1988. *Linguistics in Context.* Norwood, N.J.: Ablex.
Thompson, Sandra A. 1983. "Grammar and Discourse: The English Detached Participial Clause". *Discourse Perspectives on Syntax* ed. by F. Klein-Andreu, 43-65. New York: Academic Press.
―――――. 1987a. "The Passive in English: A Discourse Perspective". *In Honor of Ilse Lehiste* ed. by R. Channon & L. Shockley, 497-511. Dordrect, Holland/Riverton, USA: Foris.
―――――. 1987b. "'Subordination' and Narrative Event Structure". *Coherence and Grounding in Discourse* (= Typological Studies in Language ed. by R. Tomlin, 11:435-54) Amsterdam & Philadelphia: John Benjamins.
Thompson, Sandra A. & Anthony Mulac. 1992. "A Quantitative Perspective on the Grammaticization of Epistemic Parentheticals in English". *Approaches to Grammaticization* ed. by E. Traugott & B. Heine. 313-30. Amsterdam & Philadelphia: John Benjamins.
Trager, George L. & Henry Lee Smith, Jr. 1957 [1951]. "An Outline of English Structure". *Studies in Linguistics. Occasional Papers 3.* Washington, D.C.: American Council of Learned Societies.
Tsui, Amy B.M. 1989. "Beyond the Adjacency Pair". *Language in Society* 18:545-64.
―――――. 1991. "The Interpenetration of Language as Code and Language as Behavior: A Description of Evaluative Statements". *Functional and Systemic Linguistics: Approaches and Uses* ed. by Eija Ventola, 193-212. Berlin: Mouton de Gruyter.
Turner, R. *Speech Act Theory and Natural Language Use.* (Cambridge: University of Cambridge, Department of Linguistics Pragmatics Microfiche 1.1:A3, 1975).
Tyler, Stephen. 1978. *The Said and The Unsaid.* New York: Academic Press.
Ultan, Russell. 1978. "Some General Characteristics of Interrogative Systems". *Universals of Human Language* (= Syntax, IV, ed by J. Greenberg, C. Ferguson & E. Moravcsik, 211-48). Stanford: Stanford University Press.
Urmson, John O. 1968. *The Emotive Theory of Ethics.* London: Hutchinson.
Van Dijk, Teun. 1985. *Discourse and Dialogue.* (= Handbook of Discourse Analysis, 3) New York: Academic Press.
Wardhaugh, Ronald. 1985. *How Conversation Works.* New York: Basil Blackwell.
Weber Elizabeth G. & Christiane A.M. Baltaxe. "Self-Initiated Repair in the Discourse of Normal, Language-Disordered, and Autistic Children". To appear in the *Journal of Autism and Developmental Disabilities.*

Weber, Elizabeth G. & Paola Bentivoglio. 1991. "Verbs of Cognition in Spoken Spanish: A Discourse Profile". *Discourse-Pragmatics and the Verb: The Evidence from Romance* ed. by S. Fleischman & L. Waugh, 194-213. London/New York: Routledge.

Weinreich, Uriel. 1980 [1964]. "Semantics and Semiotics". *On Semantics* ed. by W. Labov & B. Weinreich, 3-13. Philadelphia: University of Pennsylvania Press. [Also published in the *International Encyclopedia of the Social Sciences* ed. by D. S. Sills, 1968. 14:164-69. New York: Crowell, Collier & Macmillan]

West, Candace. 1984. *Routine Complications*. Bloomington: Indiana University Press.

Wootten, Anthony. 1981. "The Management of Grantings and Rejections by Parents in Request Sequences". *Semiotica*. 37:59-89.

# Index

## A
accessibility of information, 57, 75
accounts, 36
act, 27
act directive, 27
act elicitation, 27
adjacency pairs, 15, 34
adjacency-pair structure, general description, 13
A-events, 91, 95
agreement, general description, 35
alternate choice, 136
alternative questions, 219
analytical procedures and principles, general description, 19, 28
appender question with candidate referent, 159
appender question with wh-word, 162
arrangements, general description, 116
aspiration, 44
assertives, general description, 10
audiotape, 20, 75

## B
background information, 55
basic unit of communication, general description, 11
because, 69
B-events, 91, 95

## C
candidate substitution, 163
candidate understandings, 181
candidate understandings, general description, 115
clause + you know code, 49
clause, general description, 5
clauses, number of, 51
code identification, 49

coding procedures, general description, 46
cognitive science, 221
commissives, general description, 10
communicative function, 8, 14, 57
communicative functions, general description, 27
context, general description, 28
contiguity, 34
conversation, 20
conversation analysis, general description, 12
conversation, organization of, general description, 29
conversations, detailed, 39
criticism, general description, 117
cutoffs, 44

**D**
D-event, 194
data, general description, 39, 58
data, organization of, 22
database, 58
database, general description, 19
declarative clause, general description, 5, 23
declarative clause, marking subsequent to, 71
declarative clause, marking which occurs within, 61
declarative clause, prior, 64
declarative forms, 58
declarative questions, function, general description, 91
declarative questions, 215
declarative questions not interpretable in terms of A- and B-events, 106
declarative questions with no associated lexical or morphosyntac marker, 85
declarative questions with no associated marker, accessbility of information, 75
declarative questions, marked, 60, 80
declarative questions, morphosyntactic patterns of, 57, 59
declaratives, general description, 10
declination component, 36
delays, 35
descriptive linguistics, 220
descriptive structure, 52
directives, general description, 10
disagreement, general description, 35
discourse analysis, general description, 11
discourse function, 6
discourse marker/conjunction, subsequent, 134
discourse mode, first-pair part, 54
discourse mode, second-pair part, 55

dispreferred responses, 35
distributive facts, general description, 79
doing questioning, 13, 30
duration, 26

## E
echo questions, 31
ellipsis, general description, 123
environment, 54
ethnomethodological analytical approach, general description, 21
ethnomethodological approach, 38
ethnomethodology, 43
events, A- and B-, see also *A-events* and *B-events*, 91, 95
exclamation code, 49
exclamatory clause, general description, 6
expressives, general description, 10

## F
first-pair part, 50, 177
first-pair part, initial, code, 51
first-pair part, overlap, 54
form-content analysis, 12
form/function correlations, 212
forms, assertive, nonassertive, 33
frequency, 26
functional questions, 4, 20

## G
gesture, 57
gesture and declarative questions with no associated marker, general description, 75
goals of this work, general description, 4, 211
grammar, 7
grammatical forms, 4
greeting code, 49

## H
hearings, alternative, 43
hearings, possible, 44
hm, 129
huh, 153, 167

## I
I don't know, 206
if clause, 69, 71, 206

illocutionary force, 10
imperative clause, 25
imperative clause, general description, 6
imputations, general description, 61
inbreaths, 44
indexical nature of talk, 28
informational units, 26
insert sequences, 15, 29
inserts, 33
intensity, 26
interactional units, 11
interactions, 22
interrogative clause, 25
interrogative clause, general description, 5, 23
interrogative form, 4, 14, 58, 63
interrogative forms, prior, 66
interrogative forms, prior self-repaired, 67
interrogative words, 129
interrogative, interpretable, 25
interrogatives, 57
intonation, 1, 2, 53, 57, 73, 202
intonation contour, 7, 31
intonation contour, general description, 26
intonation, falling terminal, 74
intonation, general description, 7, 26
intonation, rising terminal, 59, 74
intonation, unambiguous question, 59
invitation code, 49

**J**
joke code, 49

**K**
knowledge gaps, general description, 113

**L**
language-in-context, 12
language-in-use, 2
laughter, 44
left dislocation utterances, 67
lengthening, 44
lexical element, prior, 133
lexical elements, 61, 192, 218
lexical marker, 62, 127, 206

INDEX 247

like what, 178
linguistic form, 14
linguistic form, general description, 1, 2
linguistics, formal, 221
loudness, 26, 44

**M**
marker, declarative questions with no associated, general description, 59
marker, discourse, 73
marker, no associated, 73
marker, prior discourse, 69
markers, 215-217
markers in declarative statements, distribution of, 205
markers of question function, general description, 191
markers, lexical, 95, 191
markers, morphosyntactic, 191
marking, 63
marking which occurs before the nonclausal form, 131
marking which occurs before the declarative clause, 64
marking, prior-lexical or morphosyntactic, 84
marking, within/prior/subsequent, 206
material, inserted, 50
methodology, general description, 39
misinterpretations, general description, 202
morphosyntactic form, 1, 57, 211
morphosyntactic form, general description, 5
morphosyntactic patterns, 55
morphosyntax, general description, 22
move types, 27

**N**
narrator checks, general descriptions, 117
negative responses, 34
news receipts, 187
next-turn repair initiators (NTRI's), 92, 152, 215
next-turn repair initiators (NTRI's), general description, see also *NTRI's*, 31
next-turn repair initiators and declarative questions with no associated marker, 77
nonclausal forms, 58, 67
nonclausal forms, completive, 189
nonclausal forms, general description, 25, 124
nonclausal forms, non-completive, 189
nonclausal questions, 216
nonclausal questions not implicated in repair, functions of, 173
nonclausal questions with no associated marker, 126, 142

nonclausal questions with no associated marker, interpretation of, 138
nonclausal questions, accessibility of information, 138
nonclausal questions, distributive facts, 138
nonclausal questions, marked, 125, 127, 139
nonclausal questions, multiple functions of, 151
nonclausal questions, NTRI's, 138
nonclausal questions: function, general description, 151
nonclausal questions: morphosyntactic patterns, 123
noncontiguity, 35
noninterrogative forms, 20
nonsentences, 123
NTRI's, 142, 169
NTRI's and preference structure, 164
NTRI's, general description, 85
NTRI's, see also *next-turn repair initiators*, 85
null context, 10

## O

offer code, 49
oh, 142, 177, 206
organization, prosodic, 22
organization, syntactic, 22
orthography, English, 43
other disciplines, general description, 15
outbreaths, 44

## P

paratones, 26
partial repeat alone, 156
participant-tracking, 27
participants' behavior, 21
particle tag, 24, 71, 135
particles, 128, 198
pauses, 44
phonetic form, 1
phonological form, 1
physical environment, 149
pitch, 1
pitch level, 26
pitch level, change in, 45
pitch prominence, 26
placement considerations, general description, 14
post insert, 50
post-expansions, 29, 33

INDEX 249

pre-announcement, 35
pre-announcements, preferred responses to, 177
pre-disagreement, 37
pre-expansions, 29, 33
prefaces, 36
preference structure, general description, 33
prior question marker/pronoun, 218
prominence, 26, 45
prosodic groups, 26
pseudophonetic system, 43

**Q**
question pronouns, 218
question, alternative, 53
question, confirmation, 53
question, general description, 4
questions, 33

**R**
real-time production, 60
really, 187
receipt, third-position, 50
records, general description, 46
referent-proposition constructions, 67
register, general description, 26
remedial exchanges, 11
repair, 67, 84
repair initiator, next-turn code, 49
repair phenomena, general description, 30
repair type, same-turn, 52
repair, fourth-turn, 32
repair, multiple, 31
repair, same-turn, 31, 52
repair, third-turn, 32
repair, transition-space, 32
repeat, partial or full, 155
repetition, 49
repetitions, general description, 93
repetitions, not NTRI's, 200
request code, 49
request for a reason, general description, 108
requests for confirmation, 85, 94, 102
requests for confirmation which have no associated marker, 102
requests for confirmation, marked in terms of A- and B-events, 96

responses, dispreferred, 35
responses, preferred, 35
rule of confirmation, 126, 142, 194
rule of confirmation, general description, 86
rule of confirmation, see also *events, A- and B-*, 94

## S
Sack's substitution principle, 93
same-turn repairs, candidate solutions to, 172
second-pair part, 50
second-pair part, initial, code, 52
second-pair part question, 51
second-pair part speaker, 51
second-pair part, overlap, 54
second-pair parts, dispreferred, 35
second-person subjects, 199
selectional criteria, general description, 20
semantic types, general description, 6
sequence structure, 31
sequence structure, general description, 29
sequence-in-time, 34
sequential position in the talk, 14, 57
sequential slot, 180
social context, 91
social setting, 39
sociolinguistic approach, 12
solicitations, topic/sequence, 173
sounds and utterances, low intensity, 45
speaker code, 54
speech act theory, 221
speech act theory, general description, 9
speech events, 12
speech exchange system, least-constrained, 30
spoken language, general description, 1
stress, general description, 45
stress, perceived, 26
stress, primary, 46
stress, secondary, 46
structural classification, 49
subject, phonologically reduced, 24
subject, recoverable, 24
subject/verb inversion, 128
subordinating sequences, 26
syllables, unstressed, 46

syntactic clauses, general description, 22
syntactic form, 57
syntactic type code, 52

**T**
tag question, 23, 24, 34, 72
tags, see also *word tags*, 216, 219
talk-in-interaction, 28
tapes, 26, 27
telephone conversations, 20
tempo, 26
temporal order, 34
tentations, general description, 61
terminal intonation, 46
then clause, 71, 142
tokens, 3
tone sequences, 26
tone units, 26
topic continuation, general description, 118
topic/sequence solicitations, 107
topicalization code, 49
transcription, 39
transcription notation, general description, 43
transcription, systems of, 22
transcripts, 26
try questions, 185
turn constructional unit (TCU), 170
turn-taking procedures, general description, 29
turn-taking system, 60
type, functional, 49
typological studies, 219

**U**
uptakes, general description, 110
usage, 22
utterances doing questioning, 20
utterances, sequential not separated by a pause, 43
utterances, simultaneous, 43

**V**
videotape, 20, 75

**W**
well, 71, 207

*wh*-word, 25, 63, 66, 129, 154, 162
*wh*-word used to request more information, 157
what, 153
word search, 172
word tag, 71, 100, 135, 195
word tags, see also *tags*, 216

**Y**
you mean, 78
you mean + candidate understanding, 156
you're kidding, 91
you're kidding, general description, 119

In the series STUDIES IN DISCOURSE AND GRAMMAR (SiDaG) the following titles have been published and will be published:
1. GELUYKENS, Ronald: *From Discourse Process to Grammatical Construction: On Left-Dislocation in English*. Amsterdam/Philadelphia, 1992.
2. IWASAKI, Shoichi: *Subjectivity in Grammar and Discourse: Theoretical Considerations and a Case Study of Japanese Spoken Discourse*. Amsterdam/Philadelphia, 1993.
3. WEBER, Elizabeth G.: *Varieties of Questions in English Conversation*. Amsterdam/Philadelphia, 1993.
4. DOWNING, Pamela: *Numerical Classifier Systems: The Case of Japanese*. Amsterdam/Philadelphia, n.y.p.